# CHRISTIAN APOLOGETICS

IN THE

# POSTMODERN WORLD

EDITED BY
TIMOTHY R. PHILLIPS
& DENNIS L. OKHOLM

INTERVARSITY PRESS
DOWNERS GROVE, ILLINOIS 60515

InterVarsity Press® is the book-publishing division of InterVarsity Christian Fellowship®, a student movement active on campus at hundreds of universities, colleges and schools of nursing in the United States of America, and a member movement of the International Fellowship of Evangelical Students. For information about local and regional activities, write Public Relations Dept., InterVarsity Christian Fellowship, 6400 Schroeder Rd., P.O. Box 7895, Madison, WI 53707-7895.

Scripture quotations, unless otherwise noted, are from the New Revised Standard Version of the Bible, copyright 1989 by the Division of Christian Education of the National Council of the Churches of Christ in the U.S.A., and are used by permission.

ISBN 0-8308-1860-X

Printed in the United States of America

**Library of Congress Cataloging-in-Publication Data**

Christian apologetics in the postmodern world/edited by Timothy R.
  Phillips and Dennis Okholm.
      p.    cm.
  Includes bibliographical references.
  ISBN 0-8308-1860-X
  1. Apologetics.    2. Postmodernism—Religious aspects—
Christianity.    I. Phillips, Timothy R. (Timothy Ross), 1950-
II. Okholm, Dennis L.
  BT1102.C48  1995
  239—dc20                                                    95-1682
                                                                 CIP

21   20   19   18   17   16   15   14   13   12   11

12   11   10   09

*We dedicate this volume to our children.*
*May God strengthen the church and*
*their faith as they face our postmodern culture*
*in the years ahead.*

---

Jubal Janos Bartley-Walsh
Carol Ruth Sire Betczynski
Charity Joy Craig
W. M. John Craig
Andrew Symes Creegan
Timothy David Creegan
Donnie Dean Ecford
Ann Elizabeth Sire Graham
Daphne Krabill Hollinger
Naphtali Krabill Hollinger
Andrew Thomas Kenneson
Peter Edwin Kenneson
Kirsten Elizabeth Lundin
Matthew David Lundin
Thomas Roger Lundin
Andrew Derek Middleton
Kevin Timothy Middleton
Ryan Beck Okholm
Emily Kristin Okholm
Varah Aleya Perkins Potter
Aaron Brandt Phillips
Eugene James Sire
Richard Walter Sire
Chastity Patrice Smiley
Devon Gordon Stackhouse
Joshua Thomas Stackhouse
Trevor John Stackhouse
Andrew Caleb Webster
Jeremy Douglas Webster
Kennerly Louise Webster

# PART I
# DEFINITIONS:
# APOLOGETICS AND
# POSTMODERNITY

# 1
# INTRODUCTION

*Timothy R. Phillips and
Dennis Okholm*

D oes anyone obey the rules anymore? It seems not. Rollerbladers ignore both prohibitions and pedestrians as they leap over concrete obstacles and nearly careen into more conventional navigators of the sidewalk. Madonna changes identities—from a virgin to a hustler, from heterosexual to bisexual—like a chameleon. Trekkies revel in the possibilities of virtual reality and time travel, thereby experiencing the same release from moral responsibility as the crew of the starship *Enterprise*, who can relive different versions of the past at will. A lesbian couple avoids nature's prescriptions by conceiving a child through artificial insemination. An environmental activist announces his moral universe by asserting, "I could no more sink the blade of an ax into the tissues of a living tree than I could drive it into the flesh of a fellow human."[1]

In reality, everyone seems to be following her own rules. Diversity of values and beliefs has become a societal virtue, infecting every part of our lives and respecting no one creed or religion. In fact, the old "rules" by which everyone seemed to play are vanishing. The very idea of an objective and absolute truth is an archaism in pluralistic American society.

In this climate Christian apologetics stands at a crucial juncture. The challenges are formidable, as some have recognized. Alarmed by polls indicating that only 28 percent of Americans have a strong belief in "absolute truth" and that a corresponding relativism is on the rise, Douglas Groothuis urges pastors to begin setting forth a "rational defense of Christianity." Yet within the very same *Christianity Today* column, he acknowledges that such arguments "seldom win a soul to Christ."[2] After presenting a rigorous critique of pantheism in his recent apologetic textbook *Reasonable Faith*, Winfried Corduan also candidly admits, "I have never been able to persuade a pantheist of . . . [its falsity] and see little hope of ever doing so."[3]

Stanley Hauerwas in *After Christendom* perceives an even more dire situation. He claims Christians are being forced to choose between an Enlightenment understanding of "truth" and "morality" and a relativistic denial of rationality and morality with its correlative reduction of all conflicts to power. In this situation, Hauerwas argues,

> The crucial question is how we can make the story we believe to be true not only compelling for us but for the whole world—a world caught between such unhappy alternative stories. In short, the challenge is how, as Christians, we can find a way to witness to the God of Abraham, Isaac, Jacob, and Jesus without that witness becoming an ideology for the powers that would subvert that witness.[4]

How *do* we convince postmodernists of the truth of the gospel? Is apologetics still *possible* in a society that no longer believes in objective truth as demonstrable by a predefined standard of rationality? How do we persuade others of the truth of the gospel in a culture where a variety of rationalities coexist?

The apologetic task is made even more critical when David Wells, Os Guinness, Chuck Colson and others argue that much of the evangelical church is more concerned to convince "cultured despisers" of the *relevance* of the church than of the *truth* of the gospel. According to their indictment, the pure proclamation of the faith once delivered to the apostles is now being accommodated to a culture that is pluralistic, consumer-oriented and infatuated with managerial and therapeutic approaches to life.[5] How do we develop an apologetic strategy that is relevant to the postmodern culture and at the same time maintains the purity of the gospel? And once we do construct such a strategy, what are the implications for the local church?

This book grew out of the 1994 Wheaton Theology Conference, which brought together representatives of various strategies for reaching this culture that has been described as postmodern.* The term *postmodern* is

---

\* This Wheaton Theology Conference was entitled "Christian Apologetics in the Postmodern World: Strategies for the Local Church" and took place April 7-8, 1994. This annual conference encourages young evangelicals to address contemporary issues from the perspective of revelation for the purpose of helping the church. This volume represents just a sampling of the papers from that conference; unfortunately we were unable to publish them all. The conference was cosponsored by the McManis Lectureship from Wheaton College; the Bible, Religion, Archaeology and Theology Department of Wheaton College and Graduate School; the Theology Committee of the National Association of Evangelicals; Faculty Ministries of

now a commonplace. Even the local newspaper advertises *Pulp Fiction* as a "postmodern movie." But what is postmodernism? If we are going to debate strategies for reaching a culture that is caricatured in movies like *Pulp Fiction, Star Trek: Generations* and *Reality Bites*, then we had better have some idea of what we are up against.

## Modernity and Postmodernity

"Postmodernism" is a reaction against "modernity" as it developed out of the Renaissance and Enlightenment. Rejecting the superstitious past as well as its "blind and bloody fanaticism," modernity attempted to establish culture and life on a universal and objective foundation. Over against the illusions, prejudices and fanaticism of the past, modernity offered Reason (with a capital *R*) to scrutinize critically every claim and to ground the edifice of knowledge. Not only would all rational beings concur in Reason, but more importantly, Reason provided a set of rules and criteria for correct thinking about Reality, thus accessing Absolute Truth. In addition, modernity proffered the hope that through Reason humans could understand the cosmos, establish social peace and improve their condition.

The modern project proposed a variety of norms for accessing Truth. Descartes highlighted the rationalist standard of clear and distinct ideas, the sciences wielded empiricist criteria, the Hegelians placed their hope in Spirit's progress in history, and the Romantics appealed to an immediate prereflective intuition. These criteria provided a universal foundation for the disciplines. As a result, claims about reality were brought under this rational set of rules, agreed to by all rational beings, critically examined and adjudicated. Assertions not warranted by these criteria were treated with skepticism and repudiated as simply superstition and subjective impulses.

The late twentieth century widely regards the Enlightenment's claims to a universally objective foundation for knowledge as pretense. Our lives

InterVarsity Christian Fellowship; and InterVarsity Press. We thank these organizations for their invaluable encouragement and support.

are fragmented by the plurality of worlds we encounter in everyday life. Even science's once normative role is dissipating and is now viewed as just one research tradition among others. Moreover, Kierkegaard, Marx, Nietzsche and Freud not only demonstrated, each in their own way, the illusoriness of modernity's claim to a universally accessible and defensible ground for knowledge; more importantly, they also demonstrated the way in which these privileged claims to Reality have been employed oppressively. For modernity beget colonialism, Nazi atrocities and urban decay, not its utopian goal, unless one mistakes the artificial construct of Disneyland for reality![6]

In contrast to modernity, postmodernism repudiates any appeal to Reality or Truth. The very attempt to propose totalizing metanarratives that define and legitimate Reality are denounced as oppressive. Once modernity's claims to universality and Reality are dissolved, the relativism of Richard Rorty and Stanley Fish emerges. For what remains is only the autonomous Self and its power of language. These are the two constitutive elements of postmodernism, as the essays in this volume reflect.

The Self is the source of truth and reality. Human knowledge is *constructed* by the whole person (the unconscious and subconscious, as well as conscious reason). What one chooses does not matter; that one is free to choose is all that matters. As a result, postmodernism is suspicious of all metanarratives that seek to name, define, legitimate and arbitrate social institutions, roles, identities and practices.[7] There are no controlling rules or norms for society; not even God has that right!

Then how can we speak of any reality outside of the autonomous Self? We create it with words. Postmodernism shares a purely pragmatic instrumental view of language. There are no true propositions. There is only the question of what words we should use. As Rorty says, "Anything can be made to look good or bad by being redescribed." Thus, in literature and media—indeed, even in politics—the lines between fantasy and fact are erased. "In postmodernism language becomes a labyrinth that has as its only referent more language."[8] James Sire argues that there is no ontological foundation for language once we assume that there is no rational structure to reality or that we cannot know it. There is simply a continuous interpretation taking place in which each person is to get an equal number of votes to determine the meaning of whatever it is we are interpreting. There are no guarantees of whose or which interpretation will predominate today.

This preoccupation with Self and language pervades our culture. In a postmodern world, society is a network of many individuals, each with his or her own sources of truth and power. The newest electronic pastime, surfing the Internet, is the prime example. One can dialogue with a Hindu, read the narrative of a lesbian's social world or download pornographic fantasies. The only limit to these alternative worlds is the surfer's initiative and imagination!

This decentralized view of an aggregate of "selves" insists upon respecting the Other. No one Self is to insist on a totalizing metanarrative that defines the Other. The result in popular culture is "political correctness" and what Allan Bloom noted as *the* characteristic of today's college student—"niceness" or "civility." All are to have equal voice, especially the marginalized and disenfranchised. The result is a fragmented, chaotic, somewhat arbitrary amalgamation of multiple selves, none with the Enlightenment's claims to universality. In epistemology and ethics, the result is relativism. In Christian soteriology, as William Craig's essay points out, religious relativism and political correctness demand universalism.

Postmodernism's pragmatic instrumental view of language is why image is everything in our culture. Language is not neutral but a tool by which those in power or in control of the media can manipulate and construct reality. Marketing is big business in the postmodern culture because it "informs" us that what we never knew we needed, we do in fact need. At least, that is the reality an advertisement constructs. As the movie *Reality Bites* suggests, the video image is more real than the events and the people it captures. In the end, language cannot authoritatively communicate reality "as it really is"; rather, it fabricates what "really is."

With this focus on the Self and the world-creating powers of language, the pragmatic postmodern seeks to manage his or her experience and environment in the interest of what Roger Lundin calls a "manipulatable sense of well-being." *Ultimate* concerns have no place here. *The* concern is self-improvement. In fact, as the American Association of University Women study on the self-image of girls and boys implied, a positive self-image is simply a matter of feeling good about oneself "all the time." Ethical ideals to live up to and the obligations of an absolute truth are disruptive in a culture that wants to create a comfortable climate. Managerial techniques and therapy become prime assets in this state of affairs.

In his engaging essay, Lundin outlines these characteristics as well as postmodernism's challenge to Christianity. The postmodernist use of language is not a morally neutral tool that Christians can employ for their own ends, for it focuses on psychological effectiveness over against the truth. The goals of manipulating the environment and making the process itself as pleasurable as possible trivialize Christian concepts of sin, forgiveness, guilt, grace, death and resurrection. As Lundin concludes, the "promise of temporary, temporal renewal through the power of radical redescription" denies the transforming power of the Word and closes off transcendent eternity. If Christians use postmodern vocabulary to communicate the gospel, the church will become the beast of burden ridden by postmodernism, a theme that is echoed by Doug Webster.

### Defending the Gospel in Our Postmodern World: Three Strategies

As Dorothy once said to Toto: "I don't think we're in Kansas anymore." Finally, the evangelical church is beginning to realize that what Stanley Hauerwas says in *Resident Aliens* has been going on since the 1960s: we are *not* in the Kansas of modernity anymore![9] And because of that fact the church must create alternative approaches for its presentation and defense of the gospel. Traditional apologetics that lined up a barrage of evidences and rationalistic arguments established the *credibility* of the Christian faith. But, as John Stackhouse illustrates in his essay, that view of apologetics is particularly narrow-sighted. The church has always used a variety of instruments for persuading its culture to notice the church and thereby gain a hearing for these evidences. More importantly, he argues that in our present culture the church cannot even begin to speak about *credibility* until it establishes *plausibility*. By elevating persuasion and plausibility over evidences and credibility, Stackhouse is reversing Aristotle's preference for *logos* over *ethos* and *pathos*. In a postmodern cultural milieu, where universal norms and totalizing metanarratives are suspect from the outset, the church must first persuade its audience that Christianity has something important to say and should be heard; only then should the church suggest that it might be true. Perhaps the old line of defense has its place. But if it does, Stackhouse argues, its place is now in the back seat.

The sheer variety of approaches offered in these essays for defending and witnessing to the Christian faith in our postmodern culture is evidence of the vitality of contemporary evangelicalism. Underlying every apologetic argument are specific epistemological assumptions and a diagnosis regarding modernity's problems and the prospect for postmodernity. In this book, the essays illustrate at least three contrasting sets of assumptions. They are offered to help Christians think through some of the basic issues which both modernity and postmodernity pose for apologetics. The goal, we envision, is a broadened and reinvigorated understanding of Christian apologetics which effectively confronts our world.

### Apologetics of Modernity

Christian apologists met the Enlightenment's challenges through a variety of strategies. Some attempted to graft Christianity onto this universal rational foundation. The early liberal theologian Schleiermacher was one of the most important representatives of this apologetic approach. Identifying the Romantics' prereflective intuition as the sense and taste for God, he encouraged the intellectual elites of his day to reconsider the claims of Christianity.

Here, according to Nicola Hoggard Creegan, is an untapped strategy that speaks to postmodernity as much as Schleiermacher spoke to the "cultured despisers" in his own day. Schleiermacher's focus on a prereflective intuition of the Infinite in the finite undercuts the plurality of viewpoints—the constructions of reality and relativities of language and culture emphasized by postmodernism. It points us toward a worldview that is shared and in which nothing has meaning unless it can be explained in relation to God and to Christ. Creegan argues that Schleiermacher so closely identified with the artists who despised Christianity that he was able to get them to look at the larger picture, see their lives in that context and sense their deprivation without it. Schleiermacher's apologetic strategy questions postmodernism's relativism just as it challenged the modernist's "disenchantment" of the universe.

As even Creegan admits, most evangelicals are uneasy with Schleiermacher's attempt to transplant Christian claims solely on this intuition. In fact, most Christian apologists attempted to meet the Enlightenment's curb on appeals to special revelation through evidentialism. Repudiating the Enlightenment's theological rationalism—the modernist view that "religious beliefs are rational if and only if one has evidence on which those beliefs are based"—evidentialism permits a category which is "above reason." Nevertheless, this category must be a reasonable and credible supplement to what reason knows about God. Claims to special revelation, as a result, must obey the laws of logic and cohere with all the facts known by experience. Using this approach, William Lane Craig concludes that there is sufficient evidence to make Christian belief rationally credible.

With this traditional approach which assumes that we have objective truth about reality and subscribes to Western rationality and metaphysics, Craig is attempting to steer an apologetic strategy from Stackhouse's back seat. Not that Craig believes marshaling evidence and arguments is the foundation of Christian beliefs. Only the self-authenticating witness of the Holy Spirit is that! But such material confirms the faith and encourages the postmodernist to consider it. He is aided in the latter endeavor by the demonstration of postmodernism's self-referential deconstructionism and arbitrary claims. Over against a broad Christian inclusivism and a postmodern universalism, Craig defends Christian exclusivism by using a traditional evidentialist and rationalist apologetic strategy that purports to refute postmodernism.

If the approaches of Creegan and Craig find acceptance, it is probably because the other side has already accepted their underlying assumptions. But what happens when social worlds with their own different values and epistemological and metaphysical assumptions enter the picture? While the self-referential argument is widely used, does it actually help nonbelievers understand the errors of their ways? Some evidentialists have acknowledged its ineffectiveness. Even though he uses the self-referential argument, Winfried Corduan admits its inability to persuade pantheists that their position is false. For the pantheist inevitably responds, "Who am I to say that a contradiction cannot be true?"[10] So how does the declaration of a self-referential contradiction help persuade the pantheist that Christianity is true? Isn't this actually a declaration of apologetic failure? Or isn't this simply acknowledging that one lacks the categories to continue a dialogue with the non-Christian? At the very least, much work needs to be done to help the Rollerbladers and New Agers understand the importance of historical evidence (and even history), as well as properly interpret the intuition of the Infinite.

### Apologetics Between Modernity and Postmodernity

In the next section, Jim Sire is not as quick to climb into the back seat as Craig and Creegan. They do find some camaraderie, however, in insisting that there is a fundamental meaning to reality—a created reality and a real Creator. Sire shares with Craig an insistence on objective truth established by logic and factual evidence. This is what he calls the centrality of the logos of John 1 over against the "antilogocentric" approach of postmodernism.

While they all reject postmodernism on that score, Sire parts company with Creegan and Craig on the degree to which language *does* shape the way we think and construe reality. Sire accepts much of the postmodern critique of the pretentious Enlightenment rationalism that assumed that people could grasp the Truth truly and with certainty if they only exercised their ordinary mental faculties. Of course, Sire insists that sin has something to do with this; it is not just a case of postmodern intellectual humility.

As a result, Sire readily acknowledges that a variety of social worlds exist. We cannot assume that a Christian framework is a given. Rather than placing all of our apologetic bets on the evidences for Christianity's credibility, we must first persuade nonbelievers of the plausibility of Christian presuppositions. Christian apologists are not confined to the old apologetic bag of evidences. They must branch out and meet nonbelievers where they are, not remaining within their own social world but uncovering beliefs and concerns shared with the nonbeliever. Using that newly discovered common ground, the apologist can then persuasively show the credibility of Christian belief. To the environmentalist, for example, the rhetorical question "Is green enough?" is a beginning point for making the connection between ecology and an ethic that acknowledges the Creator. To the New Ager, the concept of love can provoke dialogue and differentiations between Jungian and Christian understandings of true love.[11] Simply put, evangelical apologetics *must* attend to both reason *and* rhetoric, with as much emphasis on the latter as the former in order to make reason relevant and help people see the truth.

However, this apologetic strategy resembles a high-wire act. Failures are easy and catastrophic. Unless rhetoric has equal billing with reason, this position collapses into an "apologetics of modernity," as Philip Kenneson argues in his essay. But on the other hand, rhetoric easily devolves into "selling" the gospel. The rhetorical injunction "May the Force be with you" is nothing less than a perversion of the gospel. What then are the boundaries for rhetoric?

## A Postmodern Apologetic

While authors in the second category reject central features of postmodernity, those in the third category are much more willing to gain helpful insights from some of the concerns and emphases of postmodernity. Philip Kenneson insists that postmodernity can be embraced to a large extent for the purpose of defending Christianity, while Brian Walsh and J. Richard Middleton try to answer on its own terms some of postmodernism's criticisms of Christianity.

Running headlong into the strategies advocated by Craig and Sire, Kenneson celebrates postmodernism's attack on "objective truth," for it shows the church that it cannot rely on a correspondence theory of truth for its witness—any more than it should have relished the cozy Constantinian reliance on the state. This gives the church the opportunity to explore other paradigms without being fixated on such matters as objective truth and evidentialist and rationalistic justifications for that truth. Kenneson thinks that eliminating the idea of objective truth will force the church to take responsibility for the way it sees and understands the world. In the end, by listening to postmodernism's critique of modernism, the church may learn that it is not "objective truth" which gives its testimony authority and intelligibility, but the fact that the church lives its life in a way incomprehensible apart from the God to whom it witnesses.

For their part, Walsh and Middleton question whether Christianity can escape the postmodernist critique of totality thinking and metanarratives, particularly since Christianity itself presents a total worldview rooted in the biblical metanarrative. But when they look more closely at the biblical metanarrative with postmodernist sensitivities, they discover that it contains at least two antitotalizing dimensions: the rootedness of the narrative in the experience of suffering—from the exodus to the cross—and God's overarching creational intent which delegitimizes any violent and oppressive use of the story.

But how far can we as Christian apologists accept postmodernism without selling our theological birthright? Can the Christian completely escape the accusation of oppression and violence? For Jesus Christ warned of a future righteous judgment, where some will be "thrown into the outer darkness" (Mt 8:12), excluded from the eschatological kingdom. The post-modern critique, by contrast, seems to require some form of universalism. In addition, must not the apologist insist that Christian language conveys Reality more accurately than any alternatives do? Is that possible to do in postmodernism?[12]

### The Church in a Postmodern Setting

It is one thing to suggest alternative strategies from the vantage point of the ivory tower. That contribution is crucial and eventually trickles down (to borrow a phrase paradigmatic of postmodern language use) to the popular culture. But any strategy conceived in the marketplace of ideas must be lived out in the marketplace of everyday commerce if it is to be a viable strategy for reinforcing Christian belief in *this* culture. That is to say, apologetics must be seen as an ecclesial practice. Accordingly, three essays close our survey, written by those in the trenches and on the front lines who understand the postmodern culture both intellectually and existentially.

Ronald Potter observes that the social-economic realities of American life make Christian belief problematic more often than do the traditional intellectual challenges to the faith. While Christian apologists have engaged the intellectual "spirit of the times" with their scholarly counterattacks upon Hume and company, they have largely bypassed the lived world of most Americans. This predicament, Potter provocatively suggests, simply reflects the way in which our modern world—specifically, professionalization, careerism and specialization in academia—has co-opted Christian apologetics. Taking a missiological approach, Potter calls for an apologetic that engages our contemporaries in their own social world by speaking to their plight of angst, despair, meaninglessness and spiritual homelessness. To do this effectively, Potter notes, apologetics must be centered in the church and praxis-oriented. If our apologetic cannot deal with the realities of AIDS and moral breakdown in our communities, it is impotent and irrelevant. The church cannot neglect his prescription, namely that Christian apologetics must address the sociological as well as the intellectual realities of our contemporary culture.

While sharing Potter's concerns, Dennis Hollinger works with Peter Berger's concept of a plausibility structure (see also Stackhouse's essay) which maintains and legitimizes the discrepant views of reality and value systems in our pluralistic culture—concepts of truth that are regarded as local and parochial. For the Christian worldview, this plausibility structure—that is, the social group with its social constructs that gives flesh and life to the group's worldview—is the church. Traditional apologetics has tried to articulate the biblical story of creation, fall, redemption and consummation by using rational arguments to individuals who stand apart from the Christian plausibility structure. But as we have spelled out above, postmodern people are reluctant to accept totalizing metanarratives that define reality and truth for them. In a way that is compatible with Kenneson's essay, Hollinger argues that the church must make the biblical story manifest in its entire life. The church as apologetic is a social reality which can give coherence and meaning to the Christian "life world" in a more fully orbed way—that is, through narrative, rational discourse, symbol or ritual, life experience and moral behavior. In a culture where there is growing skepticism of rationality, this approach has the advantage of recommending to the whole postmodern self a consistent, coherent worldview which can explain life as humans know it. And on this point it would appear that Creegan's commendation of Schleiermacher might find a friendly advocate.

Doug Webster's social location differs from the previous two authors, and while Hollinger might readily align himself with Kenneson in the third camp of apologetic strategies, Webster would echo Roger Lundin's concern about postmodernism. Finding himself among mainline Protestants and market-driven evangelicals, Webster is disturbed by the type of evangelism he sees occurring in a postmodern, post-Christendom culture. Pluralism and pragmatism have secularized the church; mainliners seek cultural respectability and political correctness, while marketers seek popularity. We are becoming secularized by the culture we are trying to reach with the gospel, and in this respect mainliners and evangelicals look alike. Mainline Protestantism offers a highly politicized ethic controlled by the dictates of enlightened secular culture, while market-driven evangelicalism offers a psychologized gospel conditioned by self-centered, consumer-oriented, media-induced felt needs. Webster argues that the Protestant church itself is in need of evangelization, since it has been heavily influenced by radical pluralism, individualism and relativism. The place to begin is with a deeper awareness of our sinfulness, a call to a life of obedience in Christ and a new emphasis on the inseparability of law and gospel. Failing this the church will lose her distinctive voice and merely echo the culture. Loss of cultural respectability and popularity should not concern a church that ought to be more worried about losing its soul than about gaining the whole world.

The essays that follow, then, are meant to *open* a discussion. While all the authors in this volume make passionate appeals for their point of view, none would pretentiously claim to have the last word. Indeed, these are first words about apologetics in a postmodern world. And perhaps if the discussion is joined *now* by many other voices, the church will not find itself panting to catch up to a culture that, like the Rollerblader, passed it when it wasn't looking, but will indeed find an effective strategy to convince postmodernists that not only are there rules everyone must play by, but the only game in town is the gospel of Jesus Christ.

We gladly acknowledge the help of Andrew Derek Chignell in editing this volume and of Kristy Lee Odelius in compiling the index. Their efficient work under pressure made this publication possible.

# 2
# THE
# PRAGMATICS
# OF
# POSTMODERNITY

*Roger Lundin*

Thing are in the saddle and ride mankind," complained Ralph Waldo Emerson a century and a half ago. Like his disciple and Concord neighbor Henry David Thoreau, Emerson was vexed by the ironies of modern history. Technologies like those that had ushered in the industrial revolution were intended to free the men and women of the modern world from poverty, from bondage to servile labor and from subjection to the vagaries of nature. But instead, Emerson, Thoreau and others feared, technology had brought bondage of a new kind.

To Emerson and Thoreau, technology mastered its users in several ways, not the least significant of which was its capacity to fascinate people with means rather than ends. Long before Albert Einstein made his pithy remark about the modern age being an era of perfected means and confused ends, Emerson and Thoreau had identified the problem. "Our inventions are but improved means to an unimproved end," Thoreau observed. "We are in great haste to construct a magnetic telegraph from Maine to Texas; but Maine and Texas, it may be, have nothing important to communicate. We are eager to tunnel under the Atlantic and bring the old world some weeks nearer to the new; but perchance the first news that will leak through the broad, flapping American ear will be that the Princess Adelaide has the whooping cough."[1] If Thoreau had misgivings like that about the telegraph, what would he have thought about trucking down the information superhighway or channel-surfing his way through the five hundred stations beamed down from the heavens to his hut on the banks of Walden Pond?

There is a disturbing parallel to Thoreau's fears in a work written by one of his contemporaries, Frederick Douglass. In his *Narrative of the Life of an American Slave,* Douglass writes of the irony that even here, in the ultimate relationship of user and tool—that of master and slave—the master became mastered and the user used. Douglass relates that he was at one point transferred from a plantation to a family in Baltimore. His new mistress, Mrs. Auld, "had never had a slave under her control previously" but "had been dependent upon her own industry for a living." He explains that he "scarcely knew how to behave towards her," because her kindness and respectful attitude toward him made her "entirely unlike any other white woman" he had ever known.

But all that quickly changed, once what Douglass calls "the fatal poison of irresponsible power" came into Mrs. Auld's hands. He laments the fact that "slavery soon proved its ability to divest her of these heavenly qualities. Under its influence, the tender heart became stone, and the lamblike disposition gave way to one of tigerlike fierceness." Having rendered black men and women into things, white slaveholders found themselves, according to Douglass, in the same state as their peers who worshiped new technologies. "Slavery proved as injurious to her as it did to me," he concludes.[2]

### The Legacy of Romanticism

To reassert the superiority of spirit over matter, of the human will over the tools it uses—to put humankind back in the saddle, that is—Emerson and his fellow Romantics elaborated their doctrines of the innocent, infinite and divine self. What makes the sadness of Emerson and Thoreau both ironic and pertinent to the study of postmodernity is the clear line of descent running from these apostles of Romanticism to the contemporary purveyors of postmodernism. Emerson, Thoreau and Margaret Fuller paved the way for the likes of Richard Rorty and Stanley Fish. Like the nineteenth-century transcendentalists, the late-twentieth-century American postmodernists focus on the self and the powers of language. Contemporary pragmatists share with their Romantic forebears an essentially optimistic understanding of human nature and a breezily upbeat view of the human condition.

The Romantics and postmodern pragmatists differ dramatically, however, in their estimation of the ultimate significance of that condition. To Romantics such as Emerson and Thoreau, the innocent, infinite American self was still an actor in a great spiritual drama; when Emerson wrote that the "ancient precept 'Know thyself' and the modern precept 'Study nature' become at last one maxim," he was articulating a deeply felt Romantic conviction that the law of God permeated both the self and the natural world.[3] The Romantics believed that when language was employed intuitively and creatively, it could reveal the mysteries hidden away within nature and the self. "The world being thus put under the mind for verb and noun, the poet is he who can articulate it," asserted Emerson in "The Poet." "We are symbols and inhabit symbols," he explained in that essay. But in Emerson's words, because we are "infatuated with the economical use of things," we cannot hear the symbols speak to us. Nevertheless, "the poet, by an ulterior intellectual perception, gives them a power which makes their old use forgotten, and puts eyes, and a tongue, into every dumb and inanimate object."[4]

In American postmodernism, the moral and metaphysical foundations of Romanticism simply drop away, leaving the self driven by the single engine of desire. Postmodernism in America is Romanticism stripped of its pretensions. Marx, Nietzsche and Freud materialized and demystified the transcendent self celebrated in the Enlightenment and Romanticism. In light of what Paul Ricoeur calls the "hermeneutic of suspicion," it is hard for the unaided, unimpeded self to claim direct access to God or the eternal truth of things. All that language can reveal, the postmodern argument concludes from its loss of Romantic faith, are the self's desires—desires for sexual gratification, economic gain, pleasure and power. "All preferences are principled," writes Stanley Fish, one of the mavens of literary and legal postmodernism, and "all principles are preferences. . . . In short, one person's principles are another person's illegitimate ('mere') preferences."[5]

## Implications of the Postmodern Vocabulary
What Fish and Rorty say in the works they have published over the last two decades should give pause to all who believe that Christian apologetics might eagerly appropriate a postmodern vocabulary. They make it clear that the language of postmodernism is anything but a morally neutral tool that people of any persuasion might pick up and use to some anointed or

appointed end. Instead, that vocabulary commits the one who would use it to a specific vision of the self, truth and the ethical life. This vision, in turn, is fundamentally at odds with basic affirmations of the Christian creeds.

As Fish puts it, the vocabulary of postmodernity is committed to promoting a vision of humans as the species *Homo rhetoricus* rather than *Homo seriosus*. To define *Homo rhetoricus*, Fish quotes Richard Lanham, a theorist of rhetoric: "[*Homo rhetoricus*] assumes a natural agility in changing orientations. . . . From birth, almost, he has dwelt not in a single-value structure but in several. He is thus committed to no single construction of the world. . . . He accepts the present paradigm and explores its resources. Rhetorical man is trained not to discover reality but to manipulate it. Reality is what is accepted as reality, what is useful." Picking up the argument on his own, Fish explains that "rhetorical man manipulates reality, establishing through his words the imperatives and urgencies to which he and his fellows must respond." Perhaps the most important thing to understand about *Homo rhetoricus* is that "by exploring the available means of persuasion in a particular situation, he tries them on, and as they begin to suit him, he becomes them."[6]

That is the key admission—"as they [the available means of persuasion] begin to suit him, he becomes them." For a Christian professing a gospel of truth beyond contingency or a divine imperative beyond the desires of the moment, the rhetoric of postmodern pragmatism makes for an ill-fitting suit. That suit cramps and confines. Or to drop the metaphor, postmodernism's language creates a moral universe in which the self that would use language to "help get us what we want"—in Rorty's phrase— discovers itself brought into bondage by the very tool it sought to master. And though this mastery extends even to those who employ such a vocabulary for unabashedly postmodern ends, my argument in this essay has to do with the devastating irony that confronts any who would appropriate this vocabulary for Christian apologetic purposes.

Those who adopt the language of postmodern pragmatism because they see it as a useful technology with apologetic power are likely to arrive at an updated version of Emerson's conclusion: "Words are now in the saddle and ride mankind." Christian apologists may dream of harnessing the vocabulary of postmodernism to help the church corral the wandering herds of the MTV generation; but if they dream about such possibilities, it is inevitably only a matter of time before they awaken to discover that they themselves have become beasts of burden, consigned to carry the postmodern cargo to market.

To be certain, melancholy of the kind I have just evoked does not issue from many contemporary American postmodernists. Rather than bewailing the tragic ironies of human efforts to master our destiny, they laud the newly discovered powers of the post-Romantic self and its linguistic tools. Rorty, for instance, depicts that self as a dynamic, creative agent wielding words to get what it wants, striving to "transform things until they mirror his power," as Nietzsche puts it.[7]

According to Rorty, the modern self has been freed by the legacy of Romanticism to assume a thoroughly pragmatic, instrumental view of language. Our present vantage point allows us to see that contemporary pragmatism has its origins in the battle between science and literature that began with the Romantics. Rorty acknowledges that the Romantic movement started as an effort to salvage the spiritual legacy of Christian faith by planting the sources of that faith within the self. To make this move, the Romantics relied upon the innocence of the self and the power of the imagination. They fully believed that the virtuous power in the self corresponded to the virtue and power of God. William Butler Yeats, who spoke of himself as the "last Romantic," succinctly expressed this Romantic faith:

All hatred driven hence,
The soul recovers radical innocence
And learns at last that it is self-delighting,
Self-appeasing, self-affrighting,
And that its own sweet will is Heaven's will.[8]

Rorty argues that the logic of Romanticism eventually drove its heirs to abandon their metaphysical pretensions—all this nonsense about "its own sweet will being heaven's will." We now realize that the true meaning of "Romanticism" is "the thesis that the one thing needful [is] to discover not which propositions are true but rather what vocabulary we should use." The Romantics, of course, did not know that this was what they meant. "Reason cunningly employed Hegel, contrary to his own intentions," writes Rorty, "to write the charter of our modern literary culture." It turned Hegel's "historical sense of the relativity of principles and vocabularies to a place and time" into a "romantic sense that everything can be changed by talking in new terms." The literary culture to which Hegel gave birth is one "which claims to have taken over and reshaped whatever is worth keeping in science, philosophy, and religion—looking down on all three from a higher standpoint."[9]

Rorty applauds the transformation of Romanticism by pragmatism. Having turned to the will as the source of virtue and divine truth, Romanticism finds that refuge in the will transformed into a rationalization of whatever the will prefers—"All principles are preferences" and "all preferences are principled." In arguing, as Rorty does, that "anything can be made to look good or bad by being redescribed," contemporary pragmatists assume that the creative, willing self has the power to acquire or accomplish what it wishes. In a sense, that self can even cheat death of its power. In *Contingency, Irony and Solidarity,* Rorty lauds the Nietzschean self, which "would seek consolation, at the moment of death, not in having transcended the animal condition but in being that peculiar sort of dying animal who, by describing himself in his own terms, had created himself."[10] Thus, the most deft of pragmatists will be able, by using language as a kind of gigantic crowbar, to roll away the stone of his or her inherited contingencies—even the most weighty ones of sin and death.

### Pragmatics and Therapeutics

When viewed in one way, the conclusions that Rorty and others make seem like the latest developments in a philosophical narrative stretching back

for centuries. Looked at in another light, however, the postmodern pragmatists might seem to be little more than apologists for a therapeutic
society. In speaking of the *therapeutic* in this way, I am referring to what
Philip Rieff has brilliantly described as "the unreligion of the age, and its
master science." According to Rieff, in a therapeutic understanding of the
world there is "nothing at stake beyond a manipulatable sense of well-being."[11] A therapeutic culture is one in which questions of ultimate concern—about the nature of the good, the meaning of truth and the existence
of God—are taken to be unanswerable and hence, in some fundamental
sense, insignificant. Instead the therapeutic culture focuses upon the management of experience and environment in the interest of that "manipulatable sense of well-being" described by Rieff and celebrated by Fish and
Rorty.

According to Rieff, few things suit the therapeutic ideal better than the
"prevalent American piety toward the self. This self, improved, is the
ultimate concern of modern culture."[12] In one of the central texts of the
postmodern movement, Jean-François Lyotard defines the movement as
"simplifying to the extreme, . . . incredulity towards metanarratives."[13]
Skeptical of all narrative frameworks that might impose upon or define
the autonomous self, the postmodern self seeks to be liberated from the
imprisoning confinement of the historical or communal narratives that
make a claim upon it. The *therapeutic* self considers itself free of the
obligations of truth and the claims of ethical ideals. "In our culture," argues
Alasdair MacIntyre, "truth has been displaced as a value and replaced by
psychological effectiveness."[14]

Therein lies the danger of appropriating the vocabulary of postmodernism in proclaiming the gospel. It is simply the wrong tool for the job.
The language of postmodern pragmatics can imagine no goal for human
striving beyond that of Rieff's "manipulatable sense of well-being." To
appropriate its images is to accept its vision of life as a process without a
goal beyond that of perpetuating the process and making it as pleasurable
as possible. In asking you to assume that language is nothing more than a

tool to employ for private purposes and the perpetuation of practices, postmodern pragmatism makes you a tool of its vision of the world.

### Hamlet and the Power of Thought

Words are indeed in the saddle and ride mankind. You pick up the language of contemporary pragmatism, thinking of it as a net to cast across the waters for a great catch; you find, instead, that you get hopelessly entangled in its never-ending web of words. Or, to use an image brought into common use by Shakespeare, the Christian who adopts postmodern language is likely to find himself "hoist[ed] with his own petard."

Hamlet employs that image when alluding to the trick he has played upon the courtiers Rosencrantz and Guildenstern. These two have been enlisted by Hamlet's uncle, King Claudius, to escort the prince to England, where he is to be killed according to instructions that Rosencrantz and Guildenstern carry with them. While they are at sea, Hamlet steals the instructions and replaces them with a directive that demands that the English put to death immediately the two bearers, Rosencrantz and Guildenstern themselves. Of his uncle's plans to use the courtiers, Hamlet says:

> Let it work,
> For 'tis the sport to have the engineer
> Hoist with his own petard, and 't shall go hard
> But I will delve one yard below their mines
> And blow them at the moon.[15]

It is especially instructive that Hamlet utters these words about the ironies of human intentions, because earlier in the same play he says something to Rosencrantz and Guildenstern that might easily lead one to assume him to be an originator of the postmodern pragmatic viewpoint. When the courtiers question Hamlet's designation of Denmark as a prison—"We think not so, my lord"—he responds by saying, "Why, then 'tis none to you, for there is nothing either good or bad, but thinking makes it so. To me it is a prison."

But there is a vast difference between Hamlet's observation that "there is nothing either good or bad, but thinking makes it so" and Richard Rorty's assertion that "anything can be made to look good or bad by being redescribed." And that distinction makes clear the difference between a Christian apologetic that engages the postmodern world seriously but critically and one that capitulates to that world by appropriating its vocabulary and assumptions.

Hamlet's claim about the power of thought acknowledges the constitutive role of the human mind without claiming that the mind creates the world about which it thinks. As he agonizes over the consequences of the vengeance he has been called upon to exact on behalf of his murdered father, Hamlet is paralyzed rather than liberated by the range of his thoughts, which repeatedly deliver him to the tragic ironies of the human condition. For Rorty and Fish, the gaps between human intentions, actions and consequences can be bridged by the human will and its power to wield language to its own purposes—by proclaiming all preferences to be principles or by overcoming irony and tragedy through redescription.

The key insight of tragedy—which it shares with a Christian conception of sin—is that we never span the chasm yawning between our intentions and our actions, between our actual behavior and the ideals we profess. Yet for Rorty redescription spans the gap: "A human life [is] triumphant just insofar as it escapes from inherited descriptions of the contingencies of its existence and finds new descriptions. This is the difference between the will to truth and the will to self-overcoming. It is the difference between thinking of redemption as making contact with something larger and more enduring than oneself and redemption as Nietzsche describes it: 'recreating all "it was" into a "thus I willed it." ' "[16]

Unlike the postmodern pragmatists, Hamlet understands the tragic and ironic limitations of this newly discovered way of thinking about thinking. "To be or not to be—that is the question," he asserts in the play's most famous speech. Yet by the end of that speech, Hamlet is so stymied by his weighing of options and consequences that he laments:

Thus conscience does make cowards of us all,

And thus the native hue of resolution
Is sicklied o'er with the pale cast of thought,
And enterprises of great pitch and moment
With this regard their currents turn awry
And lose the name of action.[17]

As the play draws to its tragic close, Hamlet confides to Horatio what he has learned about the limits of calculation and redescription:

Rashly,
And praised be rashness for it—let us know,
Our indiscretion sometime serves us well
When our deep plots do pall, and that should learn us
There's a divinity that shapes our ends,
Rough-hew them how we will.[18]

What is at stake here in the debate over postmodernism's vocabulary is ultimately our vision of the truth and moral order. Postmodern vocabulary assumes a naturalistic view of the created order and a preferential view of the moral life. To adopt its language is to trivialize Christian conceptions of sin and forgiveness, guilt and grace, death and resurrection. By holding out the promise of temporary, temporal renewal through the power of radical redescription, it denies the transforming power of the Word and closes off the eternity to which the entire drama of the life, death and resurrection of Christ points the way.

### Lifestyles and the Loss of Eden

Two illustrations may clarify the matters at stake. The first has to do with an essay question on a test I gave about ten years ago. It asked students to describe the consequences of the Fall as John Milton depicts them in *Paradise Lost*. Most answers focused upon the discord that came to Adam and Eve's relationship, their shame and their drastically altered view of God. But several began with a surprising thesis statement similar to this: "The major effect of the Fall was to make Adam and Eve change their lifestyle."

What has concerned me over the years has been the inability of many students, when I have related this story to them, to understand the dangers inherent in reducing the expulsion from Eden to a change in lifestyle. A world in which every action manifests nothing more than an individual's flair, his or her peculiar "style," is a world in which there is no difference in choosing between gods to worship and ice-cream flavors to consume. In March 1994, *The New York Times* reported that the local chapter of the National Abortion Rights Action League (NARAL) was mounting a public service ad campaign to counter the highly publicized De Moss foundation ads carrying the theme "Life. What a Beautiful Choice." The NARAL ads turn things around: "Choice. What a Beautiful Life." The *Times* story reports: "The spot centers on personal preferences in areas like food, religion, and hair styles, then segues into the issue of 'Whether you have a baby—or an abortion.' "[19] Chinese food or French cuisine, Jesus or Nostradamus, permed or straight, life or death: they are all the same. What you choose does not matter, only your freedom in choosing.

The ironic complexities of these issues were brought home to me early in 1994, when I read a *Newsweek* account of plans for a movie version of Nathaniel Hawthorne's *The Scarlet Letter*. In the climactic scene of that novel, Hester Prynne urges Arthur Dimmesdale to flee with her and throw off the burdensome beliefs that afflict the two of them. When Arthur tells Hester of the agony of his sin—because of the tragic and ironic "contrast between what I seem and what I am!"—she replies, "Your sin is left behind you, in the days long past." Hester urges the father of her child to "leave it all behind. . . . Meddle no more with it! Begin all anew!" She begs him to toss down this sin-stained and weary identity of his and to "exchange this false life of thine for a true one. . . . Preach! Write! Act! Do any thing, save to lie down and die!"[20]

Hester is a forerunner of the postmodern Richard Rorty, for like him she believes that moral quandaries are not resolved by repentance, but by relocation or redescription. Not much distance separates the romantic who believes that "seven years' weight of misery" can readily be exchanged for a future "full of trial and success" from the pragmatic postmodernist who writes that "all any ironist can measure success against is the past—not by living up to it, but by redescribing it in his terms, thereby becoming able to say, 'Thus I willed it.' "[21]

Arthur is beguiled by Hester's pleas, yet he finds comfort and strength in the same theological system that Hester would have him abandon. Puritan covenantal theology crushes him with the guilt it induces, but it also supports him with the consolation and meaning it imparts to his life. Furthermore, Dimmesdale discovers that without the constricting framework of his beliefs, his moral life turns into a confusing array of destructive impulses.

Hawthorne remained doubtful about the possibility of forgiveness and convinced of the destructive force of unfettered liberty. So, shortly after Dimmesdale's forest encounter with Hester, Hawthorne has him offer an ambiguous public confession of his sin before dying in his lover's arms. Tragic ironies and ambiguities abound at the novel's close.

That was not to be the case with the new movie. *Newsweek* reported that the director had said that "he wants the audience to understand [Dimmesdale's confession and death] as just a metaphor for Dimmesdale's liberation, an interpretation that allows the movie to end on the less depressing note of Dimmesdale and Hester riding off together to start a new life." According to a version of the script obtained by *Newsweek*, "As they reach the edge of the forest, Hester . . . unfastens the scarlet letter, letting it fall by the wayside. The rear wheel of the wagon rolls over it, partly burying it in the mud."[22]

Whether it manifests itself in the highest elite reaches of postmodern theory, in the recent attempts of a Presbyterian task force to redescribe fornication and adultery as possible displays of "justicelove" or in the slick productions that cascade down upon us from Madison Avenue, contemporary American pragmatism is market driven. In a passage that all who believe that George Barna holds the key to the church's future ought to cut out and plaster on their refrigerator doors, Jerry Adler writes in the

*Newsweek* story: "A century and a half ago, in the years before audience research, Hawthorne had composed his somber psychological drama with no way to know if readers might prefer a French and Indian War bodice-ripper instead. With nothing at stake but his own immortality, he could make his book as downbeat as he liked, but director Roland Joffé isn't about to take that chance with a $40 million movie."[23]

In the moral universe celebrated by this new film script, Hester and Arthur's wagon wheel rolls over much more than a discarded letter. It also buries and leaves behind them the possibility of their assuming a satisfying role in a vast cosmic drama in which their sin might be forgiven and their mortal bodies raised to eternal life. "The abdication of Belief / Makes the Behavior small," wrote Emily Dickinson more than a century ago in a poem about the loss of faith in God's sovereignty.[24] Postmodernism holds out the promise of boundless liberty; it creates a world so profoundly trivial that it starves and stifles the spirit.

More than fifty years ago, W. H. Auden imagined the contours of a postmodern moral universe, one which represented "the ultimately liberal condition." It is a world filled "with promiscuous pastures where the minotaur of authority is just a roly-poly ruminant and nothing is at stake." In this world, "Liberty stands with her hands behind her back, not caring, not minding *anything*." Finally, Auden writes, "your existence is indeed free at last to choose its own meaning, that is, to plunge headlong into despair and fall through silence fathomless and dry, all fact your single drop, all value your pure alas."[25]

Nothing that I have said in this essay should be taken as a call for Christians to abandon engagement with postmodernity or to shun the study of its thought. To respond to the pragmatism of our contemporary world, we must understand it as fully and fairly as possible. But that understanding involves more than the reading of essays and books by Richard Rorty, Jacques Derrida and Stanley Fish. It also involves situating American postmodernism within the history of this culture, its thought and social practices. Jonathan Edwards, Ralph Waldo Emerson, Emily

Dickinson and William James are every bit as important for our understanding as are the latest theoretical treatises emanating from Berkeley,
Durham and all points in between.

For an understanding of postmodernism, as in so many other ways,
Dietrich Bonhoeffer provides provocative guidance. "During the last year
or so," he wrote to Eberhard Bethge in July 1944, "I've come to know and
understand more and more the profound this-worldliness of Christianity."
But, he says, "I don't mean the shallow and banal this-worldliness of the
enlightened, the busy, the comfortable, or the lascivious, but the profound
this-worldliness characterized by discipline and the constant knowledge
of death and resurrection." This means, for us in a postmodern world,
"living unreservedly in life's duties, problems, successes and failures,
experiences and perplexities." It means sharing the "sufferings of God in
the world—watching with Christ in Gethsemane." Bonhoeffer asks, "How
can success make us arrogant, or failure lead us astray, when we share in
God's sufferings through a life of this kind?"[26]

This is the point at which our apologetic efforts might begin. With
cunning, passion, sincerity and perseverance, the church must bring to
postmodern culture the good news of a gospel that completely inverts the
categories of that culture. To an age that believes that freedom makes you
true, the church must respond with a more ancient message: "You shall
know the truth, and the truth will set you free."

# 3
# FROM ARCHITECTURE TO ARGUMENT
## Historic Resources for Christian Apologetics

*John G. Stackhouse Jr.*

Let your light shine before others,
so that they may see your good works
and give glory to your Father in heaven. (Mt 5:16)

Apologetics, like its cousin the philosophy of religion, is a type of Christian theology. Standard historians of apologetics like J. K. S. Reid and Avery Dulles assume this truism.[1] Other great figures in the history of Christian thought such as F. D. E. Schleiermacher, B. B. Warfield and Paul Tillich agree.[2] It would therefore be presumptuous indeed to suggest that to construe apologetics as a branch of Christian theology and philosophy is to drastically narrow its scope and effectiveness and thereby compromise the witness of the church.

I shall be presumptuous. I shall presume that in our time—as in every time—only a minority of persons are interested in theological and philosophical ideas, yet a larger number do concern themselves on occasion with the question of the truthfulness of religious claims. I shall also presume that the church is to meet that question in a manner appropriate to each person's authentic need and that doing so is the essence of the apologetic task. I shall further presume that God furnishes the church with the resources necessary to accomplish this mission. And I find that the history of the church offers a wide range of intriguing and exemplary modes of apologetics if we look beyond the confines of theology and philosophy.[3]

## Architecture

The Merriam-Webster dictionary company doubtless represents the common mind of our culture when it gives as its first definition of the word *church* "a building for public and especially Christian worship."[4] Christians know that the primary definition of church according to the New Testament is the congregation of Christians, the people themselves. Yet the public image of the church in general and of individual congregations is very much defined by physical plants.

Christians throughout history, therefore, have wisely paid attention to the erection of structures that would convey a particular message to the community. Medieval cathedrals spoke eloquently of the devotion of princes, clergy and townspeople to God—and to civic and personal pride.

The images in carved stone, paint and stained glass were the "books of the illiterate," joining with sermons and seasonal mystery and miracle plays to educate the masses in the Christian faith.

But the cathedrals played a crucial apologetic role as well. The populace of Europe needed to be impressed deeply with the authority and the power—and thus the credibility—of the church by every means possible. This was because, as Jean Delumeau and others have argued, medieval Europeans clung to their tribal religions while understanding little and observing less of the Christian faith until well into the Reformation period.[5] The cathedrals bore witness to the grandeur of the medieval God, his daunting Son Jesus and his glorious mother Mary. Thus they testified to the spiritual authority of the church, the church that figuratively and literally occupied the high ground.

A similar motive inspired Protestants to erect their own versions of cathedrals in nineteenth-century Ontario. As William Westfall has demonstrated, Anglicans joined with Presbyterians, Methodists and even Baptists in constructing church buildings that asserted the moral status of Christianity in an increasingly materialistic culture. Each of these groups looked back to the image of the medieval cathedral, and they together produced what Westfall calls a distinct architecture—"Ontario Gothic."[6]

In the United States, Christian institutions have used architecture to assert to themselves and others their place in the culture. Many Christian colleges as well as churches, for instance, have used Colonial or Gothic architecture to affirm that they are, as it were, pillars of society. Oral Roberts University and Robert Schuller's Crystal Cathedral dramatically exemplify a different approach, declaring in their "space-age" architecture of sharp-angled steel, concrete and glass that they are at America's sophisticated cutting edge. Willow Creek Community Church in suburban Chicago, to select just one more example, deliberately chose a physical plant that looks like the well-manicured office park in which the members of its target audience spend much of their week.[7]

The same principle applies to more modest buildings as well—buildings that are appropriate to their environment and ministry, whether the urban storefront church or the suburban church "bungalow." In each case, the church speaks to all who pass by. "Take us seriously," it says. "Don't discount us as eccentric. We belong here."

## Literature

Apologists love to speak and write: words are their stock-in-trade. Yet some of the most eminent apologists have realized that straightforward, prosaic argument may well be inferior to other genres of literature in making a way for the gospel in the hearts of many. Many contemporary Christians know at least some of the works of C. S. Lewis (1898-1963), for instance. Lewis was a noted scholar of English literature, yet his international fame rests largely on the wide range of fiction he wrote. Lewis composed children's stories, the Chronicles of Narnia, a science-fiction trilogy and a retelling of Greek myth in *Till We Have Faces* (1956). He addressed theology more directly (but still in allegory and meta-phor) in *The Great Divorce* (1946) and, perhaps his most-read book, *The Screwtape Letters* (1941). Lewis also was a master essayist, and his popular *Mere Christianity* (1952) and other collections of essays are in print to this day.

The heritage of writing Christian apologetics in a variety of genres stretches back centuries, however. One can see apologetics as a prime motive in Eusebius's *Ecclesiastical History* (A.D. 323), in Augustine's auto-biographical *Confessions* (397-98), and in Erasmus's satire, *The Praise of Folly* (1511). Søren Kierkegaard (1813-1855) wrote profound philosophy, but he also addressed the masses through his provocative journalism. For some minds, Christianity has become more plausible because of sublime poetry that speaks a Christian worldview. In the English language, for example, there is a very rich tradition which includes Edmund Spenser, John Donne, George Herbert, John Milton, William Cowper and Gerard Manley Hop-kins.[8] And what can be said of word-artists can also be said of artists in other media such as that of paint, sculpture, dance, music and so on.

Perhaps no single other apologist was so versatile as G. K. Chesterton (1874-1936). He did write direct apologetics, some of which profits readers almost a century later: *Heresy* (1905), *Orthodoxy* (1908) and *The Everlasting Man* (1925) particularly come to mind. But Chesterton also wrote history that lifted up Christian themes and ideals, notably in his biographies of Francis of Assisi (1924) and Thomas Aquinas (1933). He wrote explicitly Christian verse, some of it doggerel but some of it still quite moving, sprightly and often savage commentary in column after column of newspaper,[9] and some very popular fiction, particularly in the unlikely genres of thriller (*The Man Who Was Thursday* [1908]) and mystery story (featuring his Roman Catholic priest/detective, Father Brown).[10]

Christian apologetics, then, has long been the concern of a broad spectrum of authors, complementing and widely extending the ideas of the theologians and philosophers.

### Worldly Knowledge and Wisdom

This sort of apologetic makes contact with people's immediate, secular concerns. In the case of knowledge, Christians offer expertise that others find valuable and that prompts them to consider seriously what Christians have to say about spiritual matters.

Matteo Ricci, the Jesuit missionary to China, marvelously exemplified this. Ricci taught the Chinese a system for effective memory by building mental palaces, pavilions and divans. "To everything that we wish to remember," wrote Ricci, "we should give an image; and to every one of these images we should assign a position where it can repose peacefully until we are ready to reclaim it by an act of memory." These mental constructs provided storage for the "myriad concepts that make up the sum of our human knowledge." As Jonathan Spence explains,

> The family that Ricci was seeking to instruct in mnemonic skills stood at the apex of Chinese society. Governor Lu himself was an intelligent and wealthy scholar who had served in a wide variety of posts in the Ming dynasty bureaucracy. . . . Now he had reached the peak of his

career, as a provincial governor, and was preparing his three sons for the advanced government examinations; he himself had passed these exams with distinction twenty-eight years before, and knew along with all his contemporaries that success in the exams was the surest route to fame and fortune in the imperial Chinese state. Thus we can be almost certain that Ricci was offering to teach the governor's sons advanced memory techniques so that they would have a better chance to pass the exams, and would then in gratitude use their newly won prestige to advance the cause of the Catholic church.[11]

So-called tentmaking missionaries go beyond mere self-support in precisely this way, using their special abilities to bring plausibility to their convictions about the gospel. Christian scientists, soldiers, musicians, explorers and industrialists have used the platforms they have earned through their particular worldly successes to testify to their Christian faith. Indeed, these are the forebears of today's Christian heroes, athletes and pop singers. Sophisticates may grimace at this, but many people have claimed that they were encouraged to think again about whether Christianity is "just for losers" when these "winners" were gladly endorsing it.

Wisdom is a second dimension of this apologetical resource. Christians contribute as they can—in neighborhood associations, in the workplace, on school boards, in mass media forums and in government—to the public conversation. Such Christians bring the wisdom of the Christian tradition to bear on matters of societal concern, and they do so in such a way that those who do not share Christian presuppositions can nonetheless appreciate and benefit from this wisdom. Education, financial responsibility, marriage and child-rearing, conflict management, ecological stewardship, racial justice and a host of other generically human concerns have all been discussed by Christians in public language. Beyond the important intrinsic benefits of such "salting" and "lighting" of one's culture, Christians hereby construct reputable standpoints from which they can share more specifically Christian convictions.

## Power Events

The mention of "winners" brings forward a distinguished, if sometimes eclipsed, tradition in Christian apologetics. Indeed, it goes back to Christianity's Jewish heritage and the famous confrontation between Yahweh's prophet Elijah and the prophets of Baal on Mount Carmel. When called upon to display his power, Baal was silent, embarrassingly so. When it was his turn, Yahweh answered with a roar of fire (1 Kings 18). Other wondrous signs pointed to divine blessing upon the work of many people in the Bible, most notably the ministry of the Lord Jesus himself.

Subsequent church history treasures its lore of amazing events and dramatic confrontations. The entire genre of hagiography, the lives of the saints, is preoccupied with these attestations of God's power. One of the most effective missionaries in the early church became known as Gregory Thaumaturgus, the "Wonder-Worker."

Among the most impressive stories of all is the tale of Wynfrith of England, better known under his later name of Boniface, apostle to the Germans (680-754). K. S. Latourette tells what happened in 723:

> Following the advice of some of the most stalwart of his converts, he went to Geismar and, in the presence of a large number of pagans, began cutting down a huge ancient oak held sacred to Thor. Before he had quite completed the task a powerful gust of wind finished the demolition. The tree crashed to the ground and broke into four sections. The pagan bystanders, who had been cursing the desecrator, were convinced of the power of the new faith. Out of the timber Boniface constructed an oratory to St. Peter. The Geismar episode may well have proved decisive evidence in terms which the populace could understand of the superior might of the God of the Christians. Presumably, too, it helped to wean from pre-Christian magical practices many of the nominal converts who observed the rites of both the new and the old faith.[12]

As other observers have noted, these power events are reported much more frequently by missionaries and others on the edges of Christian evangelistic advance than among the populations of settled Christians. As the "Christian West" becomes less and less Christian, though, it may be that this mode of apologetics will become more useful here as well.[13]

## Justice and Charity

Cutting down a sacred tree displays courage and power and helps to liberate people from the bondage of superstition. The Christian religion, though, is about more than that. And missionaries more typically have demonstrated the authenticity of the message of God's love through acts of justice and charity. Pope Gregory the Great (c. 540-604), for instance, earned lasting respect and loyalty to his office by interceding for the city of Rome with barbarian invaders and by spending church money on massive relief for the poor when the political leaders failed to help. The generosity of monasteries as places of refuge, healing and nourishment redounded greatly to the credit of the church in the Middle Ages. The work of William Wilberforce (1759-1833) and the Clapham Sect against slavery in Britain and the many other worthy causes championed by nineteenth-century evangelicals on both sides of the Atlantic burnished the image of the Christian faith in those societies. In our own day, the work of organizations like World Vision and individuals like Mother Teresa shuts the mouths of those who would accuse the church of otherworldly irrelevance.

Perhaps no movement in church history, though, was as sweeping in its attempt to provide for human needs as was Pietism under the leadership of A. H. Francke (1663-1727) in eighteenth-century Germany. With the support of Pietist leader P. J. Spener (1635-1705), Francke moved to Halle and became a pastor and professor of biblical languages and theology. These duties were not enough for the indefatigable Francke. He organized the establishment of the famous Halle *Stiftungen* ("institutions"), and historian Howard Snyder makes an impressive list of them.

Most of these institutions were started partly in response to needs in Glaucha and the surrounding area after the plague of 1682-83, which reportedly reduced the population of the town by two-thirds. Francke was so moved by the ignorance and poverty of the children of Glaucha that in 1695 he began a school for the poor which soon grew to over fifty students. This led to the founding of an orphanage in 1696, and eventually to a whole series of interrelated and mutually supportive institutions. These included a *paedagogium* for the sons of the nobility (which the young Count Zinzendorf attended for six years), a Latin school to prepare students for the university, and German schools designed to provide a practical secondary education for boys and girls of ordinary citizens. In addition to the orphanage and schools, Francke founded a home for poor widows (1698), a bookstore, a chemical laboratory, a library, a museum of natural science, a laundry, a farm, a bakery, a brewery, a hospital, and other enterprises. He was instrumental also in founding the Canstein Bible House which was lodged in the new orphanage building, completed in 1698. By 1800 the Bible house had distributed nearly three million Bible and Scripture portions in several languages.[14]

Francke explicitly embraced a reform vision. "He saw his schools as means for infiltrating all levels of society with Pietist influence. His educational methods and ideas were in fact applied very widely due to the success of the Halle schools."[15]

Second, however, Francke's institutions served as examples of Pietist Christianity that impressed many people well beyond the boundaries of Germany, reaching even to the hinterland of Puritan New England through Francke's correspondence with Cotton Mather. As another scholar puts it, Francke was the "originator, founder, and lifelong head of a charitable enterprise which has caught the imagination . . . of people the world over. Nothing like it could be found in the long history of the Christian church."[16]

The apologetic of good deeds was commanded in the Sermon on the Mount, and the history of the church is full of instances of noble Christian obedience to it.

## Christian Community

If a pragmatic test is applied to the Christian truth-claim, it ought to show whether Christianity delivers what it promises. Among the most basic assertions of Christianity is the declaration that Christ established a community of believers that would be characterized chiefly by worship of him and love for each other (Jn 13—17). The inquirer therefore is entitled to ask whether such communities exist. He or she may want to know, after all the demonstrations of power and prestige and integrity and charity, whether or not Christianity does transform individuals, decisively reorient them toward Christ and integrate them into a community of love.

Monastic renewal movements understood this, and so they planted new communities of faith to initiate and sustain Christian testimony throughout Europe. Mass evangelists in our own era wisely pay attention to what they call "follow-up" so that the fire of revival can be sustained in the fireplaces of existing or newly founded churches once the tents have been folded up or the stadiums have emptied. Contemporary theologians of the church across a very wide range of viewpoints agree that the spiritual health of the church is a critical factor in the success of evangelistic effort.[17]

John Wesley (1703-1791) stands as an exemplar of this sensibility, devoting enormous energy to structuring a variety of small groups to lead people into a maturing Christian faith. For all of the spectacular successes of Methodist oratory, Wesley believed that it was in these intimate meetings of earnest fellowship, rather than in the general preaching services, that the great majority of conversions occurred. Indeed, he early resolved not to preach anywhere he could not follow up by establishing such groups with adequate leadership.[18]

Attention to this crucial, if basic, point leads us to consider several issues germane to this matter of varieties within Christian apologetics.

### The Problem of Plausibility
Apologetical theology and philosophy have traditionally preoccupied themselves with the problem of *credibility*: Is Christianity, or one of its particular truth-claims, believable? For some time, though, sociologists

of religion like Peter Berger and Thomas Luckmann have been pointing to the problem of *plausibility: could* it be true?[19]

My sense is that Christian witness faces several giant obstacles in this regard. First is typical North American ignorance about the Christian faith. Sociological studies confirm what many of us have encountered firsthand: most people know scarcely anything about the Christian faith. Most cannot name the Ten Commandments or the books of the Bible—even the Penta-teuch—or the disciple who denied Jesus.[20] It is certainly doubtful that most people could explain the foundational truths of justification by faith, the atonement or the Trinity.

I once sat beside a woman of my age on a flight to Minneapolis from Chicago. As we talked, it emerged that she had earned a B.A. from prestigious Dartmouth College and an M.B.A. from the University of Chicago's famous School of Business. But when I talked of my own job and jokingly complained that many of my introductory students couldn't put "Paul" and "Jesus Christ" in the correct chronological order on a test, she floored me with the straightforward question, "Who is this 'apostle Paul'?" This ignorance among the educated is a sign of the times.

Yet this problem of ignorance is compounded by a second problem: people's common supposition that they *do* understand the Christian faith—or at least enough of it to feel justified in dismissing it. Many North Americans have had some contact with the church, whether as children or in the company of pious relatives or by attending weddings and other rites of passage. They may not know much Bible history or Christian doctrine, but they think they know *some* things: Christianity is old-fashioned, bor-ing, irrelevant and intellectually second-rate. In many respects, sadly, these friends of ours are right. What they encountered probably *was* old-fash-ioned, boring, irrelevant and intellectually second-rate. Their mistake lies only in believing that this sort of experience constitutes sufficient grounds for rejecting the Christian faith *in toto*.

Third, many Christian leaders have made the faith not only unattractive but positively repellent. Sexual abuse, particularly by homosexual and pedophiliac Roman Catholic priests, has badly hurt the image of the church. So-called mainline Protestantism is less visible in the scandal pages, but it continues to endure its own costly time of reckoning. Evangelical Christianity, for its part, has been trammeled by the two Jimmys, Bakker and Swaggart, and their ilk.

We fail to appreciate the scope of this problem, though, if we limit it to the spectacular public failures. Evangelicals in particular have a terrible "image problem" in North America. It begins with the "holy roller" stereotypes from the nineteenth-century camp meetings and continues with the "fighting fundies" of the 1920s. Now we have a wide range of slick television preachers who work themselves into an embarrassing frenzy over (a) healing, (b) money, (c) sex, (d) money, (e) prophecy, (f) money, (g) American patriotism and (h) money. Indeed, Billy Graham has profited through his career from the fact that he is not as extreme as people expect him to be.[21] The problem, of course, has been getting them interested in attending a meeting in the first place—*this* is the problem of plausibility.

Finally, we as evangelical Christians must bear some responsibility for this ourselves. The times our friends in the community notice us, the times we do something public and impressive, are usually either in the service of direct evangelism or in protesting something we do not like in schools, hospitals, the courts or the government. Yet this does nothing but perpetuate the stereotype that evangelicals are always trying to bag converts or impose our morality on others, always telling others that they are wrong and need to change to our way of thinking.

The challenge, then, is to complement our proclamation of the gospel and our resistance to evil with winsome public demonstrations of God's care for the earth, for the financially and socially needy, for beauty and joy and for the intellectual life. We must demonstrate our worthy citizenship if we are to overcome the plausibility problem today. The examples of Christian endeavor we have considered in this essay, then, can inspire us. And we must understand thereby that it is authentic for us to embrace this wide agenda, not just as something we "put on" strategically for the sake of evangelism but as cooperation with the God who is at work to redeem the whole world.[22]

This contention might well strike home more powerfully if one considers the counterfactual situation: what if the church did *not* have these other resources? What if church architecture was nondescript and merely functional as a meeting space—or stood out oddly, incongruously in its community? What if the only Christian literature was theology and philosophy? What if Christians had nothing useful to offer others except Christian ideas? What if Christians entirely avoided power encounters? What if Christians spent all of their energies in theological and philosophical pursuits? What if Christian fellowship consisted entirely of academic conferences? As valuable as theological and philosophical apologetics undoubtedly are, it seems unlikely that many people would consent to sitting still for them if all of these other confirmations were absent.

### Applications to the Present

It may be, in fact, that it is precisely for lack of sufficient "corollary apologetics," as we might call them, that so many people in our communities today generally are *not* deeply interested in what Christians have to say theologically and philosophically. Reviewing the several categories of such apologetics might suggest lines for further reflection.

The realm of *architecture* draws us to consider the broad issue of physical space and the even broader issue of visual presentation. We do not have to explore semiotics very far to learn that every artifact is a text, a sign.[23] What, therefore, are we saying by the physical spaces in which we present the Christian message? What is the floor plan, what is the lighting and the furniture and the décor, what is the message we are sending? This concern extends to the physical appearance of the human presenters as well. Clothes, haircuts and jewelry all speak quite powerfully about class, profession, authority, sophistication and one's relation to the audience.

Consideration of architecture also points us to the vexed question of the

interpretation of signs, the ambiguity of symbols. However glorious cathedrals might appear to some, for instance, others see in them only the
wasteful use of resources to indulge and glorify the rich. If apologetics
matters to Christian individuals or groups, they will try to ascertain
carefully what crosses, ICTHUS-fish, mahogany paneling, business suits
or earrings signify to each of those they are trying to contact.

Various genres of *literature* prompt us to consider the broad issue of
rhetoric and the even broader issue of communication theory and strategy.
However cogent our arguments, they cannot effect anything if no one
listens. Are there other ways to proclaim the Christian message that will
attract a wider hearing? More to the point in many evangelical circles is
whether we will support artists in poetry, fiction, television, movies, music
and other media—even if they are our own congregants and spouses and
students and children. Or will we continue to suspect and denounce them
as worldly, compromising and superficial compared to the solid, stolid
work of preaching, teaching and writing Christian theology?

Yet another consideration that arises in this context but pertains also to
others of these modes is the question of the usefulness of one or another
piece of literature in a particular situation. Just as some philosophical
apologetics have value only in certain cultures and among certain people,
so a particular poem or novel or song or picture might well convey an
appropriate Christian message in some cases but might alienate people in
others. Sexism in Christian writing, for instance, has been pervasive
throughout history and renders much formerly acceptable literature simply unusable in some contexts today. Once again we must keep clearly
before us not only what message we think we are sending, but what
message is likely to be understood by the recipients.

*Worldly knowledge* is something evangelicals have long appreciated and
exploited. We do not have to look only at celebrated "winners," however,
to judge the merits of this form of apologetics. Any important work done
well is an effective apologetic, especially as integrity in service continues
to erode in our society. A Christian plumber who answers calls promptly,

fixes problems quickly and thoroughly, and charges a fair price for time and materials makes a powerful impression upon every customer. A Christian manager who sets out clear expectations, listens attentively to complaints and suggestions, and responds with evident thoughtfulness and wisdom elicits respect that strengthens any explicitly Christian testimony he or she might render. Good, skillful service thus casts threads around others that connect them to us, even bind them to us in a relationship of mutual respect within which spiritual conversation may take place.

The danger always lurks, however, that Christianity will be misunderstood as guaranteeing success in worldly affairs. It can be a short step from the testimonies of local celebrities at a Billy Graham crusade to the "health-and-wealth" message of the heretics on the evangelical fringe. As Christians thus appeal to worldly talent, wisdom and accomplishment in order to overcome the prejudices of others, they need deep roots in biblical teaching like 1 Corinthians 1:26-29:

Consider your own call, brothers and sisters: not many of you were wise by human standards, not many were powerful, not many were of noble birth. But God chose what is foolish in the world to shame the wise; God chose what is weak in the world to shame the strong; God chose what is low and despised in the world, things that are not, to reduce to nothing things that are, so that no one might boast in the presence of God.

It may well be, that is, that such Christians must engage in the paradox of exploiting their worldly status in order to win a hearing for a gospel that subverts precisely that status under the grace and glory of God.

The so-called signs and wonders movement champions *power events* as apologetics, implicitly opening up the issue of the miraculous and the even broader issue of power as an appropriate symbol for Christianity. As in biblical times, Christian wonder-workers today continue to face the problem of the correct interpretation of such signs: do the wonders lead people out of preoccupation with their own needs to discipleship and community, or do such blessings ironically confirm people's selfish individualism, as in "What's in it for me?" The challenge now as then is to use the medium of power to convey the Christian message of devotion to God and others, not a message of "God on call" to serve our whims.

A similar hermeneutical problem regarding power and the gospel comes into focus as we consider a typical form of contemporary apologetics, the public debate. When the Christian apologist squares off against his opponent (and I use "his" because I do not know of a single female apologist in this mode—are there grounds here for a feminist critique of this method?), it may appear that this is primarily an intellectual dialogue the purpose of which is to clarify and test various ideas. Of course, this is not so. Instead, we have here fundamentally a power encounter between champions. The typical pattern of enthusiastic attendance at debates versus the smaller attendance at the same apologist's individual lecture the next day indicates that something more elementary is taking place than a lofty exchange of views.

This construal of such events helps to explain why winning is so palpably important. A mere intellectual exchange could be considered worthwhile if everyone left with clearer, truer ideas and a fresh determination to inquire further. But in power events, there must be victor and vanquished. The dangers in such a simple dichotomy are several. Each side is sorely tempted to glorify itself as entirely right and true and to demonize the other as evil and false. Each side is sorely tempted to cheer without reflection any point made by its champion and to denigrate immediately any idea advanced by the opponent. It is bad enough, then, that each side is thus tempted to intellectual polarization with little chance to benefit from the differing views of the other. Worse, though, is the social polarization, with hostility being the only emotion remaining for the other. Worst of all is the spiritual polarization, with the dualism of "we = good" and "they = evil" leading directly to the deadly sin of pride. It may be that debates do not have to reduce to these dynamics, but the question is clear: how can this medium of power convey the gospel of grace?

Consideration of power points us toward acts of *justice and charity* and raises the broader issue of integrity and the even broader issue of moral stature. Consider the Salvation Army's image in the minds of North Americans. Quaint as their uniforms and brass bands may appear, they have a solid reputation for social service that shields them from ridicule and gives them a basis upon which to speak. Mother Teresa has also acquired this moral capital. Again, these two examples remind us we love our neighbor out of obedience to God, not merely as a means to an evangelistic end. Still, acts of justice and charity do indeed express the good news of God's love, and they create grounds upon which Christians can go on to explicitly set out that message.

Finally, the *church* itself as a community stands for the broader category of Christian institutions and points to the overarching question of what Berger calls *plausibility structures*. If churches, parachurch organizations, house fellowships and families are clearly devoted to Christ and Christian fellowship and live out their Christian calling with integrity (with the previous categories of "corollary apologetics" in view), they accomplish something deeply important.[24] These social structures, these created environments, are places in which people can consider the Christian truth-claims as if those claims really might be true. Once inside such structures, inquirers will be able to hear theological and philosophical apologetics because they have been welcomed into a context in which those arguments are now at least incipiently interesting, intelligible and *plausible*.

Apologetics is a matter of theology and philosophy. Quite so: the intellectual defense of the faith has a long and distinguished history and is a continual challenge in the present. Yet since the Christian message is fundamentally an invitation extended to human beings—not just human brains—to encounter the person of Jesus Christ rather than to adopt a doctrinal system or ideology, it is only obvious then that establishing the plausibility and credibility of that message will depend upon more than intellectual argument. It will depend instead upon the Holy Spirit of God shining out through all the lamps of good works we can raise to the glory of our Father in heaven.

# PART II
# THE
# APOLOGETICS
# OF
# MODERNITY

# 4
# SCHLEIERMACHER AS APOLOGIST
## Reclaiming the Father of Modern Theology

*Nicola Hoggard Creegan*

S hall the tangle of history so unravel, that Christianity becomes identified with Barbarism, and science with unbelief?" The apologetic passion of the man who mused on this question, Friedrich Daniel Ernst Schleiermacher (1768-1834), goes largely unheeded today. Still, in the postmodern world of megachurches and television preaching, it is plausible to argue that visible Christianity has indeed become identified with barbarism and science with unbelief. This essay will examine the apologetic vision of the man who thought it possible that the course of history might have been different, even while fearing that it would not be so.

Schleiermacher's theology differed from older Protestant pre-Enlightenment theology in daring to start with human experience and in deemphasizing the fatal fallenness of our reason and passions. While Calvin begins by pointing out the providence of the Creator, even "an awareness of divinity"[1] by which nature instructs us, he nevertheless insists that we cannot know God this way and turns to Scripture as our only point of revelation. Schleiermacher starts with the subject in the world and asserts its dependent nature. Hence we know God as God, not as Redeemer. This is what makes sense of our experience in the world. Where Calvin asserts the broken *imago dei*, Schleiermacher begins with the fragile, corruptible but nevertheless present god-consciousness in all.

In acknowledging this relationship with God through god-consciousness there is a mystical reorientation. The world is not inert but holds the supernatural within it. Human nature is not barren but holds within it the seeds of god-consciousness, which in turn points toward the great incarnation, the full god-consciousness of Christ. From the historic Christ all humanity is then divided into those assumed with him into the corporate body of blessedness and those still encompassed in the corporate body of sinfulness. Thus, subjective consciousness leads us to the incarnation, which in turn leads us to the church. In the church the incarnation is continued by the Word, and the Word proclaimed in the world converts. The vision is an interrelated one, but by beginning with human god-consciousness Schleiermacher has often been accused of anthropomorphizing

God. More recently, however, the considerable theocentrism and christo-centrism of Schleiermacher's work has become evident.[2] So also has the great "paradigm shift" his theology represents, a shift described by George Newlands as largely untapped, yet "in large measure not destructive of the tradition of the gospel, but an instrument of its renewal."[3]

Jaroslav Pelikan, in an essay on Schleiermacher as apologist, argues that betrayal is one of the characteristics of an apologist.[4] Schleiermacher is always almost betraying his cause; he is a betrayer for the cause of the gospel. His forays into the corporate world of sinfulness claim an identi-fication with that world, which he then reorients to the service of his own ends. This betrayal has been taken by his successors and developed into a theology of culture. Schleiermacher's passion for apologetics has been ignored by those who, like him, still desire to convert the world.

## Postmodernity

How is this relevant to the postmodern world? Postmodernity has been described negatively as a time when all absolutes and universals have been lost. It is a time when pluralism has led to relativism in epistemology and in ethics. The great changes of postmodern life and the technological colonization of our culture have led to the marginalization of huge num-bers of people living without natural or well-founded ties or identities. It is a time of drifters. More positively, postmodernity is described as an ethos which has urged tolerance and a voice for all. This ethos has incorporated a more holistic approach to knowledge and has emphasized the role of language in forming and destroying identity. In the postmodern world there is a confusion about how the individual relates to the community. We recognize, as we did not in the modern world, the priority of community and language over the individual. Ironically, we recognize the binding of social constructions of reality, even at a time when more organic human communities are eroding. While the emphasis on the individual is decreas-ing, the individual is still isolated in the postmodern world and is longing for a community which does not exist.

Schleiermacher, despite being the first great theologian of the modern world, seems to speak to postmodernity. His vision is one which explains how the Christian worldview holds together, and this vision and its challenge are still viable within the language of postmodernity. His apologetic undercuts the plurality of viewpoints and constructions of reality. At the same time it immediately points toward a worldview which is corporate and in which nothing has meaning unless it can be explained in relation to God and to Christ.

## Schleiermacher's Speeches

Schleiermacher begins his own early apologetic work with a stunning indictment of unbelief which is still applicable:

> The life of the cultivated person is removed from everything that would in the least way resemble religion . . . in your tasteful dwellings there are no other household gods than the maxims of the sages and the songs of the poets, and humanity and fatherland, art and science have taken possession of your minds so completely that no room is left over for the eternal and holy being that for you lies beyond the world. . . . You have succeeded in making your earthly lives so rich and many-sided that you no longer need the eternal, and after having created a universe for yourselves you are spared from thinking of that which created you.[5]

The work was entitled *On Religion: Speeches to Its Cultured Despisers* and was first published in 1799. This book had its inception in a surprise birthday party for the twenty-nine-year-old Schleiermacher, then a pastor in a remote town and grieving over a broken romance. The party was given by three of his friends, including the Romantic poet Schlegel. They found the faith of their friend to be enigmatic and appealed to him to write a defense.

Schleiermacher had been raised in a deeply pious Moravian community and had already survived a crisis of faith in his late teens. This crisis had left him determined that faith must be rethought in each generation, as each brings its new experience and new questions to old formulations and confessions. He was familiar with Kant and with Enlightenment rationalism, but equally at home with the more artistic style of the new poetic Romanticism. By this stage in his life he had already published treatises on happiness and on freedom, interacting critically with Kant. He was an ordained pastor in the Reformed Church, but was deprecatory of its institutional manifestations and its links to the state.

Thus he wrote the apology, articulating his unique blend of piety, anticlericalism and apologetic zeal. Reflecting on the extent of clerical corruption and the magnitude of misunderstanding of his faith he insists:

> All this I know and am nevertheless convinced to speak by an inner and irresistible necessity that divinely rules me. . . . It is a divine calling; even if it were neither suitable nor prudent to speak of religion, the thing that thus drives me crushes these petty notions with its heavenly power.[6]

In this apology Schleiermacher goes on to respond to the dilemma he articulated at the beginning. How can the church speak to those who feel no need for religion, find it intellectually dishonest and conceive of it only in terms of caricatures? How can the apologist respond to those who see Christianity as too particular an answer amid the diversity and infinity of life and art?

His solution, in this early work, was twofold. He tried both to draw a bridge between the artistic spirit and the religious one and to give a stunning indictment of institutional Christianity and its ties to the state. The famous central thesis of the book is that "true religion is sense and taste for the Infinite."[7] "The contemplation of the pious is the immediate consciousness of the universal existence of all finite things, in and through the Infinite, and of all temporal things in and through the Eternal."[8] "Piety," he reiterates in his later work *The Christian Faith*, "considered purely in itself, [is] neither a knowing nor a doing."[9] It is not primarily morality. It is not primarily speculation or dogma, though thought reflecting upon faith, in the context of the Word, will lead to both. The sense and taste of which Schleiermacher speaks are not a feeling in our modern sense, so much as an intuition, arising from a preordained human capacity for discerning the Divine within the finite.

Schleiermacher continues his argument, claiming that it is precisely this sense of the Infinite which is present also in artistic endeavor. Hence, art and religion should be fellow travelers, not enemies. Those with more artistic spirit, he declares, in "every flight of their spirit to the infinite . . . must set down in pictures or words the impression it made on them. . . . They must . . . represent for others what they have encountered as poets and seers, as orators or as artists. Such people are true priests of the Most High."[10]

This is Schleiermacher the betrayer, identifying so closely with his audience that he seems to side with them against the church. But a similar argument has been made more recently by Diogenes Allen, when he claims that purity, which is a part of God, is what counters evil, and this purity is to be found in those, for example, who study the world, in scientists, and presumably in artists also.[11] Schleiermacher identifies with and applauds his fellow artists for much the same reasons; he senses the power of purity.

The burden of his argument, then, is that there is a connection between the aspirations of the artist and those of the religious spirit. Why does he start with religion and not with Christianity? This was a pattern he was to follow in his magnum opus, *The Christian Faith.* Schleiermacher judges that in the cultural climate at the turn of the nineteenth century, the possibility of *any* type of religion is at stake. In the larger scheme of things Schleier-macher believes that true knowledge of religion requires the particular apprehension of sin and grace in Christian faith. He is not attempting in this work to prove Christianity true. He doesn't really think you can get from "a sense of the Infinite" to the Christian God. He does attempt to push the cultured despisers to look at the greater picture, to see their work within the wider context of meaning which religion would bring and to sense their deprivation without it.

But even these parallels only go so far, as Schleiermacher points out "Religion and art" may "stand beside each other like two friendly souls,"[12] but without religion art must lead to vanity:

Imaginative natures are lacking in penetrating spirit, in the capacity to lay hold of the essential. An easy alternating play of beautiful, often enchanting, but always merely incidental and completely subjective combinations satisfies them and is their highest end; a deeper and more inward connection offers itself in vain to their eyes. They actually only seek the infinity and universality of enticing appearance.[13]

Here Schleiermacher could be referring to postmodern scholarship, to the fascinations of a video culture, to the relentless changing of technologies or simply to the sensory experience of life in a city. It is this very enticing, changing, interplay of art, technology and technique which constitutes the modern world and which tires us so thoroughly, while constantly promising some false resolution. Schleiermacher shows us that that which is beautiful or pure or fascinating, that which is always changing, always promising resolution but never resolving, may be important but also ultimately illusory and false.

In the context of his larger works it is clear that Schleiermacher believes that the Word proclaimed in the church first converts and then brings forth piety, which is then reflected upon in the context of the Word. This reflection leads to morals and doctrine. The problem with the cultured despisers of religion, then and now, is that they fail ever to hear the Word, and so they regard religion as intellectually indefensible. This early work can be seen as an attempt to reorient the unbeliever toward the source of truth. Schleiermacher seems to start with piety, but piety in itself is not ever considered to be the beginning or cause of belief.

### Christmas Eve

The *Speeches* were an attempt at an apology for Christianity, directed very much at individual unbelievers, and barely challenging their highly individual and subjective ethos. But the other side of faith is always the community, that irreducible corporate Word-inspired and inspiring body which cannot be reduced in itself to speeches or to arguments. The *Speeches* did make quite clear that Schleiermacher regarded much of what went on in the institutional church and in its ties to the state as despicable. But the heart of faith lay not in dry secular institutions, nor in individual speeches, but in the corporate life of faith. In a sense, then, the short fictional work *Christmas Eve: Dialogue on the Incarnation* can be seen as complementing the *Speeches*.[14] Written as a Christmas gift for his friends on Christmas Eve, 1804, it portrays the Christmas Eve celebration of a middle-class pious German family and their friends as they exchange gifts, conversation and joy. The star of the early evening is a precocious child, Sophie, who makes music, explains her homemade crèche and muses articulately on the nature of happiness. Eventually the men begin a discussion of the incarnation, someone brings up biblical criticism, and others respond. In the end it is Schleiermacher as Joseph who enters late, reprimands his friends and suggests that they all retire to the piano to sing that which cannot be fully spoken.

At one level this dialogue can be seen as a recommendation of doubt or contentious christology. At a more important level it displays faith as rooted in reflective and rhetorical Word and in the joy shared by that Word. The pious mind was bound to reflect upon the joy, and piety was born of the Word. The evening held what Schleiermacher considered to be a perfect balance of joy, born of a nurturing in the Word, leading to fellowship and discussion and ending in praise.

### The Christian Faith

If we had at hand only the *Speeches*, and even *Christmas Eve*, we would know a very different Schleiermacher. *The Christian Faith*, first written in 1821, represents Schleiermacher the teacher. It is his magnum opus, a systematic work of Christian doctrine, albeit in a different form. It is written for the church but maintains a strong apologetic function. Like Calvin, Schleiermacher seeks to reconcile the Creator God with the Redeemer God. Again like Calvin, Schleiermacher begins with the world and God's creation and preservation of it.

This work is a reflection upon Christian self-consciousness as mediated through the church and its confessions. Schleiermacher debated reversing the usual order of a systematic theology which starts with doctrines of God and proceeds to deal with Christ. In his *Letters to Lücke,* however, he makes clear that he maintained the original order for apologetic reasons.[15] He knew that Christianity was in imminent danger of being threatened by scientific ideologies, and he felt he needed to anticipate and deal with this threat, especially as it pertained to the notions of God and creation and preservation.

### Absolute Dependence

Central to *The Christian Faith* is the idea of absolute dependence, already developed in embryo in the *Speeches,* where he posits our intuition of the Infinite in the finite. We find ourselves always relatively dependent on the world, Schleiermacher claims. We sense that we are both free and passive relative to the world. But in our self-consciousness we intuit also an absolute dependence on a Being over against which we have no freedom. This he refers to as the absolute dependence of ourselves and all life upon God:

> Our whole existence does not present itself to our consciousness as having proceeded from our own spontaneous activity. . . . But the self-consciousness which accompanies all our activity, and therefore . . . accompanies our whole existence, is itself precisely a consciousness of absolute dependence; for it is the consciousness that the whole of our spontaneous activity comes from a source outside of us. The self-identical essence of piety is this: the consciousness of being absolutely dependent, or which is the same thing, of being in relation with God.[16]

This, of course, is the insight which has associated Schleiermacher with the notoriety of subjectivism and anthropomorphism. I would argue, on the contrary, that Schleiermacher is unambiguously positing the existence of the objective God. He is not saying that we can know God this way, or that we can get to God by self-reflection. He is pointing out that our experience fits with the reality that God is there, but that sometimes we need to be shown that it does. All our experience, if observed, points to such a God. The feeling of absolute dependence is the sense which we make of the Absolute God impinging upon our limited reality.

Schleiermacher's claim about an intuition of God is one which is posited as preceding any particular language or culture. Traditionally, Schleiermacher's theology of absolute dependence is seen as leading inevitably to the theories of Feuerbach, Freud and Weber; we project upon the deity our own desires and wishes, individually and corporately. I would argue rather that it undercuts these conceptions. The intuition of which he speaks is one ontologically prior to culture and desire. It cannot be a projection or a wish-fulfillment because it has no content of that kind. And although many have objected to various formulations of this intuition, it is nevertheless of enormous importance to a postmodern apologetic, one which must contend with the relativities presented by multiple viewpoints and constructions of reality. Schleiermacher's answer would be that one can at least know one is absolutely dependent, that this does not require any particular language or culture. God is the prior reality behind all such constructions and entanglements of history.

Absolute dependence and relative freedom are also more generally important as answers to modern assumptions about autonomy. But again, the insight about absolute dependence is gleaned from a position inside the circle of belief. Schleiermacher is not asking an unbeliever to come to God this way. He is trying to show from inside the circle of belief that faith is not subjective, but dependent upon the radically Other, God.

Nor should the emphasis upon absolute dependence be thought of as being experientially based in the way some modern theologies are. Schleiermacher was always insistent that theology not speculate beyond the limits of our experience-based language. We cannot know, for example, what it would have been like to be Adam or Eve because we are separated existentially from them by sin. But he is not arguing here for a theology based upon hegemonic experience. He is intending, at least, to be reflecting upon actual Christian consciousness and hence positing the reality of the

Other, the God on whom all existence depends. The theologian of experience was in fact to write one of the most profound treatises ever written against a doctrine of free will based on our feeling or experience of radical human freedom.[17] One can speculate, then, that Schleiermacher might say of theologies which do begin with hegemonic experience, that although this experience is vital to the church, it must be interrogated by the Word and by reason, rather than acting alone as a hermeneutical standard for the Word.

### The Supernatural in the Natural

Schleiermacher's other central task in *The Christian Faith* was to question the boundaries of the supernatural and the natural. Nature was not to be thought of as dead, inert, mechanical stuff, broken every now and then by miracle or arbitrary intervention and separated starkly from the whole realm of the spiritual. Creation and incarnation may have had extraordinary inceptions, but they continue as naturally or supernaturally as God's order does.[18] Schleiermacher thus spoke of the supernatural in the natural. Here Schleiermacher was not positing an impotent God, a God who does not act, but one who acts constantly in maintaining life and consciousness. He was not positing a God without transcendence, but a God who is immanent in the sense in which Christ said that he lives in us.

One of the legacies of the modern to the postmodern world is a radical disenchantment of nature. Schleiermacher challenges us to reenchant the world, to remythologize the Word. He protests against proof of faith based only on miraculous intervention rather than on contemplation of the wonder of preservation in all its day-to-day manifestations. This emphasis is of course thoroughly Reformed. Calvin or Jonathan Edwards could have made a similar argument. But Schleiermacher's arguments are directed specifically at the intellectual forces emerging in his day which were to continue to affect us deeply into the twentieth century.

Schleiermacher preceded Darwin by a generation, but evolution was already in the air, requiring only the notion of survival of the fittest as its mechanism. Darwin, with his alternative explanation of origins, made explicit and popular the picture of the world as a wound-up clock. With Darwinian evolution, science succeeded in orienting intellectual discussion toward origins. These were then bracketed or explained in terms of survival of the fittest. Schleiermacher reorients us back toward the continuing miracle of the preservation of life.

That Christianity demands such a remythologization is evidenced by the popularity of Christian fantasy; in C. S. Lewis and in Tolkien trees have spirits and animals talk. And the reaction to radical disenchantment is seen in the growth of nature mysticism, the popularity of writers like Matthew Fox and religious movements like Wicca.

### Word and Church

In the second half of *The Christian Faith*, Schleiermacher deals last with what comes chronologically first, the Word, the church and the Redeemer.

Schleiermacher stands in the line of the Protestant Reformation when he describes the church as born of the Word, first in Jesus who communicated to his disciples, then in ever-radiating circles from these first believers through the centuries.

> Now in the first disciples both [conversion and faith] were effected by the Word in its widest sense, that is by the whole prophetic activity of Christ. And we must be able to understand this that we have in common with them. . . . The constant factor is above all the divine power of the Word . . . by which conversion is still effected and faith still arises.[19]

Everywhere the Word is proclaimed the church is formed. The "totality of those on whom preparatory grace is at work," he says, "is the outer fellowship, from which by regeneration members pass to the inner, and then keep helping to extend the wider circle."[20] Schleiermacher also believes that the ministry of the Word, though centered in the preaching ministry, is common to all Christians as they share the Word with each other, the stronger helping the weaker. The experience of sin and grace and the priority of the Word are the cornerstones of faith for Schleiermacher, but of particular, experiential faith in Jesus Christ. This is not where he begins, because he is always making connections with everything else, with the human being in a state of unbelief, with nature and with art.consciousness. Schleiermacher was

Schleiermacher's theology of Word has weaknesses, but it is a powerful expression of what it means to live within the space of the Word, to be drawn in by its power, to be converted and to live within it—no longer passively being acted upon but actively proclaiming. He gives us a convincing theology of Word-as-community and of the laity-in-proclamation. He emphasizes theologically what contemporary sociologists and theologians like Bellah and Lindbeck have insisted upon: to reclaim the world, to make faith a participant in the postmodern dialogue, we must recover the Word as life-forming; we must live within its contours and teach it to our children.[21]

## Schleiermacher's Despisers

The postmodern world is nothing if not rhetorical, and Schleiermacher would be the first to insist that we interrogate him. We might ask of his theology whether it does justice to sin and depravity. And is the notion of absolute dependence really as free of cultural preconditioning as Schleiermacher claims? These are complex questions, each demanding yet another paper in response. Only a schematic answer can be given here.

First, then, does Schleiermacher underestimate sin and depravity? Does the postmodern person require a strong conviction of sin or an affirmation of god-consciousness in order to be converted? The true Calvinist, of course, would spurn any thought of unfallen god-consciousness. Schleiermacher was a hopeful and irenic man. Affirmation may be central in his apologetic theology, but he does not underestimate sin. He details the multiple ways in which god-consciousness can be twisted.[22] He understands the structural and corrupting nature of sin in his designation of the corporate world of sinfulness, and he chides parents to remember to instruct their children not to rely on the false righteousness of good behavior.[23] But nowhere is his acceptance of depravity more evident than in his insistence—in his later theology, at least—of the need for conversion from the state of sinfulness to the corporate world of blessedness. In *The Christian Faith* he emphasizes:

> In the condition left behind, the stirrings of a self-consciousness suffused with a consciousness of God were never determinative of the will, being but causal and fleeting; the sensuous consciousness alone was determinative. When life is linked to Christ it is the other way about, and this change is expressed by the term "conversion." . . . Conversion, the beginning of the new life in fellowship with Christ, makes itself known in each individual by repentance, which consists in the combination of regret and change of heart; and by Faith, which consists in the appropriation of the perfection and blessedness of Christ.[24]

Schleiermacher then goes on to warn of the dangers of Pelagianism and naturalism in not defining a boundary between belief and unbelief. And he concludes that "in the unenlightened man who has only an outward connection with Christianity we may indeed trace many a Christian feature, which nevertheless is not in him a thing of living power, but merely the reflection of what is present as a reality in others."[25]

Second, how can we answer the claim that Schleiermacher's "absolute dependence" is merely a social-cultural construction of reality masquerading as a bedrock prelinguistic experience? This charge is all the more confusing because it is taken in two different ways. Liberal theology, stemming from the nineteenth century, sees in the social constructions of reality a deception that undermines all religion. But George A. Lindbeck, in the twentieth century, seeks to reclaim the integrity of theology over time by emphasizing the linguistic-cultural construction of all religion over against any prelinguistic experiential-expressive conceptions.

Schleiermacher, does, of course, claim that "absolute dependence" is prelinguistic, but not that it can be accessed prelinguistically. "Piety," he says, "is a matter of feeling, sense, or logic distinct from and prior to concepts of belief."[26] The feeling of absolute dependence, however, is said to be "awakened . . . by the communicative and stimulative power of utterance."[27] And his description of "absolute dependence" is manifestly couched in the language of the Reformed community of faith, the philosophical and scientific conceptions of causality, and the emerging mathematical language of infinity. If we were to describe breathing, though it be beyond our conscious control, it would similarly require a sophisticated scientific, consciously manipulated language. But the breathing itself is not thereby the construction of this language. "Absolute dependence" may, of course, be a projection of our wishes, a construction of reality or an experience shaped by a particular language community. But Schleiermacher goes to great pains to use it apologetically, to point out how this dependence functions in the languages of science and arts, and how it is at this point that bridges are possible with the language of theology. Much of this theology is directed at explaining how "absolute dependence" fits with the language of the confessions of Christian belief throughout history.

The ubiquitous nature of this "absolute dependence" lends plausibility to the argument that if there is any reality, Holy Reality, or bedrock behind language—and Schleiermacher believes that there is—then this absolute dependence does indeed point to such a Reality. If there is any movement at all from reality or prelinguistic experience to language, then "absolute dependence" is behind such a movement.

On the other hand the overall thrust of Schleiermacher's theology, as noted above, can be seen to be much more cultural-linguistic than Lindbeck might suggest. Schleiermacher does see faith as a language, but his overall vision is of a movement in two directions, from experience to language and back again. "Christianity has created language," he says. "From its very beginning it has a potentiating linguistic spirit, and it still has."[28] If, however, there is any point at which the prelinguistic modifies the linguistic, it is in the sense of absolute dependence.

## Conclusion
Schleiermacher, like any great theologian, will at times be exasperating, at

times blinded by the biases of his time. But the coherence of his overall vision is strong enough to take a rhetorical criticism and to yield wisdom in the postmodern world.

In a world in which the center so often fails to hold, Schleiermacher's immense contribution is in giving a comprehensive view of how the believing world hangs together, how the individual relates to the church and to the unbeliever, how the individual relates to God, and how Christ, Spirit and Word are church and body forming. He makes sense of our capacities for freedom and creativity, of our finitude while searching for infinitude and of our grappling with sin and grace, with barbarism and with unbelief. He understands the purity of the cultured unbeliever's calling even while he demonstrates its final falsity. And he demonstrates the imperative that each generation is called anew to conversion and to the reexpression of the Christian gospel.

# 5
# POLITICALLY
# INCORRECT
# SALVATION
*William Lane Craig*

Diversity" is the shibboleth of the postmodern age. Nowhere is this more so than in the realm of theology or religious studies. Harvard theologian Gordon Kaufman, observing that throughout most of Christian church history "the fundamental truth of the basic Christian claim was taken for granted, as was the untruth . . . of the claims of the church's opponents," says that by contrast today there has been "a striking change" among many Christian theologians:

> Instead of continuing the traditional attempts to make definitive normative claims about "Christian truth" or "the Christian revelation," many now see the plurality among religious traditions . . . as [itself] of profound human meaning and importance: what seems required now, therefore, rather than polemical pronouncements, is careful and appreciative study, together with an attitude of openness to what can be learned from this great diversity.[1]

According to Kaufman, religious diversity calls for a response of openness, and openness is incompatible with normative truth claims and polemical pronouncements (that is, apologetics). Why is this so? Allan Bloom, I think, puts his finger on the answer when he observes that there is a pervasive conviction in our culture that "relativism is necessary to openness; and this is the virtue, the only virtue, which all primary education for more than fifty years has dedicated itself to inculcating. Openness—and the relativism that makes it the only plausible stance in the face of various claims to truth . . . is the great insight of our times."[2] Religious diversity thus calls for a response of openness, and a necessary condition of openness is relativism. Since religious relativism is obviously incompatible with the objective truth of Christianity, religious diversity implies that normative Christian truth claims can be neither made nor defended.

Thus, we are led to the paradoxical result that in the name of religious diversity traditional Christianity is delegitimated and marginalized.

### Religious Diversity and Objective Truth
But why think that the alleged links between religious diversity and

openness on the one hand and between openness and relativism on the other are so firmly forged? Why cannot someone who believes in the normative truth of the Christian worldview, as it comes to expression in the catholic creeds, for instance, be open to seeing truth in and learning from other world religions? Arthur Holmes has taught generations of Wheaton College students that "all truth is God's truth," regardless of where it is to be found. The orthodox Christian has no reason to think that *all* the truth claims made by other world religions are false, but only those that are incompatible with Christian truth claims. So why must one be a relativist in order to be open to truth in other world religions?

No doubt the postmodernist answer to that question will be that the openness I contemplate here is insufficient; it opens the door only a crack. But religious diversity beckons us to throw open the doors of our minds to the legitimacy of religious truth claims logically incompatible with those of the Christian faith. Religious diversity requires us to view these supposedly competing claims as equally true as, or no less true than, or as equally efficacious as, Christian truth claims.

But why does religious diversity imply *this* sort of openness? The postmodernist is advocating much more than mere intellectual humility here. The postmodernist is not merely saying that we cannot know with certainty which religious worldview is true and we therefore must be open-minded; rather he maintains that *none* of the religious worldviews is objectively true, and therefore none can be excluded in deference to the allegedly one true religion.

But why think such a thing? Why could not the Christian worldview be objectively true? How does the mere *presence* of religious worldviews incompatible with Christianity show that distinctively Christian claims are not true? Logically, the existence of multiple, incompatible truth claims only implies that *all* of them cannot be (objectively) true; but it would be obviously fallacious to infer that not one of them is (objectively) true. So why could it not be the case that a personal God exists and has revealed himself decisively in Jesus Christ, just as biblical Christianity affirms?

More than that, it needs to be seriously questioned whether the post-modernist, pluralistic position even makes sense. Here we need to ask ourselves what it means to say that an assertion is true and how we may test for truth. A statement or proposition is (objectively) true if and only if it corresponds to reality, that is to say, if reality is just as the statement says that it is. Thus, the statement "The Cubs won the 1993 World Series" is true if and only if the Cubs won the 1993 World Series. In order to show a proposition to be true, we present evidence in the form of either deductive or inductive arguments which have that proposition as the conclusion. In both sorts of reasoning, logic and factual evidence are the keys to showing soundly that a conclusion is true. Since a proposition that is logically contradictory is necessarily false and so cannot be the conclusion of a sound argument, and since a proposition validly inferred from factually true premises ought to be regarded as factually true, one may generalize these notions to say that a worldview ought to be regarded as true only if it is logically consistent and fits all the facts known in our experience. Such a test for truth has been called *systematic consistency*: "consistency" meaning obedience to the laws of logic and "systematic" meaning fitting all the facts known by experience.[3] Although such a test *precludes* the truth of any worldview which fails it, it does not *guarantee* the truth of a worldview which passes it. For more than one view could be consistent and fit all the facts yet known by experience; or again, a view which is systematically consistent with all that we now know could turn out to be falsified by future discoveries. Systematic consistency thus underdetermines world-views, and so (as in the case of all inductive reasoning) we must be content with plausibility or likelihood, rather than rational certainty.

Now under the influence of Eastern mysticism, many people today would deny that systematic consistency is a test for truth. They affirm that reality is ultimately illogical or that logical contradictions correspond to reality. They assert that in Eastern thought the Absolute or God or the Real transcends the logical categories of human thought. They are apt to interpret the demand for logical consistency as a piece of Western imperialism which ought to be rejected along with other vestiges of colonialism.

What such people seem to be saying is that the classical law of thought known as the Law of Excluded Middle is not necessarily true, that is to say, they deny that of a proposition and its negation, necessarily, one is true and the other is false. Such a denial could take two different forms. (1) It could be interpreted on the one hand to mean that a proposition and its negation *both* can be true (or both false). Thus, it is true both that God is love and, in the same sense, that God is not love. Since both are true, the Law of Contradiction, that a proposition and its negation cannot both be true (or both false) at the same time, is also denied. (2) On the other hand, the original denial could be interpreted to mean that of a proposition and its negation *neither* may be true (or neither false). Thus, it is not true that God is good and it is not true that God is not good; there is just no truth value at all for such propositions. In this case it is the classical Principle of Bivalence—that for any proposition, necessarily that proposition is either true or false—that is denied along with the Law of Excluded Middle.

Now I am inclined to say frankly that such positions are crazy and unintelligible. To say that God is both good and not good in the same sense or that God neither exists nor does not exist is just incomprehensible to me. In our politically correct age, there is a tendency to vilify all that is Western and to exalt Eastern modes of thinking as at least equally valid if not superior to Western modes of thought. To assert that Eastern thought is seriously deficient in making such claims is to be a sort of epistemological bigot, blinkered by the constraints of the logic-chopping Western mind.

But this judgment is far too simplistic. In the first place, there are thinkers within the tradition of Western thought who have held the mystical views in question (Plotinus would be a good example), so that there is no warrant for playing off East against West in this matter. Second, the extent to which such thinking represents "the Eastern mind" has been greatly exaggerated. In the East the common man—and the philosopher, too—lives by the Laws of Contradiction and Excluded Middle throughout everyday life; he affirms them every time he walks through a doorway rather than into the wall. It is only at an extremely theoretical level of philosophical speculation that such laws are denied. And even at that level, the situation is not monochromatic: Confucianism, Hinayana Buddhism, pluralistic Hinduism as exemplified in Sankhya-Yoga, Vaishesika-Nyaya and Mimasa schools of thought and even Jainism do not deny the application of the classical laws of thought to ultimate reality.[4] Thus, a critique of Eastern thought from within Eastern thought itself can be—and has been—made. We in the West should not therefore be embarrassed or apologetic about our heritage; on the contrary, it is one of the glories of ancient Greece that its thinkers came to enunciate clearly the principles of logical reasoning, and the triumph of logical reasoning over competing modes of thought in the West has been one of the West's greatest strengths and proudest achievements.

Why think then that such self-evident truths as the principles of logic are in fact invalid for ultimate reality? Such a claim seems to be both self-refuting and arbitrary. For consider a claim like "God cannot be described by propositions governed by the Principle of Bivalence." If such a claim is true, then it is not true, since it itself is a proposition describing God and so has no truth value. Thus, such a claim refutes itself. Of course, if it is not true, then it is not true, as the Eastern mystic alleged, that God cannot be described by propositions governed by the Principle of Bivalence. Thus, if the claim is not true, it is not true, and if it is true, it is not true, so that in either case the claim turns out to be not true.

Or consider the claim that "God cannot be described by propositions governed by the Law of Contradiction." If this proposition is true, then, since it describes God, it is not itself governed by the Law of Contradiction. Therefore, it is equally true that "God can be described by propositions governed by the Law of Contradiction." But then which propositions are these? There must be some, for the Eastern mystic is committed to the truth of this claim. But if he produces any, then they immediately refute his original claim that there are no such propositions. His claim thus commits him to the existence of counterexamples which serve to refute that very claim.[5]

Furthermore, apart from the issue of self-refutation, the mystic's claim is wholly arbitrary. Indeed, no reason can ever be given to justify denying the validity of logical principles for propositions about God. For the very statement of such reasons, such as "God is too great to be captured by categories of human thought" or "God is wholly other," involves the affirmation of certain propositions about God which are governed by the principles in question. In short, the denial of such principles for propositions about ultimate reality is completely and essentially arbitrary.

Some Eastern thinkers realize that their position, as a position, is ultimately self-refuting and arbitrary, and so they are driven to deny that their position really is a position! They claim rather than their position is just a technique pointing to the transcendent Real beyond all positions. But if this claim is not flatly self-contradictory, as it would appear, if such thinkers literally *have no position*, then there just is nothing here to assess and they have nothing to say. This stupefied silence is perhaps the most eloquent testimony for the bankruptcy of the denial of the principles of logical reasoning.

This same debate between certain Eastern mystical modes of thought and classical logical thinking is being replayed in the debate between modernism and radical postmodernism. I want to say clearly that I carry no brief for Enlightenment theological rationalism. According to this modernist viewpoint, religious beliefs are rational if and only if one has evidence on which those beliefs are based. While I am convinced that there *is* sufficient evidence to make Christian belief rational, I do not believe that such evidence is necessary for Christian belief to be rational.[6] Not only is theological rationalism predicated on an epistemological foundationalism which is overly restrictive and finally self-refuting, but the Christian belief system itself teaches that the ground of our knowledge of the truth of the Christian faith is the self-authenticating witness of the Holy Spirit (Rom 8:15-16; 1 Jn 5:7-9). Argumentation and evidence may serve as confirmations of Christian beliefs and as means of showing to others the truth of those beliefs, but they are not properly the foundation of those beliefs. In a sense, then, my own religious epistemology could be called postmodern, and the provisional character of systematic consistency accords with the intellectual humility advocated by postmodernism.

But radical postmodernists would scorn these sops. They would regard me (perhaps justifiably!) as hopelessly premodern. They reject altogether Western rationality and metaphysics, claiming that there is no objective truth about reality. "The truth," as John Caputo says, "is that there is no truth."[7] But such a claim falls prey to precisely the same objections that I raised above.[8] Indeed, the postmodernist claim is not really distinguishable from certain Buddhist philosophies. To assert that "the truth is that there is no truth" is both self-refuting and arbitrary. For if this statement is true, it is not true, since there is no truth. So-called deconstructionism thus cannot be halted from deconstructing itself. Moreover, there is also no reason for adopting the postmodern perspective rather than, say, the outlooks of Western capitalism, male chauvinism, white racism and so forth, since postmodernism has no more truth to it than these perspectives. Caught in this self-defeating trap, some postmodernists have been forced to the same recourse as Buddhist mystics: denying that postmodernism is really a view or position at all. But then, once again, why do they continue to write books and talk about it? They are obviously making some cognitive claims—and if not, then they literally have nothing to say and no objection to our employment of the classical canons of logic.

### The Offense of Christian Particularism

So I ask again: Why could not the Christian worldview be objectively true? Here we come to the nub of the issue. The problem seen by postmodernists is that if the Christian religion is objectively true, then multitudes of people belonging to other religious traditions find themselves excluded from salvation, often through no fault of their own but due simply to historical and geographical accident, and therefore destined to hell or annihilation.[9] Many theologians find this situation morally unconscionable and have therefore abandoned the objective truth of Christianity in favor of various forms of religious relativism.

My own doctoral mentor John Hick is illustrative. Hick began his career as a fairly conservative Christian theologian. Then he began to study more closely the other world religions. Though he had always had, of course, an awareness of these competing worldviews, he had not come to know and appreciate their adherents personally. As he learned to know some of the selfless, saintly persons in these other traditions, it became unthinkable to him that they should all be condemned to hell. These religions must be as equally valid channels of salvation as the Christian faith. But Hick realized that this meant denying the uniqueness of Jesus; somehow he and his exclusivistic claims must be got out of the way. He therefore came to regard the deity and Incarnation of Christ as a myth or metaphor.[10] Today Hick is no longer even a theist, since what he calls "the Real," which is apprehended in the various world religions under culturally conditioned and objectively false religious paradigms, has objectively none of the distinctive properties of the God of theism.

Universalism is thus the raison d'être for the response of openness to religious diversity thought to be required by postmodernist thinkers.[11] Total openness and religious relativism spring from an abhorrence of Christian particularism.

The situation is not, however, so simple as it might at first seem. There are a number of distinctions that need to be made here which are often blurred. On the one hand there is the distinction between universalism and particularism of which I have spoken. *Universalism* is the doctrine that all human persons will partake of God's salvation; *particularism* holds that only some, but not all, human persons will partake of God's salvation. Particularism ranges between *broad* and *narrow* versions, one extreme being that scarcely any shall be lost in comparison with the saved and the other extreme that scarcely any shall be saved in comparison with the lost.

A second set of distinctions needs to be made between *pluralism, inclusivism* and *exclusivism*. Christian exclusivism is the doctrine that salvation is appropriated only on the basis of Christ's work and through faith in him.

Although exclusivism is most naturally associated with particularism, this is not necessary: Thomas Talbott, for example, would be one who is both a Christian exclusivist and a universalist, holding that hell is at worst a purgatory through which people pass until they freely place their faith in Christ and are saved.[12]

Christian inclusivism is the doctrine that salvation is appropriated only on the basis of Christ's work, but not necessarily through explicit faith in him. The term *inclusivism* has been misused to denominate the doctrine that salvation is *available* to all persons on the basis of Christ's work, but not necessarily through explicit faith in him.[13] Analogously, *exclusivism* has been misused to refer to the doctrine that salvation is *available* only on the basis of Christ's work and through faith in him. These represent a misuse of terms, because on these definitions those who are saved could be extensionally equivalent—that is, the very same persons—whether inclusivism or exclusivism is true.[14] For clearly, that salvation is *available* to more people under inclusivism than exclusivism, so defined, does not imply that more people actually *avail* themselves of salvation under inclusivism than under exclusivism. It seems perverse to call a view inclusivistic if it does not actually include any more people in salvation than so-called exclusivism.

Rather, the distinction that has been mislabeled here is between what may be more appropriately dubbed *accessibilism* and *restrictivism*. Restrictivists typically maintain that salvation is accessible only through the hearing of the gospel and faith in Christ. Accessibilists maintain that persons who never hear the gospel can avail themselves of salvation through their response to God's general revelation alone.

Genuine inclusivists believe that salvation is not merely accessible to but is actually accessed by persons who never hear the gospel. Inclusivism may be broad or narrow, ranging all the way from universalism to narrow particularism.

Although a broad inclusivism has become increasingly popular among Christian theologians who want to maintain the truth of Christianity in the face of religious diversity, the view faces severe biblical and missiological objections. Biblically, the teaching of the New Testament and of our Lord himself seems to be that while the harvest of redeemed persons will be multitudinous, the number of the lost will be also and perhaps even more multitudinous (Mt 7:13-14; 24:9-12; Lk 18:8). In particular, the fate of those who have not placed their faith explicitly in Christ for salvation seems bleak indeed (Rom 1:18-32; Eph 2:12; 4:17-19).

Missiologically, a broad inclusivism undermines the task of world mission. Since vast numbers of persons in non-Christian religions are in fact already included in salvation, they need not be evangelized. Instead missions are reinterpreted along the lines of social engagement—a sort of Christian peace corps, if you will. Nowhere is this reinterpretation of missions better illustrated than in the documents of the Second Vatican Council. In its *Dogmatic Constitution on the Church,* the council declared that those who have not yet received the gospel are related in various ways to the people of God.[15] Jews, in particular, remain dear to God, but the plan of salvation also includes all who acknowledge the Creator, such as Muslims. The council therefore declared that Catholics now pray *for* the Jews, not for the *conversion* of the Jews, and also declares that the church looks with esteem upon Muslims.[16] Missionary work seems to be directed only toward those who "serve the creature rather than the Creator" or are utterly hopeless. The council thus implied that vast multitudes of persons who consciously reject Christ are in fact saved and therefore not appropriate targets for evangelization.

Unfortunately, this same perspective has begun to make inroads into evangelical theology. At a meeting of the Evangelical Theology Group at the American Academy of Religion convention in San Francisco in November 1992, Clark Pinnock declared, "I am appealing to evangelicals to make the shift to a more inclusive outlook, much the way the Catholics did at Vatican II."[17] Pinnock expresses optimism that great numbers of the unevangelized will be saved. "God will find faith in people without the persons even realizing he/she had it." He even entertains the possibility of people's being given another chance after death, once they have been freed from "whatever obscured the love of God and prevented them from receiving it in life." This move leads immediately to universalism, as Talbott recognizes, since once people are free of everything that prevented their receiving salvation then, of course, they will receive it! Pinnock poses the question whether his inclusivism does not undermine the rationale and urgency of world mission. No, he answers, for (1) God has called us to engage in mission work and we should obey. But this provides no rationale for why God commanded such a thing and so amounts to just blind obedience to a command that has no rationale. (2) Missions is broader than just securing people's eternal destiny. True enough; but with that central rationale removed we are back to the Christian peace corps. (3) Missions should be positive; it is not an ultimatum "Believe or be damned." Of course; but it is difficult to see what urgency is left to world missions, since the people to whom one goes are already saved. I must confess that I find it tragically ironic that as the church stands on the verge of completing the task of world evangelization,[18] it should be the church's own theologians who would threaten to trip it at the finish line.

Finally, *pluralism* is the doctrine that salvation, or what passes for salvation, is appropriated by persons through a multiplicity of conditions and means in various religions. One would naturally associate pluralism with universalism, but that is not strictly necessary, for a religious pluralist could regard some religions—say, those that focus on human sacrifice or cultic prostitution—as not furnishing legitimate avenues of salvation, if salvation is defined solely in "this-worldly" terms (for example, the production of a saintly character). If the pluralist is motivated to solve the problem of persons' being excluded from salvation by historical or geographical accident, however, then he must hold that salvation is accessible through every religion. Otherwise the unfortunates who languish in degenerate religions would be excluded from salvation.

### The Problem with Christian Particularism
Now with those distinctions in mind, let us examine the problem before

us more closely. What exactly is the problem with Christian particularism supposed to be?

Is it simply that a loving God would not consign people to hell? It does not seem to be. For the New Testament makes it quite clear that God's will and desire is that all persons should be saved and come to a knowledge of the truth (2 Pet 3:9; 1 Tim 2:4). He therefore draws all people to himself by his prevenient grace. People who make a free and well-informed decision to reject Christ thus seal their own fate: they are self-condemned. In a sense, then, God does not send anybody to hell; rather people send themselves.

In response to these considerations, Marilyn Adams complains that damnation is so inconceivable a horror that human beings cannot fully understand the consequences of choosing for or against God.[19] She infers that they cannot exercise their free choice in this matter "with fully open eyes" and intimates that they should not be held fully responsible for such a choice. She goes on to argue that the consequences of sin (namely, hell) are so disproportionate to the sinful acts themselves that to make a person's eternal destiny hinge on refraining from such acts is to place unreasonable expectations on that person. God's punishing people with hell would be both cruel and unusual punishment: cruel because the conditions placed on them are unreasonable and unusual because *any* sin, small or great, consigns one to hell.

A great deal could be said about Adams's reservations, but a little reflection shows most of them to be simply inapplicable to the situation as I envision it. First of all, Adams seems to assume that the consequences of sin are optional for God, that he could have simply chosen to absolve and sanctify everyone if he pleased. But for God simply to pardon all sin regardless of the response of the perpetrator would be for God merely to blink at moral evil. If God left the impenitent sinner unpunished, his holiness would be compromised and he would not be just. And even if God determined to absolve everyone, how could he sanctify the impenitent without violating their free will? So long as God respects the human freedom he has bestowed, he cannot guarantee that everyone can be made willing and fit for heaven. Thus, the consequences of sin are not arbitrarily up to God. They follow from the necessity of his moral nature and the character of human agency. The question, then, is really whether God was being cruel in creating significantly free creatures at all.

I do not think that Adams's argument shows that he was. Her argument concerns the undue burden laid on people by God's placing them in a situation in which they will go to hell unless they refrain from every single sin, no matter how small. But this is not our situation as I understand it. The orthodox Christian need not hold that every sin merits hell or has hell as its consequence; rather hell is the final consequence (and even just punishment) for those who irrevocably refuse to seek and accept God's forgiveness of their sins. By refusing God's forgiveness they freely separate themselves from God forever. The issue, then, is whether the necessity of making this fundamental decision is too much to ask of a human being.

We may agree with Adams that no one fully comprehends the horror of hell—or, for that matter, the bliss of heaven—and therefore fully grasps the consequences of his decision to accept or reject God's salvation. But it does not follow that God's giving people the freedom to determine their eternal destiny is therefore placing too heavy a responsibility on them. One need not understand the *full* consequences of heaven and hell in order to be able to choose responsibly between them. It is not unreasonable to expect of people that they should be able to decide *a fortiori* between infinite loss and infinite gain simply on the basis of their comprehension of the choice of enormous loss versus enormous gain. To deny to humanity the freedom to make this decision would be to side with Dostoyevsky's Grand Inquisitor in holding that God ought to have given us earthly bread and circuses rather than the Bread of Heaven because we cannot bear so dread a freedom.[20]

Moreover, Adams has left wholly out of account what I conceive to be an absolutely crucial element in this story: the prevenient grace of God mediated by the Holy Spirit. God has not left us to make this momentous choice on our own; rather it is the work of the Holy Spirit to convict people of sin and righteousness and judgment (Jn 16:8) and to draw them to himself (Jn 6:44). God lovingly solicits and enables the human will to place its faith in Christ. The exercise of saving faith is not a work we perform for salvation, but merely the allowing of the Holy Spirit to do his work in us. Far from making unreasonable expectations, God is ready to equip anyone for salvation. We have only not to resist. When someone refuses to come to Christ and be saved, therefore, it is only because he has willfully ignored and rejected the drawing of God's Spirit on his heart. Therefore, I cannot see that in providing us with the freedom to determine our destiny by deciding for or against Christ, God has placed an unreasonable demand upon us.

Well, then, could the problem with Christian particularism be that God would not consign people to hell because they were uninformed or misinformed about Christ? Again, this does not seem to me to be the problem. For here the Christian may advocate some form of accessibilism. We can maintain that God does not judge those who have not clearly heard of Christ on the same basis as those who have. Rather we can, on the basis of Romans 1—2, maintain that God judges persons who have not heard the gospel on the basis of God's general revelation in nature and conscience. Were they to respond to the much lower demands placed on them by general revelation, God would give them eternal life (Rom 2:7). Salvation is thus universally accessible. Unfortunately the testimony of Scripture is that people do not in general live up to even these meager demands and are therefore lost. No one is unjustly condemned, however, since God has provided sufficient grace to all persons for salvation. Perhaps some do access salvation by means of general revelation, but if we take Scripture seriously we must admit that these are relatively few. In such a case, at most a narrow version of inclusivism would be true. Thus, given accessibilism, I do not see that Christian particularism is undermined simply by God's condemnation of persons who are not clearly informed about Christ.

Rather the real problem with Christian particularism is much more subtle. If God is all-knowing, then presumably he knew the conditions under which people would freely place their faith in Christ for salvation and those under which they would not.[21] But then a very difficult question arises: why does God not bring the gospel to people who he knows would accept it if they heard it, even though they reject the general revelation that they do have? Imagine, for example, a Native American—let us call him Walking Bear—who lived prior to the arrival of Christian missionaries. Suppose Walking Bear sees from the order and beauty of nature around him that a Creator of the universe exists and that he senses in his heart the demands of God's moral law implanted there. Unfortunately, like those described by Paul in Romans 1, Walking Bear chooses to spurn the Creator and to ignore the demands of the moral law, plunging himself into spiritism and immorality. Thus suppressing the knowledge of God and flouting his moral law, Walking Bear stands under God's just condemnation and is destined for hell. But suppose that if only Walking Bear were to hear the gospel, if only the Christian missionaries had come earlier, then he would have believed in the gospel and been saved. His damnation then appears to be the result of bad luck; through no fault of his own he was born at the wrong place or time in history; his salvation or damnation thus seems to be the result of historical and geographical accident. Granted that his condemnation is not *unjust* (since he has freely spurned God's sufficient grace for salvation), nonetheless is it not *unloving* of God to condemn him? Would not an all-loving God have given him the same advantage that is enjoyed by that lucky individual who lives at a place and time such that he hears the gospel? Now Walking Bear's situation is essentially no different from the billions of people living today who have yet to hear a clear presentation of the gospel. Is not God cruel and unloving to condemn them?

It will be no good trying to answer this problem by any form of Christian inclusivism short of virtual universalism. The difficulty with Christian inclusivism is not simply that it goes too far in its unscriptural optimism that vast numbers of persons in non-Christian religions will be saved. Rather in truth it does not go far enough: for inclusivism makes no provision for those who do reject God's general revelation and so are condemned, but who *would have* accepted God's special revelation and been saved, if only they had heard it. Because inclusivism deals only in the indicative mood, so to speak, it is impotent to resolve a problem framed in the subjunctive mood.

## A Solution to the Problem of Particularism

Let us therefore make a fresh start on this problem. What is the logical structure of the objection to Christian particularism? The claim seems to be that Christian particularism is internally inconsistent in affirming on the one hand that God is all-powerful and all-loving and on the other that some people never hear the gospel and are lost. But why think that these two affirmations are inconsistent? After all, there is no *explicit* contradiction between them. So the postmodernist or universalist must think that these two statements are *implicitly* contradictory. But in that case there must be some hidden assumptions which need to be surfaced in order to show that these two statements are in fact inconsistent. But what are these hidden assumptions?

The detractor of Christian particularism seems to be making two hidden assumptions:

1. If God is all-powerful, then he can create a world in which everybody hears the gospel and is freely saved.

2. If God is all-loving, then he prefers a world in which everybody hears the gospel and is freely saved.

Both of these assumptions must be necessarily true if Christian particularism is to be shown to be inconsistent.

But are they necessarily true? I think not. Consider the first assumption. I think we should agree that an all-powerful God can create a world in which everybody hears the gospel. But so long as people are free, there is simply no guarantee that everybody in that world would be freely saved. To be sure, God could force everyone to repent and be saved by overpowering their wills, but that would be a sort of divine rape, not a free acceptance of salvation. It is logically impossible to *make* someone do something *freely*. So long as God desires free creatures, then, even he cannot guarantee that all will freely embrace his salvation. In fact, there is not even any guarantee that the balance between saved and lost in that totally evangelized world would be any better than it is in the actual world! It certainly seems possible that in any world of free creatures which God could create, some people would freely reject his salvation and be lost.

The possibility that the first assumption is false already invalidates the argument against Christian particularism. But there is more: the second assumption does not seem necessarily true either. Let us concede that there are in fact possible worlds in which everyone hears the gospel and is freely saved. Does God's being all-loving compel him to prefer one of these worlds to be the actual world? Not necessarily; for these worlds might have overriding deficiencies in other respects. Suppose, for example, that the only worlds in which everybody hears and believes the gospel are worlds with only a handful of people in them. In any world in which God creates more people, at least one person refuses to receive God's salvation. Now I ask you: must God prefer one of these radically underpopulated worlds to a world in which multitudes do freely receive his salvation, even though others freely reject it? I think not. So long as God provides sufficient grace for salvation to every person in any world he creates, he is no less loving for preferring one of the more populous worlds, even though that implies that some people would freely reject him and be lost.

Thus, neither of the assumptions underlying the objection to Christian particularism is necessarily true. It follows that no inconsistency has been shown in affirming both that God is all-powerful and all-loving and that some people never hear the gospel and are lost.

But we can go one step further. We can actually show that it is entirely consistent to affirm that God is all-powerful and all-loving and yet that many persons do not hear the gospel and are lost. Since God is good and loving, he wants as many people as possible to be saved and as few as possible to be lost. His goal, then, is to achieve an optimal balance between these—to create no more of the lost than is necessary to attain a certain number of the saved. But it is possible that the actual world (speaking here of the whole history of the world, past, present and future) has such an optimal balance! It is possible that in order to create this many people who are saved, God also had to create this many people who are lost. It is possible that had God created a world in which fewer people go to hell, then even fewer people would have gone to heaven. It is possible that in order to create a multitude of saints, God had to create an even greater multitude of sinners.

But then what about persons who will in fact be lost because they never hear the gospel, but who would have been freely saved if only they had heard it? The solution proposed thus far preserves God's goodness and love on a global scale, but on an individual level surely an all-loving God would have done more to achieve such a person's salvation by ensuring that the gospel reaches him. But how do we know that there are any such persons? It is reasonable to assume that many people who never hear the gospel would not have believed it even if they had heard it. Suppose, then, that God has so providentially ordered the world that *all* persons who never hear the gospel are precisely such people. In that case, anybody who never hears the gospel and is lost would have rejected the gospel and been lost even if he had heard it. In supplying such persons with sufficient grace for salvation, even though he knows they will reject it, God is already exhibiting extraordinary love toward them, and bringing the gospel would be of no additional material benefit to them. Hence, no one could stand before God on the judgment day and complain, "Sure, God, I didn't respond to your revelation in nature and conscience. All right. But if only I had heard the gospel, *then* I would have believed!" God will say to them, "No, I knew that even if you had heard the gospel, you still would not have believed. Therefore, my judgment of you on the basis of my revelation in nature and conscience is neither unloving nor unfair."

Thus, it is possible that God has created a world which has an optimal balance between saved and lost and that those who never hear the gospel and are lost would not have believed in Christ even if they had heard of him. So long as this scenario is even *possible*, it proves that it is entirely consistent to affirm that God is all-powerful and all-loving and yet that some people never hear the gospel and are lost.

Adams objects to this solution by claiming that human beings are so burdened with psychological baggage from their childhoods that even as adults they are no more competent to be entrusted with their eternal destiny than a two-year-old is to be allowed choices that could result in his or her death.[22] If God allowed people to consign themselves to hell, then he would be cruel to create people in a world with the combination of obstacles and opportunities found in the actual world, and he would bear the primary responsibility for their damnation.

It seems to me, however, that Adams has a deficient conception of divine providence. God in his providence can so arrange the world that the myriad of obstacles and opportunities in it conspire to bring about an optimal balance between saved and lost. Certainly these obstacles and opportunities are not equally distributed, but God—being just—does not require all persons to measure up to the same standards but instead judges them according to the obstacles and opportunities which he has apportioned them. Moreover, as a loving God who wills and works for the salvation of all persons, he ensures that sufficient grace is given to every person for salvation. With respect to persons who do not respond to his grace under especially disadvantageous circumstances, God can so order the world that such persons are exclusively people who would *still* not have believed even had they been created under more advantageous circumstances. Far from being cruel, God is so loving that he arranges the world such that anyone who would respond to his saving grace under certain sets of circumstances is created precisely in one such set of circumstances, and he even provides sufficient grace for salvation to those he knows would spurn it under any circumstances.

In a certain sense, then, God *is* responsible for who is saved and who is lost, for it is he who decrees which circumstances to create and what persons to place in them. But this is simply a description of divine sovereignty, and I take it to be a positive, biblical feature of this account that it affirms a strong doctrine of divine sovereignty. At the same time, it affirms that in whatever circumstances people find themselves, God wills their salvation, and by the Holy Spirit he supplies sufficient grace for their salvation, and those persons are entirely free to embrace this salvation. Should they reject God's every effort to save them, it is they, not God, who are responsible in the sense of being culpable.

In the end Adams seems to recognize that the problems she raises are soluble for one who advocates a robust doctrine of providence and prevenient grace according to which God arranges the world such that those who are lost would have been lost regardless of the circumstances under which they were created. But she claims that even if every world of free creatures which is feasible for God to create involved such impenitent persons, that still does not imply that the impenitent need be damned: they could simply be annihilated or maintained in a world like this one.[23] But this riposte strikes me as very weak. The precise form of damnation is an in-house debate among Christian particularists; the salient point is that under Adams's two proposed scenarios not everyone enjoys salvation. Moreover, she again seems to presuppose that the consequences of rejecting God's grace are to some degree arbitrary rather than necessitated by divine justice, the demands of which could well rule out scenarios like annihilation or maintenance in a world so suffused with God's common grace as this one.

Finally, I, too, must deal with a missiological objection against my proposed solution.[24] It might be said, "Why, then, should we engage in the enterprise of world mission, if all the people who are unreached would not believe the gospel even if they heard it?" But this question is based on a misunderstanding. It forgets that we are talking only about people who *never* hear the gospel. On the proposed view, God in his providence can so arrange the world that as the gospel spread out from first-century Palestine, he placed people in its path who would believe it if they heard it. In his love and mercy, God ensures that people who would believe the gospel if they heard it do not remain ultimately unreached. Once the gospel reaches a people, God providentially places there persons he knows would respond to it if they heard it. He ensures that those who *never* hear it are only those who would not accept it if they did hear it. Hence, no one is lost because of a lack of information or due to historical and geographical accident. Anyone who wants or even would want to be saved will be saved.

The solution I have proposed to the problem of Christian particularism is only a *possible* solution. But I find it attractive because certain biblical passages also suggest something very close. For example, Paul in his Areopagus address declared,

> The God who made the world nd everything in it is the Lord of heaven and earth and does not live in temples built by hands. And he is not served by human hands, as if he needed anything, because he himself gives all men life and breath and everything else. From one man he made every nation of men, that they should inhabit the whole earth; and he determined the times set for them and the exact places where they should live. God did this so that men would seek him and perhaps reach out for him and find him, though he is not far from each one of us. (Acts 17:24-27 NIV)

This passage seems very consonant with the version of Christian particularism defended here.

## Conclusion

In conclusion, then, salvation through faith in Christ alone may be and will no doubt remain politically incorrect in an age that celebrates religious diversity. But that doctrine is not therefore false. No inconsistency has been shown to exist in Christian particularism and exclusivism; on the contrary, we have seen that it is entirely consistent to maintain that God is both all-powerful and all-loving and yet that some people never hear the gospel and are lost, since it is possible that God has so providentially ordered the world as to achieve the optimal balance feasible between saved and lost in a world of free creatures and that he supplies sufficient grace to every person for salvation, ensuring that any person who would respond to the gospel and be saved if he heard it lives at a time and place in history where he does hear it. Hence, while Christians may be open to elements of truth found in non-Christian religions, their minds need not be agape to every religious truth claim, since they are under no obligation to embrace religious relativism, having rejected its raison d'être, universalism. The proper response of the Christian to religious diversity is not merely to garner the elements of truth from the world's religions but, far more important, to share with their adherents, in a spirit of love, the Way, the Truth and the Life.

# PART III
# APOLOGETICS BETWEEN MODERNITY AND POSTMODERNITY

# 6

# ON BEING A
# FOOL FOR
# CHRIST AND
# AN IDIOT
# FOR NOBODY

## Logocentricity and Postmodernity

*James W. Sire*

**Irony Contingent on Richard Rorty
(with apologies to Walt Kelly)**
O roar, O roar for Rorty,
Richard Rorty in the night,
For he has sent the Logos
Spinning silent out of sight.
O furor for our Rorty
And applaud the inky dark
Where Mene, Mene, Tekel, Parsin
Is the Strongest Poet's work.[1]

A couple of years ago, after I had given a formal presentation to graduate students at the University of Illinois-Urbana, Kerry Ulm (now Kerry Ulm Ose), a first-year graduate student in English rhetoric, asked a question: "As a Christian, how might I respond to the postmodern approaches to literary and rhetorical theory?"

I said that I thought Christians ought to respond by challenging *a*, if not *the*, central presupposition of postmodern literary theory—the idea that there is no sure ontological foundation for language. The "belief that words simply label real categories of meaning existing independently of a language" is logocentrism.[2] Postmodern literary theory is *antilogocentric*.

### Antilogocentrism and the Postmodern Project

Postmodern literary theory, as well as much contemporary human science theory, assumes that the human mind is incapable of accessing reality. In the first as well as the final analysis there either is no rational structure to reality or if there is we cannot know it. All we know is our own language. As Nietzsche said:

> What, then, is truth? A mobile army of metaphors, metonyms, and anthropomorphisms—in short, a sum of human relations, which have been enhanced, transposed, and embellished poetically and rhetorically, and which after long use seem firm, canonical, and obligatory to a people: truths are illusions about which one has forgotten that this is what they are; metaphors which are worn out and without sensuous power; coins which have lost their pictures and now matter only as metal, no longer as coins.[3]

The epistemological question (how can we know anything at all?) is predicated on the ontological question (is there any determinacy, any rationally apprehensible structure to whatever it is that is?).[4] The presupposition of much postmodern theory of all types—sociological, literary, aesthetic—is that there is no such ontological substructure or if there is it is inaccessible to the human mind.

We may take Richard Rorty's expression of this as typical, if not definitive. Rorty identifies what "ties Dewey and Foucault, James and Nietzsche, together":

> the sense that there is nothing deep down inside us except what we have put there ourselves, no criterion that we have not created in the course of creating a practice, no standard of rationality that is not an appeal to such a criterion, no rigorous argumentation that is not obedience to our own conventions.[5]

Rorty then quotes a variety of late-nineteenth- and twentieth-century philosophers—C. S. Peirce, Jacques Derrida, Wilfrid Sellars, Ludwig Wittgenstein, Hans-Georg Gadamer, Michel Foucault and Martin Heidegger—in support of this general view. Note these three examples:

> Man makes the word, and the word means nothing which the man has not made it mean, and that only to some other man. But since man can think only by means of words or other external symbols, these might turn around and say: You mean nothing which we have not taught you, and then only so far as you address some word as the interpretant of your thought . . . the word or sign which man uses is the man himself. . . . Thus my language is the sum-total of myself; for the man is the thought. (Peirce)[6]

> Human experience is essentially linguistic. (Gadamer)[7]

> Speaking about language turns language almost inevitably into an object . . . and then its reality vanishes. (Heidegger)[8]

Describing *pragmatism*, the general rubric under which his own philosophy fits, Rorty writes:

> The pragmatist tells us that it is useless to hope that objects will constrain us to believe the truth about them, if only they are approached with an unclouded mental eye, or a rigorous method, or a perspicuous language. He wants to give up the notion that God, or evolution, or some other underwriter of our present world-picture, has programmed us as machines for accurate verbal picturing, and that philosophy brings self-knowledge by letting us read our own program.[9]

In such a situation, *truth*, to the extent that one can speak of it, is "a property of linguistic entities, of sentences."[10] We grasp it only as the outcome of *"undistorted* conversation."[11]

Betty Jean Craige in *Reconnection: Dualism to Holism in Literary Study* (1988) expands the antilogocentric approach to an entire paradigm for liberal studies:

1. Things and events do not have intrinsic meaning. There is no inherent objectivity, only continuous interpretation of the world.

2. Continuous examination of the world requires a contextual examination of things. *We ourselves* are part of that context.

3. The interpretation of a text depends on the relative viewpoint and the particular values of the interpreter. To understand a text on the basis of one's life-relation to it is to have preunderstanding. Interpretation does not depend on the external text nor its author.

4. Language is not neutral but is relative and is value-laden. It is the medium through which we do our thinking.

5. Language and discourse convey ideology, and a society's intellectual discourse rests on political values and affects society in political ways.[12]

My suggestion to Kerry Ulm was that, in the light of the radically *antilogocentric* character of literary study today, as a Christian she might well reaffirm the centrality of *logos*—in particular the *logos* of John 1:1-4. As I will explain below, a reaffirmation of the reality of *logos* would bring about a return to the notion that reality is not opaque to human apprehension nor is language merely a human invention confirmed in value by convention.

But Kerry was not impressed with my suggestion. She did not say so then, but when we last talked she said that when she first encountered *antilogocentricity*, and the postmodern project in general, she recognized more than a grain of truth in it. Our language does, in fact, shape the way we think, Western approaches to the canon have been at least unconsciously if not consciously ideological, and what constitutes literature worthy of study (and what does not) has been determined at least in part by class interests. Christians should have been the first to notice this. The doctrine of the Fall, the deceitfulness of the heart, the sinfulness of all our judgments: these notions should have led Christians to be more self-critical and culture-critical.

What Kerry actually said a couple of years ago as I proposed a presentation of the *logos* of the Gospel of John was this: "My colleagues would laugh at me." I admitted that that might be so but that in the final analysis (if not in the first) a Christian will have to see that there is a fundamental meaning to reality—both the created reality of the world around us and the "final reality" of the Creator who created and redeemed us. An apologetic cannot be grounded on anything less than the notion that at least some truth of correspondence can be known. Not every story told about God (or the gods), human beings and the universe is equally true; some stories are better, truer, than others and ought to be privileged.

Kerry's response—"My colleagues would laugh at me"—however, must be taken seriously. If one's audience—even an audience of friends and colleagues—laughs at one's "apologetic," it will have little purchase power. An apologetic is effective only if one's friends, as someone once said, come "to scoff but remain to pray" or at least recognize that a serious word has been spoken, a word that has at least the potential of plausibility about it.

Does the *logocentricity* of John 1:1-4 have a plausible ring to it in today's postmodern segment (the humanities and the social sciences) of the university world? Not, I think, unless it gets some apologetic help.

After over a year of her graduate study, I asked Kerry what she might now say if she were before an audience of her fellow graduate students and professors and were asked to justify her Christian stance in the university. Challenged by this, she paused, then said, "I would point them to the *logos* of John 1 and tell them that nothing I had studied in the university, no theory I had read, had shaken my confidence in the actual truth of Christianity as traditionally understood. My Christian faith is confirmed by the reflection of my mind, the experiences I am having and the sensitivity of my heart."

This combination of an affirmation of the *logos* (as a likely story) and the personal narrative might well be effective among her academic friends, especially in a setting outside the public arena (e.g., in the department coffee room, among friends or at a backyard barbecue).

## Paradigms Lost

In the past couple of years the popularity of some postmodern theory, and "deconstruction" in particular, has actually waned. Even four or so years ago, one wag quoted by *The Chronicle of Higher Education* said, "Deconstruction is dead on both coasts but has not yet been heard of in Oklahoma." Well, it was not dead on both coasts and it had been heard of in Oklahoma. But its days of hegemony, if it ever had it, were then and are now numbered.

First, "deconstruction" has always had an ambiguous relationship to other forms of postmodern literary theory and practice. Feminism has played off the "deconstruction" of texts it considers paternalistic. Marxist criticism has benefited from its "deconstruction" of texts it considers oppressive, racist or culturally privileged. In destructive critique, "deconstruction" has been a friend. But the "deconstruction" touted by Derrida and De Man is in the last analysis universal. Depending on how you shake it down, nihilism is either the legitimate father or legitimate child of "deconstruction." One can read "deconstruction" out of the texts of Nietzsche or see nihilism emerging from the practice of "deconstruction." In any case, neither feminism nor Marxism can withstand its acids. If no text is privileged, no story more "true" than any other, then every ideology fails to be grounded.

Second, Kerry notes that the younger professors, those just emerging from their Ph.D. dissertations, are more skeptical about the virtues of the postmodern project. There is a backlash against the notion that no idea, no literary text, is better than any other. And there is a return to the study of historical, social and political factors. Even authors are again becoming relevant to the study of literature.

Karen J. Winkler reports on this trend in *The Chronicle of Higher Education*:

Enter the age of post-theory.

It's a time when literary scholars are more focused on the cultures of particular racial, ethnic, or gender groups than on philosophical speculations on the reality of meaning, as much interested in literary history as in linguistic analysis.[13]

She continues on with a list of books that have effectively challenged "post-theory," then writes:

"The new faces on the block are the new historicism, cultural studies, post-colonialism, and gender studies," says W. J. T. Mitchell, professor of English at the University of Chicago and editor of the journal *Critical Inquiry.*

Those approaches to literary criticism are concerned less with philosophical questions about meaning and language, and more with culture. "Literary studies today are interested in how people define themselves—through categories such as race, class, gender or ethnicity," says Michael Denning, chairman of American studies at Yale University and a pioneer in cultural studies.[14]

Winkler then quotes Stephen J. Greenblatt, who teaches English at the University of California at Berkeley:

"It's a moment of paradigms lost," he says. "When there are no dominant paradigms, the questions that matter are what happens in practice, when theoretical concerns try to come to terms with a particular text."[15]

Insightful for us today is Winkler's assessment that "the challenge that post-structuralism offered to universal truth, for example, forced critics to look elsewhere for meaning—and they turned to history and culture."[16] While the main thrust seems to be toward politics—feminist and gender studies, Marxist and social issues—there is even thought of a new aestheticism, looking at literature as literature.[17]

The death of deconstruction has not, however, brought on a return to *logocentrism.* The postmodern paradigm in general is still intact. Much of feminist and Marxist literary study still rejects the notion that reality is determinate, that there are such things as essences, that reality as such can be accessed. Some stories, some perspectives may be better than others, but none is easily shown to be so. Harold Bloom talks of "strong poets"—like Freud—who convince us by their charismatic presence, who get us to talk about reality in certain ways by their rhetorical power. Rorty speaks of truth as the language people in an open society agree to speak.[18]

In these ideological forms, language creates reality; some human beings ("strong poets," charismatic figures, clever rhetoricians, in short, effective sophists) have charge over language. Recent attempts at social engineering (some of them successful) assume this approach. "Don't call me Negro (that's the term white people use of me); call me black (or Afro-American, or a person of color). I get to define myself." Much feminism does so as well.

Epistemology is thus a matter of power rather than of rationality. We know what we know because we participate in a language game that defines the limits of our knowledge. There is no independent reality against which the accuracy of the language we use can be measured.

David Lyle Jeffrey recently affirmed my own judgment about the reigning ideologies in English and language departments. Anyone interviewing for a job in the departments represented by the Modern Language Association must demonstrate that they are in line with the latest notion of political correctness or they will be eliminated from job consideration automatically. The chance of a dissenter getting a job is nil.

### Paradigm Regained

Does all the confusion in postmodern studies provide a context in which Christians can not just speak a prophetic word (that being no longer quite so necessary) but a prospective alternative? Do paradigms lost open the way for paradigms regained? Theologians Thomas C. Oden and Diogenes Allen think so.[19] Allen writes:

In a postmodern world Christianity is intellectually relevant. It is relevant to the fundamental questions, Why does the world exist? and Why does it have its present order, rather than another? It is relevant to the discussion of the foundations of morality and society, especially on the significance of human beings. The recognition that Christianity is relevant to our entire society, and relevant not only to the heart but to the mind as well, is a major change in our cultural situation.[20]

I certainly agree with the assessment that Christianity is relevant in the ways Allen says, but I am less sanguine about the recognition of that relevance by the graduate students, faculty and academic intellectuals themselves.

Still, if the Christian message is relevant and if God has not left himself "without a witness" (Acts 14:17), then there is hope for finding ways of breaking the blinding power of ideology—whether it be the ideology of radical secular feminism, Marxism, the anti-ideological ideology of "deconstruction" or the antipolitical political ideology of Michel Foucault.[21] In other words, there is reason to think that there are ways to get a hearing for the gospel in the postmodern university.

So let's turn to the task itself. What might an apologetic for the postmodern university world look like?

## Some Key Assumptions

No apologetic can proceed without making some assumptions about the nature of God, the nature of human beings and the role of apologetics. Here are some matters that I assume to be relatively uncontroversial among evangelicals. I do not presume to think that they will be assumed by a postmodern audience.

*1. Assumptions About God as Ultimate Reality.*

God is omniscient, omnipotent, omnipresent; infinite and personal; characterized by goodness (being what the good is) and by *logos*.

The *logos* is God (Jn 1:1); this means that God is the meaning of his own being. Since God is personal the *logos* is personal as well, lending relationality to the primal concept of meaning.

*2. Assumptions About Creation as External Reality*

The *logos* created the world (Jn 1:3); this means that the world is itself intelligible (characterized by orderliness and inherently accessible by rationality; i.e., the world is determinate and contingent [it is what it is but it could have been different], and it can be understood).

*3. Assumptions About Human Beings*

God made human beings in his image (Gen 1:26-27); this includes moral and intellectual capacities. The *logos* has "enlightened" everyone (Jn 1:9). As God is the all-knowing knower of all things, we can be (and God wants us to be) the sometimes-knowing knowers of some things.

Human beings have fallen, and every aspect of their nature, including human reason, has been marred by the results of sin; this means that our current capacity to know, discern and judge accurately cannot be trusted. While we are still able to use our minds and much of what we understand is true or at least possibly true, we are liable to make mistakes in thinking and not know it. In any case our human reason is not autonomous; it is based on our created God-likeness; there is no way for us on our own to ground our own notions of what is true.

*4. Assumptions About God's Intentions for Us to Know*

God has not left us to determine on our own the truth of the tough issues of life. The Holy Spirit is present in whatever way he wishes, and he woos us toward the truth, illuminates our mind and confirms our feeble grasping after the truth. He does this not in spite of our attempts at careful thought but through these attempts. The Holy Spirit is not a part of our arguments; he is not a "reason" for our belief. He is rather the final context in which our minds and hearts rest.

God has spoken clearly in human language through his prophets; this means that God wants us to know about himself and his guidelines for us. To this end the prophets have been given direct access to who God is, and the rest of us have been given indirect access through their writings.

The *logos* has become flesh and expressed the character of God in intelligible, incarnate, personal form.

*5. Assumptions About the Role of Apologetics*

The task of apologetics is to demonstrate that Christianity is reasonable and thus (a) to assure Christians that their faith is not idiotic and (b) to clear away the obstacles and objections that keep nonbelievers from considering the arguments and evidence for the truth of Christianity.

In general, these assumptions should, I believe, be the rock on which we see ourselves standing. They are the reasons *for us* why we should expect people to be able to grasp the truth of the Christian gospel: that God was reconciling the world to himself in Christ (2 Cor 5:19), or that in Jesus Christ the kingdom had drawn near and that all people should repent and believe the good news (Mk 1:14).

The point is this: If Christianity is true (and we think it is), then we know some things about people that they do not know about themselves. We know that they were made for fellowship with God; we know that they are alienated from him; we know that Christ has provided the foundation for their reconciliation to God; we know that God wants them to return to him and woos them by the Holy Spirit when they know it not.

All this can give us confidence that we are not butting our soft heads against a hard wall. Our task is, eventually, to challenge people with postmodern assumptions (many of which are in contrast to ours) to shift paradigms—to see the truth of the Christian faith and to become disciples of Jesus.

How might we best do this?

### Reason and Rhetoric

Evangelistic apologetics—that is, apologetics done for the purpose of conversion—must attend to two matters: both reason and rhetoric.

Honesty requires our case for the Christian faith to be free of fallacious reasoning. As George Mavrodes says, our deductive arguments must (1) be based on true premises and (2) obey the laws of logic and valid argumentation. Cheap, tawdry, slick arguments that persuade and convince but violate the principles of logic do not honor Christ. We may add to this that abductive arguments, such as those described by Basil Mitchell, must be fair in assessing the nature and weight of the evidence, not, for example, jumping to hasty conclusions or avoiding negative evidence.[22] Rhetoric without reason is reprehensible.

But reason without the convincing power of rhetoric is vacuous. Mavrodes adds two more criteria: a successful argument must (3) be understood by at least one person to meet criteria (1) and (2), and (4) be convincing.[23] Convincing! That's just the problem. And rhetoric is at least part of the solution. Rhetoric takes on the task of making reason relevant, bringing home the argument in such a way as to help people see that the conclusion is in fact true.

For many years I thought that one of a rhetorician's tasks (as delineated by classical rhetoric) was illegitimate: the invention of arguments. It appeared to me to be constructing arguments out of whole cloth, learning how to convince by clever lying. I now, however, take "invention of arguments" as a task central to apologetics.

What set of true statements, observations, identification of actual, relevant evidence, arguments and clever stories will help a person or a group of people recognize the truth—especially the truth about God and how we relate to him? Is there indeed a way to be a "fool for Christ" without being an idiot for anybody?[24]

It is this issue I want to address in relation to university-level apologetics, especially apologetics among thoughtful undergraduates, graduate students and faculty who have drunk deeply at the fountain of postmodernism.

Several approaches offer some hope of success.

## Telling a Likely Story

If a major postmodern assumption is that reality as such is inaccessible to human perception or understanding and that all we have is language, then why not tell a story that, if it were true, would make the contrary point plausible? Stories are indeed a major postmodern way of communicating.

One such story is the theistic "story" summarized *biblically* in the flow of history from creation through the Fall, through redemption and on through the end times and *theologically* through the Christian assumptions listed above. The key issue that this would identify is the postmodern assumption, not just that the human mind cannot access reality itself but the more basic point that no God of any kind exists. What if a theistic God did exist?[25] Raising such a point shifts the ground away from language as such to the fundamental issue of the nature of "final reality."

On this ground Christians have a chance of making some headway by pointing out that

1. the assumption of atheism is just that—an assumption;

2. arguments for any view of ultimate reality require assumptions; there is no neutral ground that is self-evident;

3. there is in fact evidence for the existence of a personal God (e.g., Jesus himself; the internal coherence of the Christian worldview and its explanatory power; and the testimony of believers);

4. there are good rejoinders to objections to the notion of such a personal God, for example, to the problem of evil.

The point of this approach is to encourage the postmodern person to consider the possibility that God might really exist. With that accomplished, traditional apologetic approaches can be used.[26]

Kerry Ulm Ose fears that such a likely story will, however, be ignored unless it is placed in the context of a Christian's personal story. The story of the big picture can best be told through a narrative of a little picture—the intimate picture of someone's personal life. Many academics know—or think they know—the big story a Christian wishes to tell. So if one tells only the big likely story without the context of the intimate personal story, they will probably, as Kerry says, "just nod and change the subject."

### Asking Why Anyone Should Believe Anything at All

This amounts to asking the postmodern person to reflect on first things: what lies at the bottom of their belief system? Do the reasons they come up with satisfy even themselves and why? Which of these reasons for believing what they believe can also legitimately undergird Christian beliefs?

Over the past twelve years I have given a lecture/discussion with this title about two hundred times. The title alone has been the most effective element of advertisements for the lecture. The response of a student at Tennessee Technical University may suggest why. He came up to the InterVarsity table where a large sign read: "Why Should Anyone Believe Anything at All?" He suddenly moaned, "There's that question again. I've seen it on posters all over campus. It makes my head hurt." Then he walked away. A few minutes later he returned and the Christian students handed him a survey sheet with the question on it. "Here, why don't you write your answer down?" He looked at the paper, pondered and then said, "I can't do it. I can't do it," and walked away for good.

This question gets underneath both the bravado of students who think they "know it all" or at least "think they know what they need to know." It's a deeply troubling question for everybody: for Christian believers who may never have asked the question of themselves, for religious people dedicated to a non-Christian spirituality and for atheists.

When I give the lecture/discussion, my primary goal is to get people to realize that the best reason for them to believe anything is because they think it is true. Even relativists can be brought to see that truth is necessary—even to the case for relativism.[27] The truth question, in fact, cannot really be avoided. Much postmodern theory assumes, if it does not state, that the human mind cannot access mind-independent reality and must deal with language only. Richard Rorty is a case in point. Charles Taylor, analyzing Rorty's version of nonrealism, writes:

> Rorty offers a great leap into non-realism: where there have hitherto been thought to be facts- or truths-of-the-matter, there turn out to be only rival languages, between which we end up plumping, if we do, because in some way one works better for us than the others.[28]

Taylor rejects this nonrealism, as well as the way Rorty deals with this rejection:

> Rorty seems to think that it is essential to his position that he consider this too as falling under his non-realist regime. So that there is no truth

of the matter between us on the question whether there is a truth of the matter between views of human nature, ethics, etc.

But to believe something is to hold it to be true; and, indeed, one cannot consciously manipulate one's beliefs for motives other than their seeming true to us.[29]

Taylor's critique has not, so far as I know, caused Rorty to change his position. But in a person who does not want to be deceived, such cognitive dissonance may well trigger a paradigm shift from postmodernism to something at least potentially Christian.

The question is: Which assumptions, which systems of belief, do the best job of explaining what we would like to have explained? Those that are essentially incoherent ought not to fare well.

If postmodern people detect incoherence in the basic assumptions of their own philosophy, it should cause them at least some discomfort. In other words, one apologetic technique is to show the inadequacy of alternatives to the Christian worldview.[30] If one can show that a proposed alternative is self-stultifying, self-referentially incoherent, fails to take relevant data into account and misunderstands the data it does deal with, then the proponents of this alternative may be open to hearing how the Christian worldview does deal adequately with the facts, is self-consistent and coherent and sheds light on even the most puzzling human issues. If, in fact, we are correct that human beings can access reality, that the creation is imbued with rationality, that our minds can work rationally even though we think they can't, then we can count on producing some cognitive dissonance among those that are living and trying to think contrary to the way they were designed to live and think (and actually do function in most of their daily thoughts).

But let us return to the specific issue at hand: logocentricity. A Christian logocentric approach to the possibility of the knowledge of independent reality is not self-referentially incoherent. The postmodern assumption that we can in principle have no access to the nature of reality is, I think, incoherent. To those who wish not to be deluded or deceived, a crack has opened up. It is the apologist's task then to elucidate a Christian explanation and to begin a dialogue that may end in a saving encounter with Christ.

**Challenging the Autonomy of Human Reason and the Search for Certainty**
Postmodernism is in major part the result of the breakdown of the world-view of modernity. One fruitful way of looking at the origins of modernity is to begin with Descartes. Descartes believed in God and the existence of himself and of an external world, but he wanted to find a way to be certain about these three important things he believed. So Descartes developed the methodology of doubt. He would doubt everything he possibly could.

He concluded that he could doubt everything but the fact that he was thinking (even doubting was thinking). So he said, "I think; therefore I am." Subsequent philosophers criticized Descartes's argument, but two premises remained uncriticized and (perhaps) unrecognized. The first premise is that the search for certainty is itself a necessary project. The second closely related premise is that the human mind is capable of grounding itself (this has come to be called the "autonomy of human reason").

It is not always recognized just how radical these two premises were in their day. The seventeenth century was not without its skeptics, but the dominant worldview was Christian, and Christians began with the confident notion that God existed. So did the external world. The main question was, Who and what is it that exists? And how can we know who and what it is that exists? Epistemology was undergirded by a metaphysics of presence. God was there as both Creator and revealer. The arguments were in the details.

Descartes proposed a profound shift in priority. The first question for Descartes was, How can I be sure of anything? He answered by concluding that he could in the first instance be sure of only one thing: his own existence. And who was he? A "thinking thing."[31]

On that primary fact—the *cogito*—Descartes rested the whole of his philosophy, arguing, for example, for the existence of God as the only explanation for the *cogito*, since it did not appear to Descartes as able to produce its own existence. Countless critics from his day on raised objections to this line of thinking, but I want to focus on only one—the first of the bona fide "postmoderns"—Friedrich Nietzsche.

Nietzsche rejects human reason as paltry, arrogant and self-deluded. Moreover language is utterly inadequate to express truth about the nature of reality.[32] His treatment of "I think, therefore I am," is devastating:

[Section 16:] There are still harmless self-observers who believe that there are "immediate certainties"; for example, "I think," or as the superstition of Schopenhauer put it, "I will"; as though knowledge here got a hold of its object purely and nakedly as "the thing in itself," without any falsification on the part of either the subject or the object. But that "immediate certainty," as well as "absolute knowledge" and the "thing in itself" involve a *contradictio in adjecto* [contradiction between the noun and the adjective], I shall repeat a hundred times; we really ought to free ourselves from the seduction of words!

Let the people suppose that knowledge means knowing things entirely; the philosopher must say to himself: When I analyze the process that is expressed in the sentence, "I think," I find a whole series of daring assertions that would be difficult, perhaps impossible, to prove; for example, that it is *I* who think, that there must necessarily be something that thinks, that thinking is an activity and operation on the part of a being who is thought of as a cause, and that there is an "ego," and finally that it is already determined what is to be designated by thinking—that I *know* what thinking is. For if I had not already decided within myself what it is, by what standard could I determine whether that which is just happening is not perhaps "willing" or "feeling"? In short, the assertion "I think" assumes that I *compare* my state at the present moment with other states of myself which I know, in order to determine what it is; on account of this retrospective connection with further "knowledge," it has, at any rate no immediate certainty for me.

In place of the "immediate certainty" in which the people may believe in the case at hand, the philosopher thus finds a series of metaphysical questions presented to him, truly searching questions of the intellect; to wit: "From where do I get the concept of thinking? Why do I believe in cause and effect? What gives me the right to speak of an ego, and even of an ego as cause, and finally of an ego as the cause of thought?" Whoever ventures to answer these metaphysical questions at once by an appeal to a sort of *intuitive* perception, like the person who says, "I think, and know that this, at least, is true, actual, and certain"—will encounter a smile and two question marks from a philosopher nowadays. "Sir," the philosopher will perhaps give to understand, "it is improbable that you are not mistaken; but why insist on the truth?"

[Section 17:] With regard to the superstitions of logicians, I shall never tire of emphasizing a small terse fact, which these superstitious minds hate to concede—namely, that a thought comes when "it" wishes, and not when "I" wish, so that it is a falsification of the facts of the case to say that the subject "I" is the condition of the predicate "think." *It* thinks; but that this "it" is precisely the famous old "ego" is, to put it mildly, only a supposition, an assertion, and assuredly not an "immediate certainty." "After all, one has even gone too far with this "it thinks"—even the "it" contains an *interpretation* of the process, and does not belong to the process itself. One infers here according to the grammatical habit: "Thinking is an activity; every activity requires an agent; consequently—"

It was pretty much according to the same schema that the older atomism sought, besides the operating "power," that lump of matter in which it resides and out of which it operates—the atom. More rigorous minds, however, learned at last to get along without this "earth-residuum," and perhaps some day we shall accustom ourselves, including the logicians, to get along without the little "it" (which is all that is left of the honest little old ego).[33]

Nietzsche has, it seems to me, destroyed the value of methodological doubt. It will not work to lend certainty to any of our ruminations.

Does that mean that we now float free of any grounding or reasons for thinking and believing what we do? No. It just means that we are not going to be able to acquire philosophical certitude for any of them.

But why should we? Is not the very attempt an act of idolatry? Are we not trying to put ourselves in the place of God? Only God can know with certainty, and that is because he is omniscient; he knows everything exhaustively. Philosophic certitude remains a divine trait. Emotional or psychological certitude is as close as we can get.

Lesslie Newbigin is right about this:

The acceptance of [a particular] vision [of reality] is a personal act, an act of personal judgment to which one commits oneself in the knowledge that others may disagree and that one may be proved wrong. It involves personal commitment. But it is not therefore merely subjective. The scientist who commits himself to the new vision does so—as Polanyi puts it—with universal intent. He believes it to be objectively true, and he therefore causes it to be widely published, invites discussion, and seeks to persuade his fellow scientists that it is a true account of reality. . . . At no stage is it merely a subjective opinion. It is held "with universal intent" as being a true account of reality which all people ought to accept and which will prove itself true both by experimental verification and also by opening the way to fresh discovery. It is offered not as private opinion but as public truth.[34]

Like Newbigin, I believe that we can come to grasp some of the truth. We may make mistakes. We may have to change our mind. But our beliefs must not be relegated to the status of private opinion. The only thing worth believing is the truth. When we believe we have apprehended the truth, we must hold it with universal intent.

As apologists, we can accept much of the postmodern critique of modernity. It properly identifies and sometimes destroys the pretensions of an Enlightenment *logos*—a *logos* that assumes that people in the exercise of their ordinary mental faculties can grasp the truth truly and certainly. That kind of ability has not been ours as human beings from at least the time of the Fall.

But then we must question the "modern project" which the postmodern project has, seemingly, accepted as a proper goal, but which it recognizes as unreachable. Since it is unreachable, postmodernism falls back into despair of knowing anything approaching the truth. It's all or nothing at all. It can't be all. It will then be nothing.[35]

### Telling One's Own Story

When I asked Kerry what she would say to a room full of her graduate student and faculty friends, this was Kerry's suggestion. "What I have found," she comments, "is that a story that is infused with the personal, especially when it is a story about transcendent truth, God and spirituality, is more convincing and more rhetorically acceptable to my academic colleagues."

The basic postmodern attitude toward belief is that a belief that fits a person is fine for that person. No story is more privileged than another. This openness to the validity of the personal story of each person means that—at least in theory—anyone should be able to have her own story and should be free to tell it. In practice, however, it does not always work out that way. On any given university campus, some stories are rejected before they are told. These include not only the "politically incorrect" stories of racist, sexist and antihomosexual sentiment, but often those of Christian exclusivism as well.

Though ultramodernists (postmodernists) ought to say they never met a narrative they didn't like, it is clear that they have. Christian fundamentalist and evangelical stories are often rejected for their exclusivity. Undergraduates in the academic context are often, maybe usually, allowed to tell their stories in underclass courses, but woe to the graduate student who does so without great care and trepidation. For young academics, tenure can depend on keeping silent about one's faith.

As students have written in response to campus surveys asking, "Why should anyone believe anything at all?": It's okay to believe anything you want, just don't insist that it's true and that I should believe it. No one should be forced to believe anything.

To be coherently pluralistic every story—including exclusivist stories—has a right to be aired. It's called freedom of speech and is protected (so far at least) by the First Amendment.

The point is, however, not just to get freedom to tell one's Christian story. It is to tell that story in a persuasive way. And some ways are better than others.

### Telling the Jesus Story

I believe that the best reason for believing that Christianity is true is Jesus, and the best reason for Jesus is Jesus himself. The Gospels—the narrative of Jesus' life, teaching, crucifixion and resurrection—are the best proof for the truth of the Christian faith. "Can any good thing come out of Nazareth?" asked Nathaniel. And Philip replied, "Come and see" (Jn 1:46).

Most people who are not Christians do not have enough knowledge of Jesus to reject him or to declare that Christianity is false or not worth believing. If people will just look, just read and ponder Mark's or Luke's or Matthew's or John's account of Jesus, they will be struck by what they find. They will be brought into a direct encounter with Jesus, and they will be forced to make an existential decision about who Jesus was and is. The apologist's role ends when the person meets Jesus.

There is something inherently attractive about the story of Jesus. Years ago Bishop Fulton Sheen expressed it in the title of what become a very popular book: *The Greatest Story Ever Told*. The plot itself is archetypal: the wondrous accounts of Jesus' birth; the accounts of the stunning effect the young man had on his friends, family, ordinary people and religious and political leaders; the fascination of his stories; the depth of his moral insight; his call to be more than moral; his exaltation of the poor and dispossessed; his healings and nature miracles; the clever way he responded to questions; his struggle in the Garden of Gethsemane with obedience to the Father; his betrayal by a close disciple; his unjust trial before both religious and political authorities; his crucifixion as a criminal innocent of a crime; his resurrection and ascension. This story penetrates the psyche; it resonates with the human spirit.

But the final key to the power of the story is its chief character. There is something profoundly attractive about Jesus himself. He stands before us as the one whom deep down we know to be the True Human. We see ourselves in him but twisted, askew. He is us but not us. He is the Real Thing. *Ecce homo!* Behold the man!

We see as well that the plot fits the character. The strange events—the miracles, the transfiguration, the striking bearing—become understandable. Both the crucifixion and the resurrection become coherent in light of the person of Jesus. Of course, he is crucified. Then the shock of the resurrection, the initial disbelief that is generated by the magnitude of Jesus' reappearance after death (the same person, but somehow transformed, somehow different). In reading about it we might well see parallels with the early disciples. They could not at first believe something so astounding either. But then we awake from our intellectual slumber. Of course, of course: why did we not see it all along? *Surely this man was the Son of God.*

It may well be, of course, that a lot of confusion may need to be cleared away before a reader can see: objections to the historical reliability of the Gospel narratives, misunderstandings that occur because of modern prejudices against the possibility of miracles, failure to grant the text its own presuppositions about what is important to tell, for example. There is, in other words, a continuing role for traditional apologetics.

Still, the story itself—hearing it told, reading it in one of the Gospels—has been for many the main doorway to belief in Jesus as Lord and Savior. Because it is a true story, it is outstandingly relevant to a postmodern apologetic. One of the practical applications of this apologetic is that it encourages the reading of the Bible and the formation of inductive Bible studies to enhance the likelihood that the nonbelieving reader will pay attention. Meeting Jesus in the Gospels, many will testify, is the major factor in their conversion.

## Telling a Story Like Jesus

The story of Jesus is a story of a master storyteller. Many of Jesus' parables were not just clever stories illustrating various metaphysical, religious and ethical principles. They were instead stories that involved the audience in the telling. The tales of the good Samaritan (Lk 10:25-37), the prodigal son (Lk 15:11-31) and the two debtors (Lk 7:36-50) engaged those to whom they were told, and they engage readers today in the same way, bringing the audience before the bar of self-understanding. Just as we are being amused by how Jesus cleverly unmasked the hypocrisy of Simon the Pharisee, we are struck by the relevance to ourselves. We see ourselves being weighed and found wanting. The parables are not so much read by readers as readers are read by the parables.

I know of no modern stories that are really comparable in relevance and power to those Jesus told. What might come close is C. S. Lewis's *Screwtape Letters*. Exemplary at least in style and setting are the academic novels of David Lodge, who however over the years has moved away from traditional Catholicism toward a "demythologized, provisional, and in many ways agnostic theological perspective."[36] Lodge's *Changing Places* (1975), *Small World* (1984) and *Nice Work* (1988) are clever depictions of university life and thought, especially centering on members of the English departments. Lodge's English teachers muddle through their careers promoting and reacting to the latest fads in literary criticism. Other modern tales that sneak up on the reader, bringing plausibility to traditional Christianity, are Frederick Buechner's *Godric*, C. S. Lewis's Chronicles of Narnia and G. K. Chesterton's Father Brown stories.

Street theater can also be effective. This has been used by a number of evangelical groups, including Rob Malone's Salt Company, a troupe that works in Malta in the summers. This gets the attention of an audience—the hardest thing of all to do in evangelism—and directs it toward the gospel.

Gordon Carkner has a series of ten posters delineating ten modern myths students today often accept, such as the idea that it doesn't make any difference what religion you believe because they are really the same at heart. This series attracted so much attention—and opposition—at Swarthmore College in September 1991 that the Christian students had to defend themselves not just from criticism but from censorship. In a meeting with the deans who tried to deal with the controversy, the leader of the Christian group was asked to explain what she believed. She responded and focused her answer on the uniqueness of Christ. One dean then remarked, "Well, it's obvious to me that people who believe that don't belong here." Two days later three Christian leaders met again with three deans. Here is a direct quote from a report made later by the Christian group:

> Potentially explosive situation. The threat to "shut down" 10 MYTHS still remains. We appeal to freedom of speech rights and propose that if we have violated any campus policy or anyone's rights then "please show us where." Deans agree that we have done neither but go on to point out that our beliefs in Jesus as the only way to God inherently "demean and depersonalize other people." Agreement is reached to let 10 MYTHS continue. Sometime in the discussion a dean angrily speaks what is an enormous irony: Can't you all see that Swarthmore College has prided itself for over 100 years on being a place of tolerance![37]

Carkner now has "Under Investigation," a second series of five posters highlighting individualism, nihilism, materialism, relativism and progress.

### Providing Plausibility by Demonstrating the Relevance of the Christian Faith to the Academic Endeavor

Many Christian academics have recognized that the Christian faith has a relation to the actual content of the scholarship they do—or could do. Some Christian faculty and graduate students are members of organizations like the American Scientific Affiliation, Christianity and Literature, the Society for Christian Philosophers and so forth; these organizations serve to foster the integration of the Christian faith with their academic discipline. Their journals provide a place for dialogue on an academic level. The willingness of some well-known academics to be explicitly and publicly identified with the Christian faith also has great apologetic value. See, for example, the collection of spiritual autobiographies of eleven academics in *Philosophers Who Believe*.[38]

Major research projects predicated on approaches that are rooted in Christian presuppositions provide an even more significant witness.[39] Take, for example, *Habits of the Heart*, the work of Robert Bellah and his colleagues (perhaps some of whom might not affirm the Christian faith).[40] More obvious and explicit are the Christian assumptions underlying political scientist Glenn Tinder's *The Political Meaning of Christianity*.[41] As C. S. Lewis himself once mused, What if every time you wanted to find out some important piece of information or check on some idea you automatically turned to a publication that originated with a person whom you easily identified with the Christian faith? Wouldn't that be even a better witness than ones that were more direct and thus, perhaps, tainted with the prejudice often associated with evangelism?

As a sometime-academic myself and now an itinerant Christian apologist, I have developed a variety of lectures to give in university lecture halls and in undergraduate and graduate classes. Some of these directly take on the multi-mindsets of the "university," attempting to show how the Christian worldview sheds light on the most interesting and relevant issues being discussed today. To that end I have prepared and given the following lectures:

Why Should Anyone Believe Anything at All?[42]

The University in Two Minds: A Postmodern Condition

Reopening the American Mind (when Bloom's book was hot)

Multiculturalism: A Christian Perspective

The Unexpected Universe

Tolerance, Relativism and a Just Society (Or: "I'm Okay, You're Okay and That's Okay. Okay?" for undergraduates)

Naming the Elephant All the Way Down

Finitude and the Problem of Human Knowing (on Pascal)

Vaclav Havel: The Moral Conscience of International Politics?

Evolution and Ethics

A Foundation for Ethics: Three Alternatives

Responsible Technology: The Social Implications of High-Tech

Ecological Responsibility: Is Green Enough?

The Crisis of Belief in Existential Literature

## Providing Plausibility Through Community

The apologetic role of community can be far more important in postmodern culture at large than in a university setting. Graduate students and faculty tend to be individualistic—sometimes so much so that they know only their closest colleagues.

Nonetheless, within an academic community, Christians can become close friends with a few colleagues. The graduate student Christian fellowship surely should be a community that provides personal support for its members and their friends, especially when these friends need help in crises (deaths within their family, overwhelming academic pressure, broken and breaking relationships). A profound apologetic role is played by suffering with and for others, and by living under the ethos of the cross, as Roger Lundin remarks elsewhere in this volume.

Such a community of fellow academics announces and embodies kingdom values. And it provides a plausibility structure within the cultural boundaries of the university. It demonstrates that intelligent people don't need to throw their brains out a library or laboratory window in order to be Christians.

Local groups of Christians associated with a university can also organize Bible studies. If these studies are held on campus, the barrier of a "religious" context can be avoided. If the atmosphere of the Bible study includes the same openness to dialogue as characterizes the university at its best, another barrier is overcome—the notion that Christianity is all proclamation from an "up-front" authority.

In a broader sense (an interuniversity sense) the various societies of Christian scholars mentioned above provide a community of discourse for the scholars and a community of witness to the nonmember readership of their journals. In the academic world the valuable role played in apologetics by this sort of community should not be overlooked.

### Praying for a Paradigm Change

The role of an apologist is limited. No human being can (nor should think he or she can) force a person to either "see" or "believe." The apologist essentially says, "Come and see." The "seeing" is out of his or her control.

But praying is not. "Lord, help Judy and Jack 'see' the truth. Help them 'see' from a new perspective. Take the blinders from their eyes. Give them the grace of your illumination." Such prayers in community and in private are always appropriate. It is the Holy Spirit whose wind blows where it wills. It is marvelous when we see the field of ripening grain bend to his breath.

### A Fool for Christ

When we are known as Christians in secular universities today, we are likely also to be known as fools. If it must be, so let it be. We know better. And so will our colleagues once we get to know them and they us. But being a fool for Christ does not necessarily lead to being an idiot for anybody.

As Christians we ought not try to be just one of the gang. That may take far too much intellectual and moral compromise. We do, however, want to be accepted by our colleagues along a broad range of human issues and to a deep personal level. When we get to be known as good students, creditable faculty, productive scholars and good teachers, we will have many opportunities to be more than just a silent Christian presence.

After all, as Christian academics in a secular world we have access to the idea brokers of the future. Let us not leave them without an effective witness.

# PART IV
# THE
# APOLOGETICS OF
# POSTMODERNITY

# 7

# FACING THE POSTMODERN SCALPEL

## Can the Christian Faith Withstand Deconstruction?

*J. Richard Middleton and*
*Brian J. Walsh*

In Lily Tomlin's one-woman Broadway show *The Search for Signs of Intelligent Life in the Universe*, the first character we meet is Trudy the bag lady. As our guide through the show, Trudy explains that she is helping some aliens from outer space determine whether, in their search for intelligent life in the universe, Planet Earth might not be a likely location. The prospects do not seem too promising!

But not only do we have the aliens' unusual perspective; Trudy herself sees things aslant. Speaking of her own madness, Trudy exclaims,

> I refuse to be intimidated by
> reality anymore.
> After all, what is reality anyway? Nothin' but a
> collective hunch. My space chums think reality was once a
> primitive method of
> crowd control that got out of hand.
> In my view, it's absurdity dressed up
> in a three-piece business suit.
>
> I made some studies, and
> reality is the leading cause of stress among those in
> touch with it. I can take it in small doses, but as a
> lifestyle
> I found it too confining.[1]

Trudy figures that being "out of touch" with reality isn't such a bad idea. After all, it's less stressful. And what is reality anyway? Nothing but a collective hunch.

### Reality Isn't What It Used to Be

Or to use the title of Walter Truett Anderson's book on postmodernity, we could say that "reality isn't what it used to be."[2] Simply stated, the naive modernist confidence that we know what the world is and that we can manage and control it by our own autonomous rationality has evaporated in the heat of a postmodern culture.

To get a sense of this "evaporation"—how our perceptions of reality have changed—consider Anderson's joke about three umpires having a beer after a baseball game.[3] One says, "There's balls and there's strikes and I call 'em the way they are." Another responds, "There's balls and there's strikes and I call 'em the way I see 'em." The third says, "There's balls and there's strikes, and they ain't *nothin'* until I call 'em."

So what is reality? Are there balls and strikes out there in the world as the first ump implies? Most baseball fans and hometown commentators insist that there are, though some might side with the second ump in his honest appraisal of his own subjectivity. Many postmodern thinkers, however, wonder whether the third ump just might have the most honest position of the three. How do we know, after all, if there is anything "real" beyond our judgments?

At issue in the joke is not the particular *content* of the umpires' judgments, whether they believe the pitch is a ball or a strike, but more fundamentally, the *status* of their judgments, what sort of calls they are making. The first ump and the third may agree that the pitch should be called a strike, but the belief functions differently for each (with the second ump occupying a position in the middle). The first ump is a *naive realist*, believing that human knowing is a matter of seeking direct correspondence between the external world and epistemological judgments. The second ump knows that access to the external world is always mediated by the perspective of the knower. He might be called a *perspectival realist* (or perhaps a critical realist), since he recognizes that the way he sees the world invariably affects his epistemological judgments. The third ump pushes this perspectivalism to its extreme. His perspective is all there is, or at least all that matters. This *radical perspectivalism* epitomizes the postmodern shift. It is, if you will, perspectivalism gone to seed![4]

While there is a significant difference between the positions of the second and third umps, it is fair to say that the current predominance of these positions (both in the academy and on the street) represents the demise of the naive realism of modernity.

Although modernity has never been simply an intellectual movement, the modern project was predicated on the assumption that the knowing autonomous subject arrived at truth by establishing a correspondence between objectively "given" reality and the thoughts or assertions of the knower. To the postmodern mind, such correspondence is impossible, since we have no access to something called "reality" apart from that which we "represent" as reality in our concepts, language and discourse. Richard Rorty says that since we never encounter reality "except under a chosen description," we are denied the luxury or pretense of claiming naive, immediate access to the world.[5] We can never get outside of our knowledge to check its accuracy against "objective" reality. Our access is always mediated by our own linguistic and conceptual constructions.

Another way to say this is that it is only in terms of some *worldview*, some overarching, guiding and directing vision of life, that we experience the world. Everyone has a worldview. When we argued this in *The Transforming Vision* in 1984 it was a potentially controversial point.[6] The fact that the term *worldview* is now common in Christian literature, general academic writing and the public press is an indication of how much things have changed in a rather short period of time.[7] One of the defining features of the emerging postmodern culture is our growing awareness, with the second ump, of the perspectival character of human life and knowing.[8]

But many postmodern thinkers would go much further than admitting that life is perspectival or that reality is mediated to us by our worldview. Since we have no way of checking to see if our constructions "correspond" to anything external, there is a growing postmodern tendency to side with the third ump. While not exactly denying there is a "world" out there beyond our knowledge, postmodern thinkers typically deny that there are any features of this "world" that could function as independently existing *norms* or *criteria* for truth and goodness to which we could appeal. Any criterion we might come up with, explains Rorty, is itself a human construction, and there is "no standard of rationality that is not an appeal to such a criterion, no rigorous argumentation that is not obedience to our own conventions."[9] We are caught, then, in a hermeneutical circle and impelled toward radical perspectivalism.

While this does not mean, for Rorty, that each individual is trapped in his or her own private reality—since we can engage in conversation with one other—it does mean that rationality ceases to be a matter of universal truth. "The application of such honorifics as 'objective' and 'cognitive,'" he writes, "is never anything more than an expression of the presence of, and hope for, agreement among inquirers."[10] For either reason, then, whether reality is mediated to us by our perspective, or is purely a human construct, the naive self-assured realism of modernity is impossible to the postmodern mind.

But not only is reality a human construct, it is more particularly a *social* construct. It is always *some group's* construction of reality that invariably ends up being the dominant construction that guides social life. If what Rorty called our "chosen descriptions" of reality are, in the words of Trudy the bag lady, nothing more than collective hunches, then we need to ask, *Whose* reality? *Which* collective hunch?[11] And the answer is that it is the modern Western construction of reality (the progress myth) that has most effectively dominated the globe and defined what is rational and normative for human life. But since this dominance is not due, on any postmodern account, to strict epistemological success (as if the progress myth is demonstrably "truer" than any other construction), what *is* it due to? Trudy may well ask of modernity, "Why is it *your* construction of reality, *your* collective hunch, that rules?" Why is any one construction of reality given privileged status, thereby marginalizing all others?

### Violence and the Therapy of Deconstruction
As soon as we begin attending to the relation of reality and representation to marginalization and oppression we have entered that rarified postmodern world known as "deconstructionism."[12] Jacques Derrida, the French

philosopher most characteristically associated with deconstruction, names the realism of the dominant Western intellectual tradition a "metaphysics of presence."[13] What is assumed to be "present" in our conceptual systems of truth is a real "given" which exists prior to language and prior to thought but which we have adequately grasped by our language and thought. That is, the Western intellectual tradition, and especially Western modernity, claims to reflect and represent reality so accurately that it simply "mirrors" the way things really are. It is this "mimetic" (i.e., imitative) theory of truth, with its assumption of a substantial convergence between reality and our description of reality, that Derrida and other deconstructionists attack. It is a central deconstructionist theme that we can never get to a prelinguistic or preconceptual "reality." Instead, deconstructionism insistently attempts to show us that what is claimed to be "present" is really "absent" and that the "given" is itself a construction of human discourse. Through this analysis the "given" is dismantled and we are disabused of our reifications.

To "reify" something is to treat it as if it were a thing external to ourselves. Peter Berger and Thomas Luckman describe reification as

> the apprehension of the products of human activity *as if* they were something else than human products—such as facts of nature, results of cosmic laws, or manifestations of divine will. Reification implies that man is capable of forgetting his own authorship of the human world.[14]

By uncovering our reifications deconstruction attempts not to destroy in any nihilistic sense but to play a positive, therapeutic role in the culture of late (and decomposing) modernity. We are to face up to our constructions and to own them as such.

But the therapist cuts deep. What is concealed in the realism of the metaphysics of presence and revealed by deconstructionism is the impulse to mastery and ultimately to violence. What is really at stake in our intellectual rhetoric about scientific objectivity and nonbiased observation is nothing less than what Jane Flax describes as the typically Western desire "to master the world once and for all by enclosing it within an illusory but absolute system."[15] We desire, in other words, intellectual mastery and control. In the famous words of René Descartes, we seek to become "the masters and possessors of nature."[16]

But the claim to have grasped reality as it *really* is (beyond the contingencies of history, particularity and change) discloses our desire for another sort of mastery, that over human beings. By granting an aura of universal truth to our local conventions, the Western intellectual commitment to realism serves ideologically to legitimate Western conquest and political superiority. As Trudy's space chums put it, reality functions as a primitive form of crowd control. Thus Derrida can claim that "the entire philosophical tradition, in its meaning and at bottom, would make common cause with oppression."[17]

The realist metaphysics of presence is thus an "aggressive realism."[18] It is a metaphysics of violence. And that violence, explain deconstructionists, is the direct result of seeking to grasp the infinite, irreducible complexities of the world as a unified and homogeneous totality.[19] Since all such "totalizing" seeks to reduce the heterogeneous diversity of reality to a system which *I* (or *we*) can grasp, the deconstructionist is suspicious, explains James Olthuis, that the "unity of truth is purchased only at the cost of violence, by repressing what doesn't fit and erasing the memory of those who have questioned it."[20] Recognizing that truth is a human, social construction, deconstructionists force us to inquire about what (and who) has been left out, silenced or suppressed in all constructions that aspire toward a "total" accounting of reality. The problem with such totalizing aspirations, argue the deconstructionists, is that they necessarily result in a violent closure of human thought that denies all heterogeneous difference or dissolves it into a homogeneous unity, effectively co-opting, dominating or eliminating that which is perceived as "other."

We could illustrate the deconstructionist point by reference to traditional U.S. approaches to immigration. Anyone who is not an American is termed an "alien." For such people to cease being aliens they must become "naturalized" citizens of the United States, since presumably to be American is "natural." After this initial step, they must then find their way into the homogeneity of the American way of life by allowing their cultural difference to be dissolved in the great American melting pot.

What deconstructionists are saying is that the sort of homogenizing and naturalizing approach to otherness and difference that is illustrated by U.S. immigration policy has characterized Western thought and culture as a whole and modernity in particular. The differences of women, the otherness of non-Western cultures and the very complex heterogeneity of the world have been dissolved or repressed into a totalizing vision. Such a vision is inherently violent because it necessarily excludes not just elements of reality that do not fit, but any *person* or *group* who sees things differently. "When convinced of the truth or right of a given worldview," notes Kenneth Gergen, "a culture has only two significant options: totalitarian control of the opposition or annihilation of it."[21] Whether or not these are the *only* options, deconstructionists say this has in fact been the legacy of the last five hundred years of Western history in relation to women, to non-Western, particularly nonwhite, peoples and to the nonhuman creation itself. It is no wonder, therefore, that postmodern author Jean-François Lyotard tells us that modernity has given us "as much terror as we can take."[22] Renouncing the nostalgia for a total scheme of things because it is both unattainable and inherently violent is a characteristic postmodern theme.[23]

### Incredulity Toward Metanarratives

It matters little whether this scheme is an abstract metaphysical system or a comprehensive metanarrative of world history; both are equally suspect to the postmodern mind. It is not just "reality" that isn't what it used to be; "history" isn't what it used to be either. Most postmoderns would go along with Christian thinkers Stanley Hauerwas and Alasdair MacIntyre in their attempt to replace the modernist notion of abstract, rational, universal systems of truth with the category of "story" or "narrative," so long as this refers to the lived, embodied, humanly constructed traditions we find ourselves a part of.[24] But if story means anything more, an overarching metanarrative that purports to portray world history from *arch* to *telos* (whether this be the modern progress myth or the Christian account of redemptive history in Jesus Christ), then its totalizing aspirations are apparent. On a postmodern reading, all such "grand narratives" or "master stories" are simply temporally extended versions of the very metaphysical systems Derrida and company have attempted to deconstruct. Just as all totalizing claims about reality are regarded as inherently violent, so all grand narratives are viewed with suspicion by postmoderns. Indeed, Jean-François Lyotard *defines* postmodernity as "incredulity toward metanarratives."[25]

Viewing metanarratives as large-scale interpretations of the whole of history with purportedly universal application, Terry Eagleton says, "Post-modernism signals the death of such 'meta-narratives' whose secretly terroristic function was to ground and legitimate the illusion of a 'universal' human history."[26] No metanarrative, it appears, is large enough and open enough to include the experiences and realities of all people. Indeed, on a postmodern reading, metanarratives invariably serve to legitimate the power structures that marginalize or trivialize these experiences.

A recent example serves to illustrate this point. In the summer of 1989 Francis Fukuyama published in the neoconservative journal *The National Interest* what has become a famous and widely read article. Entitled "The End of History?" the article discussed the meaning of the demise of Soviet communism.[27] The details of Fukuyama's argument do not need to concern us here.[28] Suffice it to say that he offers an interpretation of the events in the Soviet block at the end of the 1980s that has liberal capitalist democracy as the victor in the battle of ideologies. In fact, this victory is equivalent to the "end of history" because history is, according to Fukuyama, driven by the conflict of ideologies. And since 1989 there has been nothing left to fight about. Liberal capitalist democracy is the highest ideological achievement of the race. That this is a metanarrative, there is no doubt.[29]

But Fukuyama's reading of history also demonstrates precisely the kind of violent exclusion and marginalization of other perspectives and peoples that postmodernists criticize. Not only is Fukuyama's analysis blind to the ambiguities of democratic capitalism (manifest in such things as the inequitable distribution of wealth, a geopolitical track record that tends to support authoritarian regimes that are friendly toward capitalist economic interests, and the massive destruction of the environment at the hands of industrial capitalism), but his analysis systematically rules out the insights and contribution of any peoples who are not taken up by the spirit of capitalist democracy. This latter point is especially evident when Fukuyama declares that Western liberal democracy is nothing less than "the common ideological heritage of mankind."[30] This declaration effectively excludes the vast majority of the world's population from this "common" heritage and thus constitutes an ideological form of genocide. The grand narrative of Western progress, like all grand narratives, results in the devaluation and suppression of other stories.

But beyond the ideological suppression of stories is the quite literal totalizing violence against persons perpetuated in the name of various metanarratives. Paradigm examples of such violence stretch from neo-Babylonian imperial conquest in sixth-century Mesopotamia, buttressed by the mythology of the *Enuma Elish*, which saw Babylon as the privileged dwelling of the gods and other nations as the forces of chaos, to the twentieth-century Nazi agenda for supremacy in Europe, legitimated by a narrative of blood, soil and racial destiny.[31] Alongside these examples we might cite the Christian crusades for possession of medieval Palestine, Islamic jihad against infidels, Marxist-Leninist aspirations to world domination and the consequences in Latin America, throughout this century, of the Monroe Doctrine as part of the U.S. narrative of liberal democracy.

And so we find ourselves back with Trudy the bag lady. We surmised that she might have asked the question, "Whose reality and which collective hunch gets to rule?" And we walked the deconstructive path which argues that whoever's reality and whichever hunch is on offer, if it is framed in totalizing terms it will rule violently and oppressively. And now perhaps Trudy will ask, "Whose master-story and which metanarrative gets to tell the 'truth' about world history? And who will be co-opted, excluded or oppressed?"

Now there is a great deal that Christians can be rightly critical of in the movement known as postmodernity, and in deconstruction in particular. Among other things, it is not clear that much is left after deconstruction besides anarchic pluralism, political cynicism and cultural and moral paralysis. Deconstructive therapy, in other words, is so radical that it runs the risk of killing the patient.

Nevertheless, the deconstructive critique of modernity and the postmodern awareness of the totalizing potential inherent in all metanarratives are, in our opinion, important points that Christians need to hear. So, our approach in this paper is not a frontal attack on postmodernity. That is required too (and certainly tends to be the dominant response from the Christian world). We are more interested, however, in facing the therapist—in allowing the deconstructive scalpel (to mix our metaphors a little) to do its work.

Our question, therefore, is whether the *biblical* narrative of creation, fall and redemption in Jesus Christ (the story in which we, as Christians, are rooted) has the resources to face (and survive) the postmodern charge of totalizing violence. Does the postmodern suspicion of metanarratives apply also, legitimately, to the biblical story? How are we, as Christians, to respond to this question?[32]

### The Antitotalizing Thrust of the Biblical Metanarrative

First of all, we need to admit unabashedly that Christianity is rooted in a metanarrative that makes universal claims. This is another way of saying that the Scriptures disclose a *world*view in storied form. It is difficult to see how one could take the biblical presentation of creation, fall and redemption as merely a local tale. Indeed, it is difficult to find a *grander* narrative, a more comprehensive story anywhere. Christianity is undeniably rooted in a grand narrative that claims to tell the true story of the world from creation to eschaton, from origin to consummation. So, we must admit that, yes, the Christian faith is rooted in a metanarrative of cosmic proportions. And we have no intention of giving this up and opting for a merely *local* story. That would not be the gospel.

But does this mean that the gospel, as a metanarrative, is inevitably violent and totalizing? The postmodern charge is rooted both in a systematic insight and a historical observation. The insight is that those who articulate metanarratives and worldviews are inevitably finite, fallible (indeed, fallen) human beings. Not only is it quite literally impossible for any human articulation of a metanarrative to be genuinely universal in scope (and thus not exclude, devalue, co-opt or oppress, either explicitly or implicitly), but our fallen human tendency is to use our overarching value-systems as ideologies to legitimate our own interests. The historical observation follows from this, namely that the biblical story has, in fact, often been used ideologically to oppress and exclude those regarded as infidels or heretics. In the hands of some Christians and communities, the biblical metanarrative has been wielded as a weapon, legitimating prejudice and perpetuating violence against those perceived as the enemy, those on the outside of God's purposes. There simply is no innocent, no intrinsically just, narrative, not even the biblical one.

Having said that, however, it is our contention that the Bible, as the normative, canonical, founding Christian story, contains at least two identifiable, counterideological dimensions or antitotalizing factors. These dimensions do not, of course, *guarantee* innocence (or justice, or compassion for the other) on the part of those who adhere to this narrative. But these dimensions *permit or allow* the Christian story to delegitimate and subvert violent, totalizing uses of the story by those who claim to live by it. The first of these dimensions consists in *a radical sensitivity to suffering* which pervades the biblical narrative from the exodus to the cross. The second consists in the rooting of the story in *God's overarching creational intent* which delegitimates any narrow, partisan use of the story. And these two dimensions, we submit, are intrinsic not only to the content, but also to the very structure of the canon.

### The Exodus and Israel's Sensitivity to Suffering

Our starting point is the central event of the Old Testament, the exodus from Egypt. Yahweh's deliverance of the Hebrews from Egyptian bondage and their subsequent constitution as a people at Sinai is widely regarded by Jews as the founding and pivotal event in their own narrative and by Christians as the central event in the Old Testament. But the centrality of this event is also evident in the numerous retellings of the story found within the Bible, what Old Testament scholar Gerhard von Rad called the "little historical credos," embedded in texts as diverse as Deuteronomy 26:1-11 ("A wandering Aramean was my ancestor"), the covenant renewal ceremony of Joshua 24, and Psalms 105 and 106.[33]

In these (and numerous other texts) we find fascinating evidence of what biblical scholars variously call midrash, the traditioning process or inner biblical exegesis. That is, at some later stage in a community's development, as they face a changed existential situation, that community remembers, retells and rearticulates crucial aspects of their dramatic narrative as the basis for self-understanding and renewed ethical action in that changed situation. Alasdair MacIntyre is entirely correct here: "I can only answer the question 'What am I to do?' if I can answer the prior question 'Of what story or stories do I find myself a part?' "[34] For later Israel to answer the question "What am I to do?" it had first to answer the question "Of what story am I a part?"

So the founding Torah story (the call of Abraham, bondage in Egypt, deliverance by God, the wilderness journey and the gift of the Promised Land) is retold by particular individuals and groups at later stages within the overarching biblical narrative as the explicit basis for ethical action. Even the Decalogue is predicated on the founding story. Hence the commandments open with the following words, "I am the LORD your God, who brought you out of the land of Egypt, out of the house of slavery" (Ex

20:2). In Israel's case, ethical action is narratively formed.

The significance of this founding Torah story is that Israel's narrative memory was shaped decisively by the crucible of oppressive suffering and liberation unto justice. The memory of suffering and God's desire to relieve this suffering was kept alive in the constant retelling of the story.

But it was also kept alive in the numerous psalms of lament which became part of the liturgical repertoire of ancient Israel. Lament psalms, which constitute almost one-third of the Psalter, are abrasive prayers which give voice to pain. Refusing to repress such pain in favor of business-as-usual, these psalms articulate suffering as intolerable and demand redress and deliverance from God. In other words, the paradigm of the Hebrews' agonized groaning and complaining to Yahweh about Egyptian bondage in Exodus 2:23-25 and 3:7-10 found a settled home in the genre of individual and communal lament psalms (like Psalm 22, which Jesus prayed on the cross). These psalms, sung in worship, would have reinforced Israel's exodus memory and further shaped the Israelites' sensitivity to suffering.[35]

This sensitivity to the suffering of others is further evident in the motivational clauses found in the Book of the Covenant, that collection of laws which follows the Decalogue in Exodus. Two sorts of motivational clauses stand out as the basis for doing justice to aliens, widows and orphans, that is, to those who are relatively powerless or marginal in the community. These clauses both appeal to the exodus story. One says, "You shall not oppress a resident alien; you know the heart of an alien, for you were aliens in the land of Egypt" (Ex 23:9). The other says, "You shall not abuse any widow or orphan. If you do abuse them, when they cry out to me, I will surely heed their cry" (Ex 22:22-23).[36]

What has become clear in recent biblical scholarship, especially since the groundbreaking sociological study of Norman Gottwald, is that the whole purpose of the exodus-Sinai event was for Yahweh to found a community with an ethical pattern of life alternative to that of imperial Egypt.[37] Because of the distinctive ongoing story it told, remembered and participated in, this was to be a community which refused to cause oppression and instead was committed to fostering justice and compassion toward the marginal.[38] This sensitivity to suffering is both a major thrust or trajectory within the Bible and constitutes the first of the two counterideological dimensions of the biblical metanarrative.[39]

Old Testament scholar Walter Brueggemann has referred to this biblical trajectory as the "embrace of pain," since it involves ruthless honesty about (rather than denial of) suffering. To use a postmodern metaphor, this biblical trajectory does not make false claims to "presence," but instead highlights "absence"—the absence of God, the absence of justice, the absence of shalom. Biblical texts in this trajectory thus critique the unjust status quo in the name of Yahweh, the God of justice and liberation, and call for social transformation in the name of the founding narrative.[40]

### Prophetic Discernment of the Creator's Purposes

Brueggemann also calls this biblical trajectory the "prophetic imagination," since it is the prophets *par excellence* who give voice to the suffering of the people (and also the suffering of God) and who rearticulate the founding exodus story as the basis both of their critique of later stages in Israel's story (especially the corrupt monarchy) and of their proposal of an alternative, eschatological future.[41]

It was the unanimous message of the great Old Testament prophets of judgment (Isaiah of Jerusalem, Jeremiah, Hosea, Amos, Ezekiel, etc.) that Israel (or Judah) would be judged by God for its injustice, which was rooted in idolatry, in following not the Yahweh story of exodus from bondage but the Canaanite Baal story of cyclical fertility and guaranteed security. Even when there is no explicit accusation of Canaanite idolatry, the indictment of injustice stands, injustice stemming from the royal establishment's usurpation of power at the expense of the marginal within Israel, which amounts to an abandonment of Israel's founding exodus story.[42]

Scripture testifies amply to other prophets, judged in the canonical text to be "false" prophets, who, like the canonical prophets, appealed to the founding exodus story but drew the opposite conclusion. The canonical prophets argued that just as God delivered Israel from Egyptian bondage, so God could (and would) deliver Israel over to a new bondage, the Babylonian captivity. Yahweh was against all injustice, whether Egyptian or Israelite. The status quo prophets (later judged to be false) argued, on the contrary, that just as God delivered Israel from Egyptian bondage, so God could (and would) deliver them also from the hands of the Babylonians, because Yahweh was fundamentally on Israel's side. Both sorts of prophets appealed to the same narrative, but drew contradictory implications and conclusions.

As we know, the canonical prophets, who were largely dismissed as seditious madmen (Jeremiah, for example, was imprisoned for treason), turned out to be correct.[43] Israel did go into exile and as a result suffered a fundamental crisis of story, identity and life-pattern. In this new, changed situation the dispirited exiles desperately needed a new articulation of their story that would address this crisis. So they cried out to Ezekiel by the river Chebar in Babylon: "How then can we live?" (Ezek 33:10).

And the answer was, as always, we live out of our narratives. James Sanders, a pioneer in the field known as "canonical criticism," argues that it was the experience of land-loss and exile that engendered a rehearing of the prophets of judgment who had previously been dismissed.[44] And they were reheard not just because they were factually correct or had predictive accuracy, but also because they somehow did not think that exile annulled the story that began with the exodus and the deliverance from bondage. It is not just that Yahweh would, in the fullness of time, again deliver the people from Babylonian exile. They certainly said that (or some of them did). But, more fundamentally, it was the conviction of these prophets that Yahweh's purposes were not simply to establish Israel as an alternative countercommunity to the imperial tradition of the ancient Near East. Israel's existence as a nation, even an egalitarian nation, practicing justice toward the marginal, was not ultimately what God had in mind. On the contrary, going back to God's promise to bless all nations through Abraham's seed (Gen 12:1-3), the canonical prophets discerned that Israel's distinctive practice of justice was meant to shine as a beacon in the ancient Near East, attracting other nations to the distinctive God who wills such justice.

Indeed, God's purpose in the exodus was that Israel was to be no less than the bearer of a universal, cosmic metanarrative, a drama of God's intent to mend the world, to bring justice and healing to all nations and to the nonhuman realm.[45] This was the meaning of Israel's election as a "priestly kingdom and a holy nation" (Ex 19:6). Their role was mediational; their calling was to restore the nations to God.[46]

It was not crucial that Israel was landless, that their national identity was gone, that the monarchy was ended, that the temple was destroyed, that the sacrificial system and the cultic, ritual tradition had ceased. Yahweh could sustain Israel even on the margins and he could further his cosmic purposes even through the suffering of his servant people.

The canonical prophets discerned, in other words, that Yahweh was not simply Israel's God, but the Creator of heaven and earth, who had a redemptive purpose for all peoples. This is what Sanders calls the "monotheizing" process at work in the Bible. It was the insight that *this* was the sort of God with whom the Israelites had to do that distinguished the true from the false prophets and that allowed the former to bring a message of judgment.[47] This universal perspective or monotheizing insight into God as Creator constitutes the second counterideological or antitotalizing dimension of the biblical metanarrative.[48]

## The Shape of the Canon

Two important consequences for the very shape of the biblical canon followed from this insight, argues Sanders. The first is that the Torah or Pentateuch, the first and foundational grouping of books in the Bible, ends with Deuteronomy, not Joshua. Whereas every retelling of the story within the Bible (von Rad's *credos*) contains minimally the exodus from bondage and the entrance into the Promised Land, the Torah ends surprisingly *before* the entry into the land. This should give us pause. The book of Joshua, which tells the story of the entry, is relegated to the second grouping of books, the Former Prophets or Historical Books.[49] But the Torah, the founding story, ends with the Israelites still in the wilderness, as poignant testimony to the nonessential (or at least secondary or derivative) character of Israel's settled, national identity.[50]

Just as the traditioning process of repeating the story in new situations inevitably changed the story in subtle or explicit ways (two very *different* retellings, for example, are found in Psalms 105 and 106), so the exilic retelling effected a decisive change, reflected in the final shape of the canonical text.[51] Sanders cogently argues that only a Torah story that excluded land settlement could have provided a meaningful narrative for landless exiles (especially since it was a distorted narrative of national identity and land possession that had led to exile). Israel learned that even in a chaotic, marginal state of diaspora they could still be God's people and act ethically in accordance with their story. So the first consequence for the canonical shape of this inner biblical monotheizing process (this insight into God as universal Creator) is the exclusion of land possession from Torah.

The other consequence of this monotheizing insight is the placing of the Genesis creation story as the prologue or introduction to the book of Genesis, to Torah and ultimately to the entire Bible. It is noteworthy that while none of the early retellings of the story within the canon start with creation, by the time of the exile (specifically in Jeremiah 32 and Nehemiah 9) creation is explicitly articulated at the beginning of Israel's narrative.[52] What this canonical placing of creation does is decisively to reinterpret the exodus-Sinai story in terms of a larger, more comprehensive metanarrative.[53] Israel's "election" as the chosen people, which was often treated as election for privilege and elite status (in opposition to the *goyim*, the nations), is thus reinterpreted in the context of the metanarrative as election *for service*. Although a nationalistic reading of election is possible (though not required) in terms of a local narrative of exodus to land possession, in the context of the larger metanarrative this reading is subverted. Instead, Israel is called to be the particular, historically conditioned vessel chosen to mediate a universal story of the healing of the world. As the servant of Yahweh, Israel exists for the sake of other nations.[54] It is this monotheizing metanarrative rooted in the Creator's purposes that constitutes the second of the two counterideological dimensions of the biblical story.

It is important to note, however, that these two counterideological dimensions of the biblical metanarrative do not simply exist side by side. On the contrary, they are integrally connected. It is precisely *because* Yahweh is the universal Creator and Judge of all nations, indeed of heaven and earth, that the marginal and the suffering have a normative court of appeal against all injustice.

This connection is clear in a text like Psalm 146:5-7, 9:[55]

Happy are those whose help is the God of Jacob,
 whose hope is in the LORD their God,
who made heaven and earth,
 the sea, and all that is in them;
who keeps faith forever;
 who executes justice for the oppressed;
 who gives food to the hungry.
The LORD sets the prisoners free. . . .
The LORD watches over the strangers;
 he upholds the orphan and the widow,
 but the way of the wicked he brings to ruin.

The upshot of this twofold counterideological dynamic is that God has an overarching narrative purpose alternative to the many oppressive systems and stories in which we find ourselves. Not only is this God not to be identified with such systems and stories, but as sovereign Creator, God is able to fulfill his purpose of *shalom* for his creation, a purpose which includes the liberation of the oppressed and the empowerment of the marginal. It is thus crucial to hold together *both* dimensions of this counterideological dynamic in creative interaction.

A merely one-sided emphasis on God as sovereign Creator without attentiveness to human suffering might well result in an arid, totalitarian view of deity and an ethos of legalism and blindness to the marginal.[56] Attention to pain, on the other hand, without the possibility of appeal to a sovereign Creator may result in either a disempowered theology of suffering and survival or a vengeful sectarian attempt at heroic self-assertion in the face of overwhelming odds.[57]

### Jesus and the Biblical Metanarrative

It is arguably this latter possibility which was realized in first-century Israel, with its plethora of messianic revolutionary movements seeking liberation from Roman oppression. In the tradition of the Maccabean rebels against their Seleucid overlords some centuries earlier, many Jews in the time of Jesus positioned themselves in a generalized stance of opposition not just to the Romans, but toward all Gentiles, as outsiders. Even within Israel, as Marcus Borg has shown, a complicated ritual system of clean and unclean (or same and other) was imposed on sociopolitical and economic classes of Israelites, such that vast multitudes of the poor were considered as ritual outcasts, officially non-Jewish, excluded from the benefits of the covenant.[58]

Into this situation Jesus came, mounting a scathing prophetic critique of the religious and political "center" on behalf of the excluded other—the tax-collectors, Gentiles, prostitutes and "sinners" in general.[59] This prophetic stance is pervasive in the Gospels but is indicated significantly by the almost complete absence of the popular first-century religious category "holiness" from the teaching of Jesus. Borg argues that Jesus avoided the term on principle because it had come to function as a category of self-righteous exclusion which betrayed the heart of Israel's exodus faith. Israel's election from among the nations, described in Exodus 19:4-6 as a priestly calling to be a "holy nation," was widely interpreted in the time of Jesus as election unto separation, purity and boundary setting.

Instead, taking Israel's vocation to be one of priestly reconciliation, Jesus reinterprets holiness as loving inclusion of the marginal, as seen in his replacement of the levitical commandment "Be holy, because I the LORD your God am holy" (Lev 19:2) with "Be merciful, just as your Father is merciful" (Lk 6:36), an injunction he embodied by befriending the outcasts of Jewish society.[60] It thus does not require much argument to show that Jesus clearly stands in the prophetic tradition of the "embrace of pain." As Walter Brueggemann has profoundly elucidated in his book *The Prophetic Imagination*, Jesus embodied the counter-ideological dynamic of sensitivity to suffering.[61]

But Jesus also stands in the creation tradition, as James Sanders and Tom Wright have argued. Both Sanders and Wright suggest that Jesus' essential critique of first-century Judaism was that the vision of the canonical metanarrative, which Wright calls "creational covenantal monotheism," had become compromised, being reductively replaced by a nationalistic, sectarian narrative of "covenantal monotheism" (period).[62] That is, first-century Judaism had ignored both the creational prologue to the Torah and the exclusion of land possession from the Torah, which resulted in a totalizing form of "justice" both toward Gentiles and toward the marginal even within Israel. Hence, in place of the teaching of Leviticus 19:18 to "love your neighbor" (to which some religious teachers had added "and hate your enemy"), Jesus enjoined his disciples, in a radical, antitotalizing move, to "love your enemies" (Mt 5:43-44). What is more, he specifically grounded this injunction in the example of God's universal love as Creator, who causes sun and rain to nourish both the just and the unjust, without discrimination (Mt 5:45).

That Jesus could both side vigorously with the marginal within Israel (pervasively evident in his frequent clashes with the Jewish religious and political center) and at the same time resist the allure of militant messianic movements which sought, on behalf of the marginal, the violent overthrow of Rome (evident in his persistent refusal to be acclaimed "king" by the crowds) is testimony to a profound discernment on his part of the fundamental contours and intent of the canonical metanarrative.

This discernment is illustrated in what was perhaps his most controversial and subversive action, the so-called cleansing of the temple, when he overturned the moneychangers' tables (Mt 21:12-16; Mk 11:15-18; Lk 19:45-46), an action following directly on the heels of what has come to be known as the Triumphal Entry.

As the Gospel text has it, Jesus had entered Jerusalem during the Passover week to shouts of messianic acclaim ("Hosanna! Blessed is he who comes in the name of the Lord!"). In response to the growing expectation that he would throw off the yoke of the Romans and liberate Israel (an expectation which always ran high during Passover, when Israel celebrated the original exodus), Jesus entered the temple and decisively called into question the heart of Jewish self-understanding. Whereas Israel as elect nation and the temple as symbol of that election (representing God's presence among the chosen people) were meant, in the context of the canonical metanarrative, to be a vehicle for the reconciliation of the world, both nation and temple had become impediments to this overarching narrative purpose. Quoting two Old Testament prophetic texts (Is 56:7, Jer 7:11), Jesus declared that the temple, which should have been "a house of prayer for all the nations" had become instead "a den of robbers" (Mk 11:17).[63]

Since the term *robbers (lēstai)* acquired, possibly as early as 40 B.C., the technical connotation of militant brigands or insurrectionists resistant to Roman rule, it is significant that when Jesus was crucified between two *lēstai* by a Jewish-Roman coalition, it is Barabbas, a true *lēstēs*, who goes free in his stead (Mt 26:55; Mk 14:48; Lk 22:52; Jn 18:40). It is further significant that what precipitated Jesus' arrest, leading eventually to crucifixion, supposedly on charges of insurrection against the Roman state, was precisely his challenge to Jewish self-identity in the temple.[64]

The irony is thus complete. The very one who discerned the anti-ideological thrust of the canonical story, that Israel is God's servant to bring blessing to the nations (including the Romans), and who attempted to restore Israel to that vocation, is sacrificed on the altar of Roman and Jewish self-protective ideology. Jesus quite literally suffers for the sins of the (Jewish and Gentile) world.

In this he fulfills a vocation adumbrated in the Old Testament both of Israel and the prophets as the "servant of Yahweh," rejected by those to whom they are sent. Here we have the historical basis of the New Testament claim about the atoning sacrifice of Jesus' death. It is not simply that Jesus rightly discerned the thrust of the canonical metanarrative, evident in his antitotalizing critique of the "center," but that through his passion and death he *recapitulated* in his person the suffering of the rejected prophets and of exilic Israel before him. Jesus, in other words, paradigmatically embodied the central biblical trajectory of embracing marginality and pain, on behalf of *both* the margins and the center, as testimony to his trust in the Creator of both center and margin, who is able to bring life even out of death. The person of Jesus, and especially his death on a cross, thus becomes in the New Testament a symbol of the counterideological intent of the biblical metanarrative and the paradigm or model of ethical human action, even in the face of massive injustice.[65]

But the cross of Jesus is not merely symbolic in the New Testament. Christians confess that in the death of this marginal one we find (paradoxically) the "center" of the biblical metanarrative. In Jesus' voluntary submission to death on our behalf and in his vindication by God through resurrection, the fundamental plot conflict introduced by human sin is in principle reversed. The cross-resurrection event is thus the denouement or climactic turning point of the entire story. Although the conclusion of the story is still future, Christians confess that in Jesus the Kingdom of God (decisive plot resolution) is at hand (see Mk 1:15; Mt 4:17).

## Concluding Questions

In conclusion, two potentially troubling questions raise themselves. First of all, is our reading of the biblical text in light of postmodern questions a distortion of the biblical message, a sellout to the pluralistic spirit of the age? This is a serious question, one that cannot be simply ignored. It is a question that anyone attempting to do apologetics must struggle with. In our case, we must admit that the encounter with postmodernity (not just as an intellectual movement, but by living in a postmodern culture) has indeed influenced both our reading of Scripture and our ministry in the church. Nevertheless, we believe not only that our rearticulation of the biblical story is faithful to the text and intent of Scripture, but that post-modernity has been immensely helpful in focusing our attention on dimensions of the text that we might otherwise have missed.[66]

The second question to be considered is whether we have adequately addressed the postmodern charge. Does the biblical metanarrative escape the accusation of totalization and violence? On the one hand, we believe our analysis shows that the biblical story contains the resources to shatter totalizing readings, to convert the reader, to align us with God's purposes of shalom, compassion and justice. On the other hand, however, such transformation is never guaranteed. It is not a mechanical function of the text, but depends on our response, we who claim this text as canonical. It means we must take the text of Scripture seriously, more seriously even than our theology, which is often subbiblical. It means that we must be willing for the biblical text to judge our constructions, to call us into question, to convert us. In one sense, then, the charge of totalization addressed to Christianity can only be answered by the concrete, nontotal-izing life of actual Christians, the body of Christ who as living epistles (2 Cor 3:1-3) take up and continue the ministry of Jesus to a suffering and broken world. *That* is the only postmodern apologetic worth bothering about. If our articulation of Scripture as nontotalizing and counterideologi-cal can contribute to the empowerment of the church in the exercise of its mission in a postmodern world, perhaps that is adequate.[67]

# 8
# THERE'S NO
# SUCH THING
# AS OBJECTIVE TRUTH,
# AND IT'S
# A GOOD THING,
# TOO

*Philip D. Kenneson*

The way to solve the problem you see in life is to live in a way
that will make what is problematic disappear.
*Ludwig Wittgenstein*[1]

M y hunch is that some readers are quite suspicious of my title, suspecting that the proverbial wolf in sheep's clothing has infiltrated this collection of essays dedicated to defending the gospel. Let me assure you that I am not a relativist. But the reason I am not a relativist may not bring you much comfort; it is because I *don't believe* in objective truth, a concept that is the flip side of relativism and that is necessary for the charge of relativism to be coherent. In other words, one can defend objective truth or relativism only by assuming that it is possible for human beings to take up a "view from nowhere"; since I don't believe in "views from nowhere," I don't believe in objective truth or relativism. Moreover, I don't want *you* to believe in objective truth or relativism either, because the first concept is corrupting the church and its witness to the world, while tilting at the second is wasting the precious time and energy of a lot of Christians.

### The Intellectual Origins of "Objective Truth"

Peter C. Moore did the evangelical community a great service when he helped us "disarm the secular gods."[2] He left the job unfinished, however. Some secular gods, like their ancient counterparts, rule as divine pairs. Hence, when Moore rightly unmasked the secular god of relativism, he left her consort—objectivism—fully enthroned. Therefore, the deep irony is that Moore's disarmament strategy, like that of many Christians, involves inciting domestic violence; in short, this squabble is strictly a family affair.

What defines this family as a "family" is its common roots in the European Enlightenment, especially in the intellectual heritage of Locke, Descartes and Kant. These three thinkers probably more than anyone else set the philosophical framework from which we are now only beginning to free ourselves. Locke's "theory of knowledge," Descartes's theory of mind as mental process and Kant's notion of philosophy as the tribunal of pure reason helped to produce many of the dichotomies that now appear self-evident: object/subject; realism/idealism; knowledge/opinion; fact/value; reason/faith; rational/irrational; public/private. This philosophical tradition has taught us to think of knowledge as a kind of picture or mirror of the way the world *really* is. Such a view of "knowledge," however, creates its own special set of problems—problems rooted in our anxiety that our knowledge might *not*, in fact, mirror the world as it *really* is. In order to guarantee that no wholesale slippage takes place between our view of the world and the world as it really is, what we think we need is a theory of knowledge, a method for determining true pictures from false ones. In short, this project of supplying secure foundations for knowledge, what we call epistemology, is the attempt to assure ourselves that our pictures do, in fact, hook up with the world. Within such a view of knowledge, truth (or Truth) is not so much a concept as it is an entity "out there" in the world, waiting to be discovered; Truth is merely the word for the way the world really is which we are trying to picture or mirror with our knowledge. When human beings discover this Truth, picture it faithfully in their minds and mirror it accurately in their language, we say that they have genuine knowledge. Moreover, such knowledge is "objectively true" when its status as true does not ultimately depend on the testimony of any person or group of persons. Indeed, the whole point of claiming that something is "objectively true" is to say that any person, unhindered by the clouds of unreason and the prejudices of self-interest, would come to the same conclusion.

### The Correspondence Model of Truth Is Not the Only Option

My reason for rehearsing this bit of intellectual history is to remind us that this way of thinking about knowledge, truth and reality, what is often called "the correspondence theory of truth," is not the only paradigm available. You will remember that the entire epistemological project is funded by what Richard Bernstein calls "Cartesian anxiety," a product of methodological doubt: intense anxiety naturally follows when one begins with the premise that doubt is more fundamental than trust.[3] But one may legitimately ask: Why not doubt this fundamental posture of doubt? What, for example, happens if one begins with a view of all knowledge as rooted in trust?[4] First, certain questions become central that were previously bracketed, such as: Who should be trusted? Moreover, once we leave behind the Enlightenment view of knowledge and the correspondence theory of truth, we are also free to leave behind the entire epistemological project and the seemingly endless dichotomies generated and sustained by that project.[5]

I think such a move has exciting possibilities. Part of my task, therefore, involves not so much arguing *against* the notion of objective truth as suggesting that the intellectual problems that produced the dichotomy between the "objective" and the "subjective" need not continue to preoccupy us.[6] In short, this old paradigm of knowledge and truth is a dead-end street down which we need not continue to travel. Reminding ourselves that this model of knowledge and truth is merely a model might free some Christians from one understandable reaction to my proposal: that Christians simply *cannot* abandon the idea of objective truth because to do so would be to deny something central to the gospel. But the fact that most Christians throughout most of history have done well without the concept might encourage these latter Christians to ask *why* they feel so much is at stake here.

One reason many Christians are hesitant to give up this paradigm is that they are unsure how to make sense of their own lives without it. What is the life of a Christian if not a life dedicated to "objective truth"? Moreover, many Christians fear that if they adopted the model I am proposing there would be no reason to evangelize. If what Christians believe is not objectively true, then on what basis could they possibly commend it to others? This temptation to appeal to objective truth is particularly strong among Christian apologists, who believe they strengthen their claim by insisting that their message is *objectively* true, presumably because they likewise believe that the alternative is merely saying that it is *subjectively* true: merely true for them. But here again we are reminded that the secular gods often arrive in pairs. Appeals to objective truth are attempts to bracket human beings all together, while notions of subjective truth place the responsibility for truth firmly on the individual. Both moves are equally dubious.

But someone will likely object: "Surely there are some things which are 'true' independently of what human beings believe. Your position makes it sound as if we *make* these things 'true,' as if *we* are determining reality. We believe that God exists independently of us." These are important objections, but what gives them part of their force is the old paradigm. The picture which holds us captive is that something called Truth is "out there" waiting to be discovered or represented in language. Within such a picture, my position does indeed sound as if *we* are determining the reality. But if I might paraphrase a passage from Richard Rorty,

> We need to make a distinction between the claim that the world and God are out there and the claim that truth is out there. To say that the former are out there, that they are not our creation, is to say, with common sense, that many things are brought into being by causes which do not include human mental states. To say that truth is not out there is simply to say that where there are no sentences there is no truth, that sentences are elements of human languages, and that human languages are human creations. Truth cannot be out there—cannot exist independently of the human mind—because sentences cannot so exist, or be out there. The world and God are out there, but descriptions of the world and God are not. Only descriptions of the world and God can be true or false.[7]

What I am asking you to do is to try on a different model of truth. Within such a model, truth claims are inseparably bound up with human language and are, therefore, inextricably linked to matters of discernment and judgment, which means they are irreducibly social or communal affairs. Within this model, it makes no sense to speak of either objective truth— "truth as viewed from nowhere"—or subjective truth—"truth for me."

Yet many evangelicals believe they have an enormous stake in the correspondence model of truth, as evidenced by the numerous books attacking relativism and subjectivism in the name of absolute, objective truth. As an example, let me, for a moment, pick on the work of James Sire, if only because I think he has earned the right to be taken seriously. Sire's most recent offering labels the position I have sketched above—that truth claims are inseparable from human language—"linguistic relativism."[8] While there is much to like in Sire's work, I believe he has created a bogeyman out of the "linguistic relativist." Sire's agenda is greatly shaped by questions from the previous paradigm, questions of universal systems of justification and rationality, objective truth and transcendent essences. This makes it difficult for him to assess those like Rorty and myself who no longer believe that such an agenda is worth pursuing. Sire believes that such views about the place of language in human affairs lead to a "radical relativism" where "even science has no special status,"[9] and that they leave the Christian faith in the same boat as every other religion, which means that "it can succeed in gaining converts only by making those claims in such a way that it convinces other people to speak the same language. Objective truth has nothing to do with it. Objective truth is inaccessible."[10] Had Sire said that the concept of "objective truth" was incoherent rather than that such truth is inaccessible, I would be willing to accept his description of my position and stand behind it. The problem, of course, is that Sire thinks that my position makes no sense. And of course Sire *is* right about this. My position is non-sense, that is, unintelligible, as long as one continues to evaluate it in terms of the previous paradigm. But to make such an admission in no way counts against my position, any more than the inability of Newtonian physics to make sense of Einsteinian physics counts against the latter. What is required is a willingness to shift paradigms, a shift that will bring to the foreground an entirely different set of questions.

But of course Sire does not shift paradigms. This helps explain why he believes that those like myself *must* ask ourselves whether our positions are true or accurate, whether our views hook up to reality the way reality *really* is. But this anxiety about the way language does or does not hook up with reality is precisely the anxiety I refuse to share. Contrary to Sire's insistence, Rorty does not have to ask the kind of truth question Sire believes simply must be asked.[11] Nor do I. Nor do other Christians. And my refusal to ask or answer these kinds of questions in no way makes me a relativist. Since Sire continues to insist that people like Rorty and I really are relativists even though we say we aren't, let me paraphrase a few lines of Rorty's as a response:

> "Relativism" is merely a red herring. Realists are, once again, projecting their own habits of thought upon us when they charge us with relativism. For the realist thinks that the whole point of philosophical thought is to detach oneself from any particular community and look down at it from a more universal standpoint. When the realist hears that there are those of us who repudiate the desire for such a standpoint he cannot quite believe it. He thinks that everyone, deep down inside, must want such detachment. So the realist attributes to us a perverse form of his own attempted detachment, and sees us as those who refuse to take the choice between communities seriously, as mere "relativists." But those of us who are trying on this new paradigm can only be criticized for taking our own communities *too* seriously. We can only be criticized for ethnocentrism, not for relativism. To be ethnocentric is to divide the human race into the people to whom one must justify one's beliefs and the others. The first group—one's *ethnos*—comprises those who share enough of one's beliefs to make fruitful conversation possible. In this sense, everybody is ethnocentric when engaged in actual debate, no matter how much realist rhetoric about objectivity he produces in his study.[12]

In short, because I have neither a theory of truth nor an epistemology, I cannot have a relativistic one of either. My point is that Christians need not continue to answer "the truth question," and the sooner we see that we needn't, the sooner we can get on with the business of being Christians, which in no way entails accepting a certain philosophical account of truth, justification and "reality." I hope Sire will forgive me for harping so long on his position, but it seems that his position is not only what a lot of evangelicals believe, but also what many think they *must* believe in order to remain faithful evangelicals.

### The Virtues of an Alternative Paradigm of Truth

But I don't want to stop at saying that Christians are not *obligated* to accept the old paradigm of truth. I want to argue that contemporary Christians would be *better off* without such notions, where "better off" entails having a clearer idea of what it means to be a Christian and what it means to be the church. Here are some suggestions for what the Christian life might look like within this alternative paradigm:

First, the church becomes an indispensable touchstone. Even a non-Christian like Rorty understands that if you give up on attaining a view from nowhere, "then the important question will be about what sort of human being you want to become," which will quite naturally lead you to ask, "With what communities should you identify, of which should you think of yourself as a member?"[13] In other words, once one leaves behind achieving a "view from nowhere," what comes to the foreground is the community or communities whose convictions and practices are themselves an embodiment of what they take to be good and true. This encourages us to explore further what Christians ought to have understood already on more "theological" grounds: that what it means to be a Christian is inseparable from what it means to be the church.

Within such a model, the church has a word to speak to the world not because it has a message that is objectively true, a message which could be separated from the embodied message that the church always is. Rather, the church has a word to speak to the world because it embodies an alternative politics, an alternative way of ordering human life made possible by Jesus Christ. The central practices and virtues of such a community, practices and virtues which embody—even if imperfectly—the character of the God it serves, are such things as forgiveness, reconciliation, peacemaking, patience, truth-telling, trust, vulnerability, faithfulness, constancy and simplicity of life. This suggests that evangelicals need to pay a good deal more attention to ecclesiological matters than they traditionally have.

Second, within this new paradigm, beliefs and convictions are not denigrated as second-class knowledge or opinions, but are acknowledged as all we have got and all we have ever had. This means we can stop talking about something being "merely" a belief, a locution which gains its force only when something seemingly more stable is waiting in the wings. Moreover, within this new paradigm beliefs are no longer mental states which may or may not correspond to reality; instead, beliefs and convictions are understood as habits of acting. For example, take my deeply held conviction that our twenty-year-old daughter is trustworthy. On the correspondence model this *has* to be a belief or conviction, because there is no neutral test to check to see if the proposition "My daughter is trustworthy" hooks up to reality, which is what I would need in order to say, "I *know* that my daughter is trustworthy." On such a view, my conviction is actually considered a kind of wishful thinking: "I hope my daughter is trustworthy." But if we drop the old paradigm and begin to consider beliefs and convictions as habits of action, an interesting shift takes place. My conviction about my daughter's trustworthiness becomes a kind of explanation for why I do and don't do certain things. For example, I don't check up on her all the time to see if she's doing what she's supposed to be doing. Notice that on this model it would be incoherent to say that my actions routinely contradict my deeply held beliefs, because such beliefs are themselves nothing other than habits of action. In other words, it wouldn't make any sense to say that I believe my daughter is trustworthy and yet find myself checking up on her every hour. But notice that under the old model there's nothing necessarily incoherent about my beliefs not being embodied in my actions. Believing that a certain proposition hooks up with the way the world really is does not require one to act in any certain way.

With regard to the relationship between truth and belief within this new paradigm, truth becomes internal to a web of beliefs; there is no standard of truth independent of a set of beliefs and practices. This means that instead of asking whether one's language hooks up to reality, one is encouraged to ask: What web of convictions, beliefs and practices must be in place before one can make the judgment that a certain statement is true or false?[14] For example, when someone says, "The statement 'Jesus is Lord' is true for Christians but not for others," this can be heard in two completely different ways. Under the old model, this is heard as a denial of objectivity and public truth and an affirmation of subjectivity and private truth.[15] But under the new paradigm, this sentence translates into something like " 'Jesus is Lord' is consistent with the convictions and actions of Christians, but not with those of others." In other words, how Christians view and act in the world cannot be separated from their judgments about the world, judgments which are shaped by the church's narrative and ongoing life. It simply does not make sense to think of reality as it is in itself, apart from human judgment.

Such a shift has enormous consequences for how we think about our beliefs, but they are *not* the consequences one might expect if one continued to evaluate this new paradigm by the old one. For example, if one were to acknowledge under the old paradigm that a standard of truth is never available independent of a set of beliefs, this would mean that we could *never* know for certain what is true. But under the new paradigm, such an acknowledgment entails something quite different: that we *always* know for certain what is true, because we are always in the grip of some belief. And this is the case even though what we certainly know may change if and when our beliefs change. But until they do, we will always find ourselves arguing *from* the perspective of those convictions and *for* the perspective of those convictions, telling our interlocutors what it is that we see and trying to alter their perceptions so that, in time, they will come to see it too.

In short, we will be passionately evangelistic, trying to persuade others to our beliefs because if they believe what we believe, they will see what we see; and the facts to which we point in order to support our interpretations will be as obvious to them as they are to us. Indeed, this is the whole of Christian witness, an attempt on the part of one party to alter the beliefs of another so that the evidence cited by the first will be seen as evidence by the second. In the more familiar model of apologetics the procedure is exactly the reverse: evidence available apart from any particular belief is brought in to judge between competing beliefs. This is a model derived from an analogy to the procedures of logic and scientific inquiry, and, basically, it is a model of demonstration in which beliefs or convictions are either confirmed or denied by facts that are independently specified. The model I have been arguing for, on the other hand, is a model of persuasion in which the facts that one cites are available only because certain convictions have already been assumed.[16]

There are many other ways in which this belief would serve the Christian community better. For example, such a model would seem to embody more faithfully the classic posture of "faith seeking understanding." Such a model also rightly affirms the limitations of human knowledge and the humility that is the corollary of that acknowledgment. Such a humility does not require us to remain silent altogether, but it may encourage us to brush aside certain kinds of questions. For example, once we free ourselves from the strictures of epistemology, we can learn to brush aside questions like "But how do you *know* what God wants of us?" in the same way we brush aside questions like "How do you *know* that Jones is worthy of your friendship?" or "How do you *know* that Yeats is an important poet, Hegel an important philosopher and Galileo an important scientist?" As Rorty reminds us, there is no way to silence doubt on such matters, for "those who press such questions are asking for an epistemic position which nobody is ever likely to have about any matter of moral importance."[17] In short, the position I am advocating suggests that sometimes one should avoid answering the epistemological question "How do you know?" and respond instead by asking: "Why do you talk that way?"[18] Such a move, I believe, would be a great gain for the Christian community.

Third, under this new paradigm we will be forced to find a different authorization for our witness. In the recent past, Christian apologists have often sought authorization for their projects by insisting that what they were saying was objectively true. But once we give up on the notion of objective truth, we are free to admit that our reliance on this prop in the past was a form of denial: a denial of our calling as the church. Too often appeals to the objective truth of the gospel have served as a means for the church to evade its responsibility to live faithfully before the world. In short, Christians insisted that the gospel was objectively true regardless of how we lived. The paradigm I am advocating frankly admits that all truth claims require for their widespread acceptance the testimony of trusted and thereby authorized witnesses. This is as true for the truth claims of science as it is for those of the church.[19] We trust scientists, among other reasons, because they have certain credentials, because we believe that they regularly subscribe to a method that minimizes the effects of their own idiosyncrasies and because they have been remarkably successful in predicting and controlling nonhuman reality. Whether reasons such as these are good reasons to trust the scientific enterprise is a matter for another book; for now we need only acknowledge that they provide the basis for authorizing the scientific project.[20] But when it comes to the Christian faith, the question of what authorizes the church to speak a word to the world becomes more difficult to answer.[21]

Once we give up on the notion of objective truth, it becomes clear that what is needed is a reason for non-Christians to give us a hearing. This is a question of the moral authority of the church's embodied life, a life that gives our truth claims intelligibility and credibility. Our efforts to argue people into the kingdom by insisting that what we are saying is objectively true reduce the Christian faith to a form of gnosticism, and ironically, a modernist form of gnosticism at that. If we could unequivocally prove to people that the proposition "God exists" is objectively true, the inhabitants of our culture would yawn and return to their pagan slumbers. What our world is waiting for, and what the church seems reluctant to offer, is not more incessant talk about objective truth, but an embodied witness that clearly demonstrates why anyone should care about any of this in the first place. The fact that most of our non-Christian neighbors cannot pick us out from the rest of their non-Christian neighbors—or if they can, what makes us pick-outable are matters relatively incidental to the gospel—suggests that they are right in refusing to accept what we *say* we believe but which our *lives* make a lie.

## The Apologetic Challenges Facing the Church

I realize there are plenty of Christians who think it makes good sense to say that the proposition "Jesus Christ is Lord of the universe" is objectively true; that is, our temptation is to insist that this is simply true whether we or anyone else believe it or not. But succumbing to such a temptation is deadly for the church. There is no place to stand and judge this statement as true per se. There is no view from nowhere. But neither should we say that such a statement is just one opinion among others, for such a view would also require a view from nowhere. What we forget is that the truth claim "Jesus Christ is Lord of the universe" is a sentence in twentieth-century English whose meaning, like any sentence, is not automatically perspicuous. What does it mean to say that the following sentence is "objectively true": "Jesus of Nazareth, a first-century Jew, is the promised Messiah of God who came to earth to inaugurate a kingdom over which he continues to rule, even though one must have eyes to see it"? To make such a claim intelligible, let alone true, one must have a concrete historical community who by their words and deeds narrate this story in a way that gives some substance to it. We know who Jesus is only on the basis of human witnesses to the history of God's dealings with God's people, which is mediated to us, not objectively, but through communities of human beings animated by the Holy Spirit. We cannot know what "lordship" entails apart from communities of faith who daily strive to embody the claims of this Lord on their lives. Do we really know what the coming kingdom looks like apart from communities who are themselves imperfect historical embodiments of this in-breaking kingdom? Do we really know in what sense Joshua the Anointed One rules, apart from the communities of faith who at times are given the eyes to see this ruling and participate in it? Insisting that "Jesus is Lord of the universe" is objectively true is like saying that Sultan Said is Sultan of Oman regardless of whether he has any loyal subjects who acknowledge his sultanate—he just *is* Sultan. Can one really be Sultan or Lord apart from those who acknowledge one's claim to Lordship? Isn't that part of the grammar of "Lord"?[22]

It does absolutely no good for us to sit here and insist that the proposition "Jesus is Lord of the universe" is objectively true while at the same time we live our lives in such a way that this lordship remains completely invisible. If Christians feel compelled to claim that Jesus is Lord of the universe, then that lordship must be visible somewhere; it can never be objectively true, nor should we desire it to be, for such a desire not only requires us to bow down to the modernist god of objectivity, but more importantly, it involves us in denying our very reason for being. God called the church into being to bear witness by its embodied life together that God has come to earth and dwelt among us, a mission that should not have left things the way they were.

Stanley Hauerwas has argued for some time that the church, rather than bemoaning the collapse of Christendom, might see in such collapse a providential opportunity to regain a sense of its own calling, its own identity.[23] In short, there might be reasons for Christians to celebrate the current situation in which the nation-state refuses to prop up the church. But Constantinianism dies hard, and it is difficult for those in the West to believe that they can be Christians without the nation-state's blessing and cooperation. But we can. In a parallel way, I have been arguing that the church's existence as a people set apart to witness by their corporate life to the God they confess and worship is not inextricably tied to a certain philosophical conception of truth (the correspondence theory of truth). Rather than tightly clutching this concept and insisting that the gospel can only be proclaimed faithfully within such a philosophical framework, we might take the time to explore the opportunities that present themselves once this prop is gone. I have suggested that one of these important opportunities is the way giving up on the notion of objective truth will force the church to take responsibility for its judgments about the way it sees, understands and acts in the world. This means that what will give our testimony authority will not be that what we say is "objectively true" such that any reasonable person would be required to take us seriously. Rather, what will lend our testimony authority is that by the grace of God we live in such a way that our lives are incomprehensible apart from this God. As Cardinal Suhard has elegantly argued: "To be a witness does not consist in engaging in propaganda, nor even in stirring people up, but in being a living mystery. It means to live in such a way that one's life would not make sense if God did not exist."

That is the challenge which the contemporary American church faces and the one at which we are failing miserably. I suspect that far too many of us are a long way from being living mysteries. I suspect, for example, that my neighbors have no trouble at all making sense of my life quite apart from any conception of God whatsoever. For those concerned about "how the church can make the truth of the gospel compelling in a pluralistic culture that embraces relativism," I suggest as a starting point that the church take inventory of itself and begin to examine the myriad ways it has itself become an obstacle to the proclamation of the gospel.

One of the favorite passages of contemporary Christian apologists is 1 Peter 3:15, which urges that Christians "always be prepared to give an answer to everyone who asks you to give the reason for the hope that you have" (NIV). To their credit, evangelicals, perhaps more than anyone, are poised to give answers; the problem is that no one is *asking*. Unless we are content to answer questions no one is posing, it seems to me the most urgent apologetic task of the church today is to live in the world in such a way that the world is driven to ask us about the hope we have. Until that happens, I fear all the theories in the world about apologetics are in vain, and the truth we *say* we bear witness to will be heard as falsehood.

My hunch is that when the church begins to embody its testimony to the world, when it begins to embody the character of this particular God known in Jesus Christ, when our neighbors see the Spirit alive in our common life and when our neighbors begin to ask us about the hope we have, only then will the church have something to say. *What* we will need to say probably can't be known ahead of time.[24]

I would like to end where I began, by quoting Wittgenstein. Though I doubt he had the Christian apologetic encounter in mind when he wrote, I find his warning sobering: "The truth can be spoken only by someone who is already at home in it; not by someone who still lives in falsehood and reaches out from falsehood towards truth on just one occasion."[25]

# PART V
# THE CHURCH
# IN A
# POSTMODERN
# SETTING

# 9
# CHRISTIAN APOLOGETICS IN THE AFRICAN-AMERICAN GRAIN

*Ronald Potter*

A frican-American literary and cultural critic George Kent wrote at the beginning of his powerful but little-known *Blackness and the Adventure of Western Culture* the following:

I began writing this [book] by trying to say something of conscious intentions, and of my hope that, if I had successfully fulfilled them, they would be useful in effecting some shift in the criticism of black literature. But a voice blocked me and my writing. It kept saying: "George, you are lying, man. . . . The problem is, you must say, 'I tried to do this and that, or to avoid doing this and that.' And that way you are double trapped: by a rhetoric that falsifies and confuses conscious striving. . . . So say things that you are really clear about, and that you can express simply and clearly."[1]

As I began preparing for this presentation with the desire and intention of breaking new theoretical ground and hoping to effect some shift in the discursive practices of evangelical apologists and subsequently explicate the contours of a distinctly African-American variety, a voice blocked my writing. It kept saying, "Ron, you're lying, homeboy. Don't capitulate to a rhetoric that falsifies and confuses the spiritual strivings of your people. So say things that you are really clear about and that you can express simply and clearly." I have decided not to be disobedient to the heavenly voice. This presentation will not seek to explore the dimensions of a black apologetic proper, nor will it engage in a type of prolegomenon. Rather, it will seek to challenge my white evangelical friends to "revision" (to borrow a term from Stanley Grenz[2]) the enterprise and practice of Christian apologetics.

### The African-American Grain

My challenge unapologetically is informed by the "African-American grain." This term has both descriptive and interpretive import. As a descriptive term, it attempts to depict the contours of black life in America. W. E. B. DuBois, one of the greatest American scholars of the twentieth century, more than any other thinker described accurately the identity crisis confronting African-Americans. At the beginning of this century, in his now classic text *The Souls of Black Folks*, DuBois noted that the black American

> ever feels his twoness—an American, a Negro, two souls, two thoughts, two unreconciled strivings, two warring ideals in one dark body, whose dogged strength alone keeps it from being torn asunder. The history of the American Negro is the history of this strife, this longing to attain self-conscious manhood, to merge his double-self into a better and truer self.[3]

This DuBoisian double consciousness best describes the life-world of African-Americans. To quote from black Christian thinker and social critic Cornel West: "The life worlds of Africans in the United States are conceptually and existentially neither solely African, European or American. But more of the latter than any of the former."[4]

The term "African-American grain" is also being employed as an interpretive or conceptual framework. African-Americans, like all other social and ethnic groups, have their own way of perceiving, knowing and construing reality. This reality construction represents a kind of world and life view. Ironically, this black perspective is more genuinely American than some forms of Anglo-American thought.

According to philosopher John McDermott, classic American thought has always been more pragmatic than speculative. Indeed, it has traditionally been a mode of thought that sides with experience over reflection as the primary resource in formulating beliefs.[5] One can clearly recognize this tendency in the thought of such diverse thinkers as Jonathan Edwards, Ralph Waldo Emerson, William James, John Dewey and Reinhold Niebuhr. Theoretical thought in the African-American grain is fundamentally concerned about the social utility of an idea or concept. If theoretical thought does not make a difference within the actual lived experience of African-Americans, then it must be jettisoned.

## The Apologist's Vocation

In approaching this subject, I want to take a look at how Christian apolo-

getics may be revisioned from an African-American perspective. Thus the
first item we must look at is revisioning the vocation of the Christian
apologist. The best place to start is with the most delicate and difficult of
issues: the self-image and self-identity of Christian apologists. The reason
for this is that the sense of vocation of Christian apologists sets the tone of
the discipline of apologetics.

African-American philosopher and social critic Cornel West suggests
some insightful ways in which theologians can renew their sense of calling.
West writes:

> An appropriate starting point for reform in theological education is
> seminary professors creating for themselves a sense of vocation and
> purpose that revels in the life of the mind, always in conversation with
> the best that is being thought and written regarding their intellectual
> concerns—yet puts this at the service of the people of God. Seminary
> professors must first view themselves as servants of the Kingdom of
> God and thereby resist the lucrative temptation of a flaccid careerism.
> ... Such a vocation means that seminary professors will be marginal to
> the academy. .... Need we remind ourselves that the great seminary
> professors of the past (who were neither careerists nor technicians, but
> rather ecumenical intellectual figures with which the larger culture had
> to reckon) had this sense of vocation. ... In this way, seminary professors
> can change the character of theological education by giving students a
> novel sense of what it means to have a vocation as a Christian intellec-
> tual in our time.[6]

I have quoted West at length in order to drive home the point of the
apologist's making his or her calling and election sure. Such perceptive
evangelical thinkers as David Wells, Os Guinness and John Seel have
accented this theme of vocation over against the professionalism and
"illusions of technique" that permeate much of theological education
today. These thinkers have been especially prophetic in challenging evangelicals to recognize the various ways in which capitulation to modernity
can occur. While evangelical thinkers await a frontal assault from moder-

nity via the history of ideas, the modern Zeitgeist enters from the rear through such "carriers" as professionalism, careerism and specialization.

Believing the deceptive present to be a gift from the gods, many evangelical thinkers have unwittingly brought the Trojan horse of modernity within the gates of the city of God. The consequent disintegration of ecclesiastical Troy should remind us that the apologist who trades with modernity, even on a noncognitive level, is apt to come out with a poor bargain. That is, the apologist will probably have to give up far more than he or she will get.

Russell Jacoby's splendid text of a few years ago, *The Last Intellectuals*, has great import for the task of revisioning the vocation of the Christian apologist as well as for the project of Christian apologetics. In this important and in some ways prophetic volume, Jacoby bemoans the demise of the public intellectual—the intellectual who is not inextricably tied to the academy but is one whom Cornel West refers to as an organic intellectual, tied to a community of praxis.[7]

### Public Intellectuals

Who are the "last intellectuals" amongst evangelical apologists? I would like to suggest two Christian thinkers who exemplified what it meant to be a Christian public intellectual in our time.

The first exemplar was the insightful cultural critic Francis Schaeffer. Schaeffer was American evangelicalism's quintessential public intellectual. He understood well the pastoral aspects of Christian apologetics. Moreover, Schaeffer opposed most strenuously the careerist and specialist modes that have recently emerged within evangelical discursive practices. Schaeffer believed that apologetics should not be merely an academic subject, a new kind of scholasticism; rather, apologetics should be an effective tool for communicating the Christian message within a post-Christian culture. In essence, Schaeffer's vocation as a Christian intellectual must be understood within a missiological frame of reference.

William Hiram Bentley was another person who typified what it meant to be a public Christian apologist in our time. Bentley was for many black evangelicals what Schaeffer was for many white evangelicals. He served for many years as the president and board chairman of the National Black Evangelical Association and was an adjunct professor of theology at Trinity Evangelical Divinity School. Bentley was in the beginning stages of developing what he envisioned as a black evangelical theology. His mode of theological reflection emerged within a pastoral setting. Indeed, Bentley gave new meaning to the understanding of the "pastor as apologist"—that is, one who not only confronts the so-called cultured despisers of the faith but also addresses a variety of different interlocutors. Bentley represented a long tradition of apologetics done in the service of ministry within the African-American grain.

### Three Publics

What do the examples of Schaeffer and Bentley suggest in terms of revisioning *our* contemporary context? First of all, we must recognize that we address ourselves not to one, not to two, but to actually three "publics." David Tracy in his groundbreaking book of 1981 entitled *The Analogical Imagination* deals with the publics the theologian must face—the public of the church, the public of the marketplace and the public of the academy. This understanding is grounded in the discourse of the apostle Paul in Athens in Acts 17. Most of us like to accent Paul's engagement with the cultured despisers of the faith. But a careful look at that passage indicates that Paul addressed himself to three different publics: the religious community (that is to say, to the Jews and the God-fearing Greeks—those persons who were already conversant with Jewish religion and morality), the marketplace or the public sphere (whoever happened to come by) and then, last, the Epicurean and Stoic philosophers (those who participated in what social theorist Alvin Gouldner has referred to as the "culture of critical discourse").[8]

It is to these three "publics" that we too as twenty-first-century apologists must address ourselves. Far too many Christian thinkers focus on a single public. More often than not, that "public" represents the modern and postmodern cultured despisers of the faith. Rarely do evangelical apologists have any effect within the marketplace of common public life. Evangelist and apologist Michael Green writes regarding this issue:

> Most of our apologetics is directed to those who are literate middle class rational thinkers. But the majority of our countrymen do not read books at all. They are not middle class and they are not used to abstract thinking. They are immediate visual people. The Christian presses pour out more and more books for a reading public that is, if anything, shrinking. Such books have very little impact on our society in a television age that relies less and less on the written word.[9]

I would suggest to you that the cultural and intellectual climate that we as Christian apologists face today has been grossly misunderstood. Many of us have tended to overestimate the pervasiveness and cognitive sovereignty of so-called secularized modern consciousness. All too often we speak as if the "modern scientific worldview," the "modern view of reality" and the "secularized modern consciousness" were philosophical perspectives and cognitive commitments shared by everyone within the Western world. Sociologist Andrew Greeley suggests, however, that only a very small percentage of the American population actually could be considered truly secular. Accordingly, virtually the only persons who represent so-called modern man and woman are those within the intellectual community. Moreover, not everyone within the knowledge class shares in the Weltanschauung of secular modernity. Greeley contends that empirical data simply do not support the notion that most people within American society have adopted a secular worldview.

Sciological studies do, in fact, indicate that American religious consciousness has not been appreciably affected by scientific and technological advances. Most Americans still basically affirm a traditional theism. Far too many of us have accepted the Bultmannian myth that it is "impossible" (or at best improbable) for persons to benefit from scientific and technological advances and simultaneously affirm a supernaturalist view of reality. The assumption is that those who have been exposed to the benefits of modern science and technology also accept the philosophical framework of modern science.

In reality, most Americans enjoy the benefits of advanced technology without giving a second thought to its philosophical foundations. To be sure, a consumer-oriented society is not prepared to critically think through the philosophical assumptions of advanced technology. Most Americans suffer from a mild form of religious schizophrenia. They think and live in two entirely different realms of reality: the profane reality of the ordinary world and the sacred reality of Sunday-morning religious experience. The most amazing aspect, however, is that most of them are unaware of this double consciousness.

### Inner-City Secularism
But in spite of this, there is a sense in which even segments of the urban underclass experience the "angst" of postmodern consciousness. This distinctly African-American strain of postmodernity was cogently expressed in Richard Wright's classic novel *The Outsider*, published in 1952. Wright's protagonist, Cross Damen, experiences extreme marginality. Damen is not only marginalized due to his racial and ethnic origin, but he is actually outside the religio-moral framework of both black and white Americans. Damen's secularism is not altogether attributed to his reading of French existentialist philosophers. Rather, for Damen, the actual lived experiences of African-Americans inhabiting the "underside" of modernity eventuate in a secularism-in-black!

Fundamentally, secularization for many African-Americans has generated a near-profane world and life view. This newly emergent urban ethos has been described variously as a "crisis of the black spirit" and "nihilism in black America."[10] Essentially, this new ethos is one in which reality is divested of any sacred significance. Damen's recurring phrase throughout the novel, "Man is nothing in particular," is echoed throughout the urban underclass. This profanation of human life is responsible in part for the high homicide rate in most inner-city communities. It is this postmodern angst that must gain the attention of Christian apologists.

## The Apologetic Task

Finally, I need to say a word on how I revision the apologetic task. The task of the Christian apologist, especially within the African-American grain, is not dissimilar from the ministry of Jesus as depicted in Luke 7:18-22. In that passage John the Baptist, imprisoned and about to be executed, is experiencing a moment of doubt concerning Jesus. He sends a few of his disciples to Jesus to inquire whether he is the Messiah or if they should look for another. Jesus sets forth a type of evidentialist apologetic and then says, "Go and tell John what you have seen and heard: the blind receive their sight, the lame walk, the lepers are cleansed, the deaf hear, the dead are raised, the poor have good news brought to them."

This "praxis-oriented" apologetic (to borrow a term from Nick Wolterstorff[11]) must inform our theological reflection. We must be able to demonstrate to the least of these—to the marginalized, to the urban underclass—a gospel that can communicate to them in their totality; and by that I mean a gospel that can deal with persons who are unemployed, people who are homeless. Our gospel must be able to deal with the issues of violent crime and police brutality, the moral and spiritual disintegration of our urban communities typified by drugs, AIDS and unwed juvenile parenthood, and the spirit of hopelessness and despair in our communities—or it is irrelevant and impotent. That is not to suggest that Christ is irrelevant and powerless, but that the transmitters of that transforming vision are irrelevant, impotent and ineffective.

In the midst of everything that seems so difficult, that seems so powerful, that seems so overwhelming, we are challenged to relate the transforming vision of the gospel to those on the underside of modernity, assuring them that there is a way through, there is a way to stand, there is a way to live, there is a way to hope. Don't give up!

# 10
# THE CHURCH
# AS APOLOGETIC
# A Sociology of Knowledge
# Perspective

*Dennis Hollinger*

Christian apologetics should operate with two assumptions. First, we should assume that apologetics is a contextual enterprise that seeks to respond to the questions, critiques and skepticism of a given place and time. The defense of the gospel, then, is an ongoing, ever-changing discipline that attempts to respond to challenges in ways that can be heard by the contemporary culture and the church.

Our second assumption is that there are limits to all forms of contextualization, including apologetics. If our defense of the faith distorts the very core of the gospel and the foundations upon which it rests, then the apologetic must be rejected. A case in point is Bultmann's attempts to defend the faith for modern hearers through his demythologizing agenda.

My proposal for an apologetic in the postmodern world is to understand the church itself—a visible, corporate expression of the Christian worldview—to be an apologetic. This is a contextualized approach for our own time and it is one that reinforces the core of the gospel rather than distorting it. My understanding of what is needed for our contemporaries to see Christianity as cogent, truthful, meaningful and compelling has risen both from academic study (in particular one school of sociology) and from my own experience ministering to very bright, young, driven and questioning people in our nation's capital.

Peter is one such person. He is a brilliant, well-rounded scientist in his early thirties working in a government agency. Brought up in a liberal Jewish background, Peter had an intellectual exposure both to his own tradition and to various world religions and philosophies. Though bar mitzvahed as an adolescent, he has never embraced or practiced any religion and has seen little need for it whatsoever. I met this very likable young man after he began to express some general interest in looking at Christianity to one of his colleagues, who happened to be one of our parishioners. We began to meet and talk about the Bible, the contours of Christian thinking, the relationship of Judaism to Christianity and the myriad questions that a thinking person might ask in our generation.

It was quite clear after several discussions that he was fascinated with intellectual inquiry on questions of ultimacy, but it was equally evident that he was not ready to embrace a personal faith in Christ. Assuming that his hangups (especially as a scientist) were likely the typical modern ones relative to supernaturalism, I drew on my arsenal of traditional apologetic arguments. I rehearsed all the classic defenses I could recall in an attempt to convince him that miracles are possible, a historic resurrection really happened and that Jesus of Nazareth was fully God and fully human. But Peter looked at me and said, "But those aren't the issues for me. That all makes sense and may well be true. But what I'm trying to grasp is how a Christian worldview fits with the whole of reality. What I need to see is how it makes sense and fits within both the routine and the not-so-routine, even the tragic elements of human experience." And then he added, "What has initially drawn me into exploring Christianity are my friends who have a framework for making sense of work, play, life and death. But I wish to see more of how it is really expressed in the fray of human reality; to see how and where your worldview is really manifested." Without thinking, I said, "Peter, you need to come to church." Peter's thinking and longings, like those of so many others today, call for the church itself to be an apologetic. But first, what is there in our culture that beckons such an approach?

## Pluralism and the Problem of Legitimation

One of the major characteristics of modernity that carries over into the postmodern world is pluralism, the coexistence of divergent worldviews. Postmodernity is best understood as a shift in culture or the ideational dimensions of society. In this world the societal or structural elements of modernity continue as before, but with greater intensification. One such element is this socio-cultural pluralism.[1]

Throughout much of human history people's worldviews, or "life worlds" as some sociologists put it, were minimally challenged. One rarely rubbed shoulders with people who put their world together in significantly different ways or lived their lives in accordance with significantly different values. Life was not segmented into highly differentiated components and the gap between the personal self and the public self was minimal or even nonexistent. As sociologist of knowledge Peter Berger puts it:

> Through most of human history, individuals lived in life worlds that were more or less unified. . . . Compared with modern societies, most earlier ones evinced a high degree of integration. Whatever the differences between various sectors of social life, these would "hang together" in an order of integrating meaning that included them all. The integrating order was typically religious. For the individual this meant quite simply that the same integrative symbols permeated the various sectors of his everyday life.[2]

In such a setting one's worldview—and in particular its religious dimension—was not challenged by the structural or cultural realities of society.

All of that changed with modernity and has only intensified in our present era. The fragmentation of life which began with the division of labor in the industrial revolution has only increased in our information era with its service-oriented economies. The result is loss of a unifying center to give coherence and meaning to the totality of life. The accompanying sociocultural pluralism with its multiplicity of competing value systems, meaning systems and claims to truth tends to raise questions about the validity of one's own frame of reference. The pluralistic situation multiplies the number of competing "life worlds" in such a way that they are all relativized and claims to truth are put on the defensive. In such a context it is easy to see how deconstructionist epistemologies develop; they question any ability to interpret reality or make claims to truth from an objective standpoint.

It is this pluralistic milieu above all other factors which triggers the commonly heard response that one religion or set of values is as good as any other. In this context, "Subjectively, the man in the street tends to be uncertain about religious matters. Objectively, the man in the street is confronted with a wide variety of religious and other reality-defining agencies that compete for his allegiance or at least attention."[3] The post-modern individual, somewhat unlike the modernist, is not stridently antispiritual or antisupernatural, as is evidenced by the growing popularity of New Age thinking. Rather, the postmodernist relativizes claims to ultimacy by making them all equally valid or by claiming that there are no universals whatsoever. All reality-defining agencies have become local and parochialized. Thus, the primary issue facing contemporary Christian apologetics is not naturalism versus supernaturalism; rather, it is how one specific supernaturalism can be understood as *the* way, the truth and the life amidst the plethora of choices.

In such a context, then, how do we establish legitimacy for our world-view as Christians? Peter Berger argues with his sociology of knowledge framework that in the midst of pluralism, "each world requires a social 'base' for its continuing existence as a world that is real to actual human beings. This 'base' may be called its plausibility structures."[4] A plausibility structure is very simply a social structure which manifests the worldview of a people. A particularistic, minority life world can only make sense and find legitimation in the expression of a social group that lives out, symbolizes and converses with that life world in ways that make it seem objectively and subjectively real. Thus, the firmer the plausibility structure, the firmer the view of reality on which that structure is built.

When a whole society served as a plausibility structure for a religion, as in the Middle Ages, all social processes confirmed its reality. But in the pluralistic context, plausibility structures will become increasingly sectarian as they become more expressive of distinct beliefs and values. It is even more imperative, therefore, that the plausibility structure be compelling in its legitimation of the life world, which is now viewed as one among many options. With reference to Christianity Berger writes:

> The reality of the Christian world depends upon the presence of social structures within which this reality is taken for granted and within which successive generations of individuals are socialized in such a way that this world will be real to them. When this plausibility structure loses

its intactness or continuity, the Christian world begins to totter and its reality ceases to impose itself as self-evident truth.[5]

Berger insists that all of this does not imply a social determinism, making faith nothing more than an effect of social processes. Rather, as Christians we can understand that the transcendent reality of the gospel is mediated or at least heard and seen in a social context. What is that social context or plausibility structure? It is the church.

## The Church as Plausibility Structure

Christian apologetics in the modern world was largely an atomistic or individualistic venture that assumed that a human being standing alone could be convinced by rational argumentation of the validity of Christian truth. It fit well with the Enlightenment assumptions about human beings and the priority of rationalism as a method of epistemology. While it may have worked (and that is perhaps a matter for debate) for that period of history, such an apologetic does not appear to be working for a world in which pure rationality is suspect and in which pluralism only exacerbates claims to truth.

In such a context the need for a plausibility structure to give flesh, life and meaning to the Christian worldview is heightened. And the church is the plausibility structure of the Christian faith. It is through this social reality that the Christian worldview is potentially expressed in such a way that it provides a holistic appeal to modern hearers who will not rely on one mode of reality affirmation.

The worldview or defining narrative which we seek to portray and defend is best subsumed under four categories or plots: creation, fall, redemption and consummation. These are the essential components which form the core of a Christian life world. Underlying this is of course a supernaturalist assumption which makes possible the acceptance of a God who really can intervene into the ebb and flow of human lives and history. An apologetic for postmodernity can best seek to defend this view of reality by giving visible, lucid expression to it in ways which appeal to the totality of human personhood. More specifically, I suggest that the church should embody five dimensions of human existence in its attempt to reflect coherence between the Christian worldview and expressions of that worldview.

First, there is the narrative dimension. Here we appeal to the fact that human beings are storytellers who seek to find narratives to make sense of their own lives and the saga of human history. Narrative theory has been widely utilized in varying disciplines such as literature, history, philosophy, sociology, theology and biblical studies. Though there is much variation in the way narrative is defined and used, most adherents emphasize that story is the best vehicle for interpreting reality, which is always shaped by a community sharing a common story. As applied to Christian faith, Stanley Hauerwas and David Burrell argue that "we discover our human self more effectively through . . . stories, and so we use them in judging the adequacy of alternative schemes for human kind."[6] They believe that for Christians the supreme story is the biblical story culminating in the Christ story, and that its truth is discerned not through rationality but through its resonance with our own stories and life experiences.

While narrative theology may have certain limitations,[7] the utilization of narrative forms does have some merit in defending the gospel to postmodern thinkers. When the church gathers each Sunday to worship, it is essentially rehearsing the grand story of creation, fall, redemption and consummation. And as Alan Jacobs has contended:

> An important task of contemporary apologetics is to argue that Christianity can tell a better story—that is, a more coherent narrative, one that accounts more accurately and completely for the events of our lives, one that can give our lives meaningful direction—a better story, then, than any of its rivals.[8]

A second way in which our worldview is expressed within the church is through the cognitive or discursive dimension. Though postmodernity as an intellectual movement debunks this rationalistic component, in reality its adherents and the masses continue to employ it. Even the narrative purists and deconstructionists utilize rational discourse to repudiate the traditional rational approaches to discovering and defending truth. Therefore, we need not shy away from some appeal to classical apologetics as long as it is buttressed by other modes of discourse and defense. Narrative modes of theology and apologetics alone will not suffice to answer the questions that postmoderns ask, and thus some appeal to rational argumentation may still resonate with them. However, the rational appeal will be most powerful when it is connected to a living body that expresses the Christian worldview in multiple ways, so that rationality is not severed from other dimensions of the human self.

A third means of worldview expression within the church is the symbolic or ritual dimension. Here the appeal is to the fact that humans are symbol- and ritual-makers, for anthropologists have long noted these as major vehicles through which people articulate and solidify their life world. Symbols tend to be right-brain modes of communication that enable us to see the world in highly compelling ways in their appeal to beauty, symmetry and wholeness.

It is perhaps no accident that the primary ritual of the Christian church, the Lord's Supper, has served as one of the most potent appeals for the reality of Christ's atonement and resurrection. After all, the apostle Paul wrote, "For as often as you eat this bread and drink the cup, you proclaim the Lord's death until he comes" (1 Cor 11:26). The power of the Eucharist for a proclamation and defense of the gospel was brought home to me vividly through recent conversations with a young woman. Though a believer, she was going through one of those intellectual dark nights of the soul and expressed gnawing doubts regarding the deity of Christ and even the reality of a personal God. She asked if she could come to the Lord's Table even in her time of doubt. I invited her to come with the little faith she had, knowing both the power of the Eucharist to mediate the presence and reality of Christ and her own proclivities toward ritual and symbol. Several weeks later she told me that it was her coming to the Table more than anything else that reaffirmed her faith in the living Christ.

In the postmodern world, symbol and ritual are powerful forms of communication and can be vital tools in Christian apologetics. It may well be that C. S. Lewis's greatest appeal to the postmodern mind will not be through *Mere Christianity*, *Miracles* or *The Problem of Pain*, but rather from the Chronicles of Narnia or his science-fiction trilogy. These books give a symbolic portrayal of the Christian life world, appealing to beauty, symmetry and wholeness of life.

A fourth way in which the church can express its worldview is through the life experience dimension. Here the appeal is to seeing the Christian life world in the midst of everyday realities, including both the routine and the tragic elements that face us. This expression gives flesh to the reality of a personal, transcendent God and to the supernatural dimensions of faith as they are integrated into life situations.

It seems rather odd and not very compelling that modern, rational apologetics was forever defending a supernatural worldview but tended to be skeptical of contemporary supernatural expressions within the church and personal experience. B. B. Warfield was indeed one of the great defenders of Christianity in the face of modernity, but his apprehension regarding the possibility of miracles for our own age would seem to undermine the apologetic arguments for a supernatural worldview.[9]

In my most recent conversation with Peter (the young scientist I mentioned earlier), he told me that the most compelling force in his consideration of becoming a Christian is prayer. He is now part of a small group that studies the Bible each week, shares life's stresses and strains, and prays together. At times they pray for Peter as he faces pressures at work and needs in his own life. With wet eyes he told me, "It is in those prayers that I am coming to realize that God may be more than a principle, and may indeed be personal. Those prayers are causing me to question whether the secular assumptions from which I have been operating may not teeter in the face of life experiences and intellectual quests." What Peter is coming to see in the small group, and now in occasional attendance at church, is the Christian worldview expressed in multiple ways, not least of which is life experiences.

A fifth dimension through which the Christian worldview manifests itself is that of moral behavior. This apologetic appeal is of course an old one, for it was one of the favorites of the early Christian apologists. In the face of criticism that Christians undermined the good of society, the early apologists argued that the moral behavior of Christians was a positive force within society. In our postmodern world it can again be a powerful apologetic as it seeks to show the coherence between our life-world foundations and their expression in moral and ethical living.

Within the fragmentation of our pluralistic context, one of the major problems both society and individuals are facing is the absence of a coherent foundation for ethics; we lack a language for moral obligation. As Robert Bellah and his colleagues noted in *Habits of the Heart*, for most Americans "there is simply no objectifiable criterion for choosing one value or course of action over another. One's idiosyncratic preferences are their own justification, because they define the true self. . . . The right act is simply the one that yields the agent the most exciting challenge or the most good feeling about himself."[10]

In such a world the church can make two appeals in its apologetic. One is that Christianity provides humanity with the most adequate foundation for understanding goodness, evil and human responsibility. The Christian story of creation, fall, redemption and consummation is a better story to account for life, its moral requirements and our failures than any other. The second appeal is the coherence between the Christian worldview and its expression in moral behavior. Postmoderns can best understand a holy, loving, just, forgiving, life-giving God of grace when they see a holy, loving, just, forgiving, life-giving community founded on the grace of God and made effective through our Lord and Savior Jesus Christ.

## Conclusion
In the pluralistic postmodern world, the church is the plausibility structure of the Christian life world. As Paul put it, "You show that you are a letter

of Christ . . . written not with ink but with the Spirit of the living God" (2 Cor 3:3). It is through the visible church—foibles and all—that the world can best understand and find compelling the gospel and its derivative way of life. But the appeals must be broad and must resonate with the whole of the human self, not one isolated dimension as in the modern, rationalist apologetic. Narrative, discourse, ritual and symbol, life experience and moral foundations/behavior all have potential for expressing and legitimizing the Christian view of things in a world that increasingly finds our faith foreign to its own thought-forms, values and actions. It is precisely for this reason that the worldview needs concrete, tangible expression within the church—the only institution on earth that can adequately serve as Christianity's plausibility structure. Such an approach in no way minimizes the importance of truth, but rather emphasizes that truth can be recognized and affirmed through multiple dimensions of human life and experience.

The idea of the church as an apologetic is not really new. As Robert Wilken noted, from the inception of Christianity

it had a social and ecclesiological dimension. Christians had constituted a new kind of community, one that was independent of the social and political institutions of the Roman empire; it was not territorial, i.e., defined by people or region or city, and its central rite, the Sacrifice, as it was called in Christian antiquity, embraced old and young, male and female, slave and free, gentile and Jew, rich and poor, educated and uneducated. Such a community was without precedent, and it figured large in the theological response to pagan criticism of Christianity.[11]

Unfortunately, contemporary evangelicalism has always been rather ambivalent regarding the church, finding little room for ecclesiology in either its theology or its apologetic.

In the postmodern world, says Robert Jenson, we have no common story. "Modernity was defined by the attempt to live in a universal story without a universal story-teller."[12] But in the postmodern world we no longer have even a universal story to give meaning and coherence to life.

What then shall we do? Jenson contends that "the obvious answer is that if the church does not *find* her hearers antecedently inhabiting a narratable world, then the church must herself *be* that world. . . . If the church is not herself a real, substantial, living world to which the gospel can be true, faith is quite simply impossible."[13]

With God all things are possible. But in the pluralistic, postmodern world, God's possibilities can become vivid and real to searching nonbelievers when the church itself is an apologetic, a manifestation of the good news of Christ.

# 11
# EVANGELIZING
# THE
# CHURCH
*Douglas Webster*

I first became acquainted with the phrase "evangelizing the church" through Latin American liberation theologians. Their rejection of the Roman Catholic spiritualistic and feudalistic conception of their culture revolutionized the ancient Latin Christendom model. The history of salvation became the salvation of history; the coming of Christ became the history of man-becoming. The so-called artificial barriers between the church and the world were removed, in favor of a Christendom without the name. The church announces to the world that all people are "in Christ" and the world evangelizes the church through the epistemological privilege of the poor, the social sciences, economic justice and political liberation.

This strategy of desacralizing the world and secularizing the church provides an interesting parallel to the North American scene. Mainline Protestants and market-driven evangelicals are struggling with evangelism in a post-Christian culture. It has become increasingly more difficult to draw the line between church and culture and to offer the gospel of Jesus Christ in a distinctive voice. Our evangelism sounds either like spiritualized political correctness or Christianized self-help. We have been secularized, on the one hand by pluralism and on the other by pragmatism. Mainliners seek cultural respectability and marketers seek popularity. Cultural forces shape our identity; arts and education for mainline Protestants and entertainment and the marketplace for evangelicalism. We have become secularized by the culture we are trying to reach with the gospel.

Over the past few years I have experienced both extremes. My prevailing culture has been the church, and I can testify to its need for evangelization. The very things we take pride in exhibit our cultural captivity. Mainline Protestantism offers a highly politicized ethic controlled by the dictates of enlightened secular culture, while market-driven Protestantism offers a highly psychologized gospel conditioned by self-centered, consumer-oriented, media-induced felt needs.

The postmodern world has demanded from the church a reason for its existence, and the church has answered with reasons meant more to impress than to transform. On the one hand we are for diversity and pluralism, tolerance and acceptance. On the other hand we are for self-esteem and intimacy, fun and fulfillment. Jesus helps us cope with stress and equips us for success. In commending ourselves after this fashion we hope to give the world a reason for thinking we have a place in the postmodern age.

## Mainline Ethics

For all their dissimilarities, liberal Protestantism and popular evangelicalism are more alike than they realize. Both poles of the Protestant continuum are being evangelized by the world rather than evangelizing the world.

There is a danger in overgeneralizing from one's experience, but I believe my pastoral experience is not unique. I am currently serving the First Presbyterian Church of San Diego. Twenty years ago it was known for its youth ministry and world missions emphasis. Today it is known for its Ladle Ministry, which feeds about five hundred poor people in the church's dining room every Sunday, and its outstanding classical sacred music program.

When I arrived, both the director of the Ladle Ministry and the world-class organist were gay. Some in our congregation celebrated the church's diversity, while others were concerned over the church's compromise. After several years of study, debate and open forums on the subject, our session of elders passed a resolution disqualifying those engaged in homosexual behavior from teaching or leading in the church.

In keeping with the resolution, the personnel committee began to work on a policy that would cover several important concerns, such as substance abuse, premarital sex, adultery and deceit, as well as homosexuality. The aim of the standing rule was to publicly acknowledge a standard for employees, not to come down hard on offenders. The grounds for dismissal applied to those who repeatedly and persistently practiced sinful behavior and were unresponsive to correction and counsel.

One reason for the policy was the outside legal opinion that the church was vulnerable to litigation if it did not have a written policy stating a basic moral code of conduct. Another reason was a desire to be open with prospective and current employees, who numbered around seventy.

The standing rule was presented at session for a vote shortly after I arrived. This simple, straightforward document became the flashpoint for the conflict that had been building up in the church for years. The policy came to be perceived by some in the congregation, especially some choir members, as a personal attack on the organist. It was immediately branded as "legalistic," "pharisaical" and "homophobic" and generated the strongest negative emotions I have ever experienced in any church.

The negative reaction was that of a minority, but they were strong and militant and reached out to gain support in the arts community, the gay community and presbytery. They had hoped that I, as a new pastor, would not make homosexuality an issue but would go along with the cultural trend in order to keep the peace and harmony of the church. But to do so in this case would have meant dissuading a spiritually sensitive session and ministry staff from doing what they were convinced was right and biblical.

Others in the church agreed that the homosexual lifestyle was wrong, but they said that what consenting adults do in the privacy of their homes is their own business and the church should not get involved. Others opposed the policy because it meant losing a great organist. As one member said, "I worship the music!" Still others were negative simply because they were confused by misinformation and the angry emotions of a few in the church, and they were upset to see the decorum of a traditional Presbyterian church disrupted.

Within the week the organist met with the personnel committee and tendered his resignation, effective immediately. Although he assured the committee that he had no intention of suing the church, he expressed how "stunned, shocked, and deeply hurt" he was. Even though the church had struggled with this issue for months, he claimed he never would have

\n567891011

accepted a job in a church where his sexuality would have been a problem. He clearly saw himself as suffering for the sake of the gospel and persecuted by narrow-minded, pharisaical literalists.

This continues to remain a contentious issue in our congregation. We are an embarrassment to the leadership of presbytery, and I remain uninstalled, a formality pending reconciliation with a self-designated "peace and harmony committee." Many in our congregation still want a clear biblical stand on sexual morality, but others feel this stand violates our commitment to diversity, inclusiveness and tolerance.

The elders recently debated the qualifications for elders and deacons. The debate was prompted by a description in the bulletin from the nominating committee advising the congregation regarding what to look for in a spiritual leader. For a minority of elders it sounded narrow and restrictive. One elder read from the Presbyterian (U.S.A.) Book of Order to make her point:

> The Church in its witness to the uniqueness of the Christian faith is called to mission and must be responsive to diversity in both the Church and the world. . . .
>
> Our unity in Christ enables and requires the Church to be open to all persons and to the varieties of talents and gifts of God's people, including those who are in the communities of the arts and sciences.
>
> The Presbyterian Church (U.S.A.) shall give full expression to the rich diversity within its membership and shall provide means which will assure a greater inclusiveness leading to wholeness in its emerging life. Persons of all racial and ethnic groups, different ages, both sexes, various disabilities, diverse geographical areas, different theological positions consistent with the Reformed tradition, as well as different marital conditions (married, single, widowed, or divorced) shall be guaranteed full participation and access to representation in the decision making of the Church. (G-4.0400-.0403)

The issue for us was whether the diversity commended in these paragraphs was to be defined by our culture or by the Word of God. The qualifications for elder and deacon are laid out in the Book of Order and include a personal commitment to Jesus Christ as Lord of all and Head of the church, a firm resolve to live under the authority of God's Word, a sincere acceptance of the essential tenets of the Reformed faith, an appreciation for our denomination's polity and discipline, a readiness to further the peace, unity and purity of the church, and an earnest desire to serve people with energy, intelligence, imagination and love.

It is certainly politically correct to approve gay and lesbian relationships, but it is not biblically correct. Different theological positions consistent with the Reformed tradition are quite different from different theological positions consistent with radical pluralism. Thus the tension between secularization and evangelization is fought out in the sanctuary.

Secularization within the church has led to a weakening of direct evangelistic efforts. The extent of mainline denominational evangelism reminds me of the goal envisioned by First Presbyterian's concert committee: to provide spiritual uplift and cultural enrichment. "Outreach" translates into making a name for ourselves in the community.

## Market-Driven Evangelism

Before coming to San Diego I was pastor of adult ministries at Cherry Creek Presbyterian Church in southeast Denver. Under its founding pastor, Cherry Creek experienced phenomenal growth. In many ways the church was an example of the market-driven evangelical church. Within a few years the church audience numbered in the thousands, with a highly trained professional staff, full-service programming and expansion plans for the future. The major factor in this formula for success was a slightly irreverent, very entertaining, thirtysomething pastor who preached acceptance and love. Everything he did from start to finish was high-energy. The sermon was a fast-flowing stream of consciousness. He pumped the audience up, gave them a boost, made them laugh and cry. Whenever he sensed he was coming on too strong, making a truth too definite, a conviction too strict, he interjected a joke.

He had a knack for connecting with people.

Inspired by his phenomenal popularity and the growth of the church, the pastor envisioned a new expansion plan, one church on two sites. This vision would allow him to work both audiences and shuttle between services. The core group at the original site could not imagine life without the preacher, and the preacher could not imagine staying in a sanctuary that held only nine hundred. This new site held the promise of a megachurch: thirty-eight acres of prime real estate at the crossroads of two interstate highways, situated next to the largest residential real estate development in the country. It was the modern equivalent to the ancient cathedral on the city square: excellent accessibility, plenty of room for parking, a great view of the Rockies and high visibility.

But unknown to anyone else in the church, the pastor who had generated both the popularity and the vision was talking to representatives of the largest church in the denomination. They were looking for a pastor and were already in the process of planning a major building program to service their Sunday-morning audience of five thousand. For a time the preacher kept his options open, secretly candidating for a call to the flagship church of the denomination while advocating the vision for a market-driven megachurch. Whether the resistance to his vision was too much for him or the call of a bigger church too attractive, he chose the new church over the new vision.

Here and in the case of the mainline church, we must suspect the motives and strategy for evangelism and ask some important questions. For the mainline church, does reaching out to the community mean accepting the culture on its own terms or transforming the culture on Christ's terms (Rom 12:1-3)? Doesn't preaching the gospel necessarily entail preaching against evil, urging repentance from sin and turning to Christ? In the market-driven church, outreach seems to mean competing for your market niche with the most appealing Sunday-morning performance in your region, followed up by attractive programs, support groups and youth activities through the week. May not the consequent emphasis on entertainment dilute the message of the cross?

In both the mainline church and the market-driven church, preaching has become innocuous. Whether in a boring homily or in an entertaining topical sermon, both confuse the message of the cross with preaching affirmation, not deliverance. If we want to evangelize our culture, we must begin by evangelizing our churches.

### Blessed Are Those Who Mourn

Perhaps the first step in a pastoral strategy for the evangelization of the American church is a deeper awareness of our sinfulness. The second step involves a renewed commitment to the inseparable relationship between law and gospel. Heavily influenced by radical pluralism, self-gratifying individualism and relativism, we have lost our consciousness of personal sin.

To mourn is to grieve the loss of our innocence, to lament our unrighteousness, to be filled with sorrow because of our sinfulness. The tragedy of this world is not primarily social nor political, but personal. It begins with me. British author G. K. Chesterton was asked to write a magazine article on the subject "What's Wrong with the Universe?" He responded to the editor's request with two words, "I am."

"The ethos of victimization," writes Charles Sykes in *A Nation of Victims*, "has an endless capacity not only for exculpating one's self from blame, washing away responsibility in a torrent of explanation—racism, sexism, rotten parents, addiction, and illness—but also projecting guilt onto others."[1] Sykes argues that the United States has become a nation of finger-pointers, adept at blaming their ills on society, dysfunctional families, poor education, government bureaucracy, racism, sexism or psychological maladjustment: in short, blaming everybody and everything but oneself.

Today's therapeutic culture has succeeded in raising people's expectations and sensitivities. If there is a single war cry, Sykes suggests, it might be "I deserve!" As one writer declared, "I deserve love. I deserve to be trusted. I deserve freedom. I deserve friendship. I deserve respect. I deserve sexual pleasure. I deserve happiness."[2] If there is any thought of God, it is one of disappointment. "How could God let me down? Doesn't God care?" When things go wrong, the most commonly asked question is "Why me?"

Blame desensitizes people to the root problem of evil. By universalizing victimhood our society has not gained a clearer, truer understanding of personal and social evil. Now it appears that there is no such thing as a personal moral choice for which we are responsible. We are the product of our DNA, parenting, schooling and economics.

You may recall the tragedy in New York's Central Park when thirty boys, most under the age of sixteen, went "wilding." They raped and battered a twenty-eight-year-old jogger. What caused this gang to viciously, unmercifully attack this woman? The experts spoke of alienation, peer pressure, inequality, status anxieties, television and advertising. But one of the boys blurted out the reason they did it: "It was something to do. It was fun."

"The ambition of the modern mind," writes George Will, "is to spare itself a chilling sight, that of the cold blank stare of personal evil. The modern program is squeamishness dressed up as sophistication. Its aim is to make the reality of evil disappear behind a rhetorical gauze of learned garbage."[3]

Extreme cases of the no-fault defense make the nightly news. The judges have ruled a mistrial in the Erik and Lyle Menendez trials. The juries were hopelessly deadlocked, even though the defense conceded that the brothers had premeditatively killed both their parents with a shotgun at point-blank range as they were eating ice cream and watching television. The defense attorney skillfully argued that the young men had suffered such terrible abuse from their father that they could no longer think rationally. As one legal expert observed, the defense lawyer was able to build sympathy for the boys by months of emotional exposure, so that the jury entered into Erik and Lyle's trauma and fear. Meanwhile, the prosecution could not bring the parents into the courtroom; they were no longer available to receive our sympathy. Judgment was based on feelings and appearances, prompting screenwriter Paul Ciotti to say, "If the Menendez brothers aren't guilty of murder, then no one in this country is ever guilty of anything."[4]

When the bubonic plague swept through Europe, it killed nearly 50 percent of the population by the end of the fourteenth century. The source of this Black Death remained a mystery, and "ignorance of the cause augmented the sense of horror."[5] The deadly germ actually spread to humans and animals through the bite of a flea or a rat and then spread through close human contact. But the plague bacillus remained undiscovered for another five hundred years. Some medieval doctors blamed the disease on contaminated air caused by the movement of stars and planets. Others accused the Jews of starting the plague by poisoning the city wells, and entire Jewish communities were exterminated in brutal massacres. Since the source of the contagious disease was unknown, people became fearful and suspicious of everything from the fresh air to their Jewish neighbor.

The trauma and horror experienced by medieval people because of their lack of basic biological knowledge is analogous to the despair and confusion experienced by modern humanity due to our lack of basic biblical knowledge. We are ignorant of the ancient revelations essential to dealing with evil. In an effort to cope with evil our culture has rationalized, psychologized and politicized it. In our effort to make life easier by blaming others, we end up making life impossible. We refuse to acknowledge the simple fact that we ourselves are sinners.

While what we may want is affirmation and approval, what we need is repentance and deliverance. Scaled-down forms of salvation will not work. The last thing in the world we need is to be told that we are okay; that all we are suffering from is a problem of self-esteem or boredom. This is too superficial an answer. C. S. Lewis expressed the depth of our problem when he said,

Niceness—wholesome, integrated personality—is an excellent thing. We must try by every medical, educational, economic, and political means in our power to produce a world where as many people as possible grow up "nice"; just as we must try to produce a world where all have plenty to eat. But we must not suppose that even if we succeeded in making everyone nice we should have saved their souls. A world of nice people, content in their own niceness, looking no further, turned away from God, would be just as desperately in need of salvation as a miserable world—and even might be more difficult to save.[6]

Luther used a graphic figure to depict our responsibility in the death of Christ. He said we carry around the nails of Christ's cross in our pocket. We cringe at the very thought of the crucifixion; we hardly feel responsible for spikes driven through the hands and feet of Jesus. But that is what our sins did. He "was wounded for our transgressions, crushed for our iniquities; upon him was the punishment that made us whole, and by his bruises we are healed" (Is 53:5). We prefer the role of victim; it is shocking to find out that we are not the crucified, but the crucifiers.

The comfort we really need is not a pat on the back or an affirming nod of approval. While a smile and a hug are nice and may brighten our day, the human soul longs for a deeper comfort. The comfort Jesus promises to those who mourn is much deeper than either the approval of our friends or the solace offered by our loved ones. And it certainly cannot be confused with popular psychology or public relations. His comfort is deeper and more multifaceted than the disturbing evil it promises to dispel.

I have never met anyone who mourned more painfully and in greater agony than David Conner. The lines on his face seemed frozen and contorted in a cry of pain. His eyes, swollen and red, filled with an endless supply of tears. He shivered as if he were always cold. I believe David grieved as deeply as anyone could grieve. And when I visited him in prison, even his faint smile seemed to hurt.

David was in prison because he killed a mother and child on a two-lane road in Indiana. It was a Saturday afternoon, and David had been drinking. He was impatient and annoyed at a motorcyclist who had passed him on a curve. He sped up to pass and lost control on the next curve. He hit the oncoming car head-on. The mother and child died instantly.

It was as if in the twinkling of an eye David entered hell itself. Every evil thing that he had ever done was now discharged, dumped, deposited in his despairing soul. How could a human being do what he had done? He went from being an ordinary husband, okay father and average worker to the very personification of evil. Overnight he became an object of hate in our small town, violently condemned by the victims' family. And who could blame them? Two white crosses marked the spot on the highway where the accident occurred.

Yet throughout his ordeal David reminded me of myself, of my own sin and moral culpability. He was not alone in his need. There was a glaring obviousness about his evil, but it did not obscure my own.

David honestly mourned what he had done. He tried to understand his actions, but he did not excuse them. He was filled with remorse and repentance. Did Jesus have David in mind when he said, "Come to me, all you that are weary and are carrying heavy burdens, and I will give you rest" (Mt 11:28)? Yes indeed. Was the second Beatitude intended for David—"Blessed are those who mourn, for they will be comforted" (Mt 5:4)? Most certainly.

Whether there is an empty six-pack in the trunk or some leftover crucifixion spikes in our pockets, we all need to repent and turn to Christ for forgiveness. For only then can we begin to experience the comfort we need. It was not easy for David to mourn the way he did, but anything less would have been self-defeating. Only the forgiveness and comfort of Christ turned David's mourning into rejoicing and made him a husband and father again.

## Law and Gospel

Today we are tempted to make the law the enemy of gospel. Any mention of the law is branded as legalism. Few among today's believers express an earnest desire for purity and holiness. The virtues of peace and harmony are loudly promoted, but the quest for godliness sounds archaic and quaint. The desire to be holy is sometimes even frowned upon, as if it were synonymous with a "holier than thou" attitude. There is a great deal of confusion over the believer's relationship to the law of God.

Over the course of a year I met several times for lunch with an agnostic who was seriously considering the claims of Christ. His Christian friends at work gave him books by C. S. Lewis, Chuck Colson and Philip Yancey. He followed the Sunday-morning message as closely as anyone in the congregation. When we met, our conversations centered not so much on intellectual issues of faith and reason as on ethical concerns of faith and practice. He claimed that the biggest hurdle he had to overcome was his wife, a believer. She had faithfully attended church for years and felt the problems in their marriage were rooted in the fact that he was not a Christian.

One of the first questions he asked me was, "Do you believe it is right for my teenage daughter to invite her boyfriend home to spend the night in the same bed?" Before I could answer he said, "My wife does. She believes that Jesus desires intimacy in relationships, so it's okay for my daughter to sleep with her boyfriend. I'm sorry, but I think that's wrong. What do you think?"

The longer we talked, the more apparent it became that his wife had used the love of Jesus to condone whatever behavior pattern their children had wanted to practice. Of course it is possible that the agnostic was using his wife's perspective as an excuse for not becoming a believer. Yet her feeling toward the moral law is not unusual in the American church. By claiming that the unconditional love of Jesus approves immorality in the name of intimacy, she divorced law and gospel, forgiveness and obedience. For others, the excuse is diversity or tolerance, justifying sin in the name of Jesus.

Without reservation or qualification Jesus claimed absolute loyalty to the written Scriptures, but he did it in such an extremely unusual and provocative way that no one would have escaped the significance of his words. After Jesus spoke about the law, the issue shifted in the minds of his hearers from Jesus' attitude toward the law to the relationship of the law to Jesus. He pledged undivided loyalty to the law, but in doing so he made himself central to the law's relevance. The authoritative "I" became the focus of attention. He did not come to destroy the law but to fulfill it, perfectly, in his own person.

Unknowingly many contemporary Christians favor the views of Marcion, a second-century theologian who tried to divorce the Old Testament from the New Testament. Marcion believed that the God of the Old Testament was vindictive and judgmental. He claimed that the God of the Jews performed evil acts and was self-contradictory. According to Marcion, Jesus was not the fulfillment of Old Testament messianic prophecies but was a revelation of the God of love.[7] Marcion's ancient heretical thesis is still popular today as self-designated "enlightened" Christians distance themselves from the commands of God's Word.

It is almost as if many modern Christians wished that the malicious rumors spread by the Pharisees about Jesus were true. It would be a relief for them to find that Jesus rendered the Old Testament commands obsolete. They would find it easier to believe that Jesus liberated people from the prescientific, anachronistic commands of the Bible than to think that Jesus lined up with the Law and Prophets. They confuse Jesus' resistance to the scribes and religious leaders with opposition to the moral order of the Old Testament.

It is precisely the false representation of Jesus' relationship to the Law and the Prophets that provoked his definitive reaction. Jesus declared the Law, far from being obsolete, to be absolute. "For truly I tell you, until heaven and earth pass away, not one letter, not one stroke of a letter, will pass from the law until all is accomplished" (Mt 5:18). He could not have made his point more emphatically. "Trivialize even the smallest item in God's Law and you will only have trivialized yourself. But take it seriously, show the way for others, and you will find honor in the kingdom."[8] Absolutely nothing will be left out, dismissed or rendered obsolete "until all is accomplished." Separate law and gospel, separate forgiveness from obedience, and the gospel is secularized into cheap grace, even if that cheap grace is politically correct or subjectively uplifting.

## A Pastoral Strategy

I have argued that the Protestant church is in need of evangelization and that the place to begin is with a biblical theology of evil, a clear proclamation of both the cross and the ethic of Jesus Christ. There are of course other dimensions to evangelization. The gospel shapes the worship and body life of the community of believers and inspires a deep concern for world missions. But as a pastor called to share the gospel, addressing personal sin and the life of obedience in Christ strikes me as a practical starting point. Without this we lose our distinctive voice and merely echo the culture.

At the very point of religious pride, the church reveals its spiritual need. The enculturated ethic of the mainline church and the remain-as-you-were evangelism of the market-driven church expose a fundamental need for spiritual renewal.

The inevitable loss of cultural respectability on the one hand and popularity on the other should not concern us. Both losses are necessary, and really gains, if we are to experience the power of the gospel. What is true for individuals is also true for churches. We could gain the world but lose our souls.[9]

# Notes

**Chapter 1: Introduction/Phillips and Okholm**

[1]Roderick Frazier Nash, *The Rights of Nature: A History of Environmental Ethics* (Madison: University of Wisconsin Press, 1989), p. 169.

[2]Douglas Groothuis, "Evidence That Demands a Sermon," *Christianity Today* 36 (March 9, 1992): 16.

[3]Winfried Corduan, *Reasonable Faith: Basic Christian Apologetics* (Nashville: Broadman & Holman, 1993), p. 94.

[4]Stanley Hauerwas, *After Christendom* (Nashville: Abingdon, 1991), p. 148.

[5]See David F. Wells, *No Place for Truth* (Grand Rapids, Mich.: Eerdmans, 1993); Os Guinness and John Seel, eds., *No God But God: Breaking with the Idols of Our Age* (Chicago: Moody Press, 1992); Charles Colson with Ellen Santilli Vaughn, *The Body* (Dallas: Word, 1992).

[6]For a helpful philosophical analysis of postmodernity see Richard Kearney, ed., *Twentieth-Century Continental Philosophy* (New York: Routledge, 1994), especially Thomas Docherty's essay, "Postmodernist Theory: Lyotard, Baudrillard and Others," pp. 474-501. See also James L. Marsh, John D. Caputo and Merold Westphal, eds., *Modernity and Its Discontents* (New York: Fordham University Press, 1992).

[7]Much of this description of postmodernism is indebted to John Castelein, "(Dis)locating Postmodernism," paper presented at the Wheaton Theology Conference, 1994.

[8]Ibid.

[9]Stanley Hauerwas and William Willimon, *Resident Aliens* (Nashville: Abingdon, 1989), pp. 15-19.

[10]Corduan, *Reasonable Faith*, p. 94.

[11]Robert Roberts, "Theology and Personal Maturity in Christianity and Carl Jung," *Proceedings of the Wheaton Theology Conference* 1 (1992): 56-73.

[12]Much of this paragraph is indebted to the response of Stephen Spencer to J. Richard Middleton and Brian J. Walsh, "Yes, Trudy, There Is a Metanarrative," paper presented at the Wheaton Theology Conference, 1994.

**Chapter 2: The Pragmatics of Postmodernity/Lundin**

[1]Henry David Thoreau, *Walden: Or, Life in the Woods,* in *Thoreau,* ed. Robert F. Sayre (New York: Library of America, 1985), p. 364.

[2]Frederick Douglass, *Narrative of the Life of Frederick Douglass, an American Slave,* in *The Norton Anthology of American Literature,* ed. Nina Baym et al., 3rd ed. (New York: Norton, 1989), 1:1895-97.

[3]Ralph Waldo Emerson, "The American Scholar," in *Emerson: Essays and Lectures,* ed. Joel

Porte (New York: Library of America, 1983), p. 56.

[4]Ralph Waldo Emerson, "The Poet," in *Emerson: Essays and Lectures*, ed. Joel Porte (New York: Library of America, 1983), p. 456.

[5]Stanley Fish, *Doing What Comes Naturally: Change, Rhetoric and the Practice of Theory in Literary and Legal Studies* (Durham, N.C.: Duke University Press, 1989), pp. 11-12.

[6]Ibid., p. 483.

[7]Friedrich Nietzsche, *Twilight of the Idols*, trans. R. J. Hollingdale (Harmondsworth, U.K.: Penguin, 1968), p. 72.

[8]William Butler Yeats, "A Prayer for My Daughter," in *Selected Poems and Three Plays*, ed. M. L. Rosenthal, 3rd ed. (New York: Collier, 1986), p. 92.

[9]Richard Rorty, *Consequences of Pragmatism* (Minneapolis: University of Minnesota Press, 1982), pp. 148-49.

[10]Richard Rorty, *Contingency, Irony and Solidarity* (Cambridge: Cambridge University Press, 1989), p. 27.

[11]Philip Rieff, *The Triumph of the Therapeutic: The Uses of Faith After Freud* (New York: Harper & Row, 1966), p. 13.

[12]Ibid., p. 62.

[13]Jean-François Lyotard, *The Postmodern Condition: A Report on Knowledge*, trans. Geoff Bennington and Brian Massumi (Minneapolis: University of Minnesota Press, 1984), p. xxiv.

[14]Alasdair MacIntyre, *After Virtue*, 2nd ed. (Notre Dame, Ind.: University of Notre Dame Press, 1984), pp. 30-31.

[15]William Shakespeare, *Hamlet*, ed. Willard Farnham, in *William Shakespeare: The Complete Works*, gen. ed. Alfred Harbage, rev. ed. (Baltimore: Penguin, 1969), act 3, scene 4, lines 206-10.

[16]Rorty, *Contingency, Irony and Solidarity*, p. 29.

[17]Shakespeare, *Hamlet*, act 3, scene 1, lines 83-88.

[18]Ibid., act 5, scene 2, lines 8-11.

[19]"Pro Bono TV Spot for Abortion Rights," *The New York Times*, March 1, 1994, p. C18.

[20]*Nathaniel Hawthorne: Novels*, ed. Millicent Bell (New York: Library of America, 1983), pp. 283, 288-89.

[21]Rorty, *Contingency, Irony and Solidarity*, p. 97.

[22]Jerry Adler, "Hester Pryncesse," *Newsweek*, April 4, 1994, p. 58.

[23]Ibid.

[24]*The Complete Poems of Emily Dickinson*, ed. Thomas H. Johnson (Boston: Little, Brown, 1960), p. 646.

[25]W. H. Auden, "The Sea and the Mirror," in *Collected Poems*, ed. Edward Mendelson (New York: Random House, 1976), pp. 336-37.

[26]Dietrich Bonhoeffer, *Letters and Papers from Prison*, ed. Eberhard Bethge (New York: Macmillan, 1972), pp. 369-70.

## Chapter 3: From Architecture to Argument/Stackhouse

An early draft of this paper was read to the Colloquium of the Department of Religion, University of Manitoba, March 9, 1994, and I gladly acknowledge the help of my colleagues and our students in revising it into its current form.

[1]J. K. S. Reid, *Christian Apologetics* (London: Hodder & Stoughton, 1969); Avery Dulles, *A History of Apologetics* (Philadelphia: Westminster Press/London: Hutchinson, 1971).

[2]F. D. E. Schleiermacher, *Brief Outline on the Study of Theology*, trans. Terrence N. Tice (Atlanta: John Knox, 1966); B. B. Warfield, *The Idea of Systematic Theology Considered as a*

*Science* (New York: Randolph, 1888); Paul Tillich, *Systematic Theology*, vol. 1 (Chicago: University of Chicago Press, 1951).

[3]It perhaps is worth noting that none of the categories that follow describe resources that are exclusively Christian. Other religions have their counterparts. Yet that reality does not undercut the usefulness of such apologetical resources. Just as in the case of Christian theological and philosophical apologetics that have parallels in other religions, good use of the following suggested resources can be made in comparison with the offerings of other religions.

[4]*Webster's Ninth New Collegiate Dictionary* (Springfield, Mass.: Merriam-Webster, 1990), s.v. "church."

[5]Jean Delumeau, *Catholicism Between Luther and Voltaire: A New View of the Counter-Reformation* (London: Burns & Oates/Philadelphia: Westminster, 1977).

[6]William Westfall, *Two Worlds: The Protestant Culture of Nineteenth-Century Ontario* (Montreal: McGill University Press, 1989), pp. 126-58.

[7]Ken Sidey, "So Long to Sacred Space," *Christianity Today* 37 (November 8, 1993): 46.

[8]For examples, see Donald Davie, ed., *The New Oxford Book of Christian Verse* (Oxford: Oxford University Press, 1981).

[9]For samples, see Lyle W. Dorsett, ed., *GK's Weekly: A Sampler* (Chicago: Loyola University Press, 1986).

[10]Chesterton also acquired a reputation for his art, especially caricatures. See Alzina Stone Dale, *The Art of G. K. Chesterton* (Chicago: Loyola University Press, 1985).

[11]Jonathan D. Spence, *The Memory Palace of Matteo Ricci* (New York: Viking, 1984), pp. 1-4.

[12]Kenneth Scott Latourette, *A History of the Expansion of Christianity*, vol. 2, *The Thousand Years of Uncertainty* (New York: Harper & Brothers, 1938), p. 92.

[13]See the bibliography in Gary S. Greig and Kevin N. Springer, *The Kingdom and the Power* (Ventura, Calif.: Regal, 1993), pp. 446-50.

[14]Howard A. Snyder, *Signs of the Spirit: How God Reshapes the Church* (Grand Rapids, Mich.: Zondervan, 1989), p. 87. See also Gary R. Sattler, *God's Glory, Neighbor's Good: A Brief Introduction to the Life and Writings of August Hermann Francke* (Chicago: Covenant, 1982).

[15]Snyder, *Signs of the Spirit*, p. 88.

[16]F. Ernest Stoeffler, *The Rise of Evangelical Pietism* (Leiden: E. J. Brill, 1971), p. 31; quoted in Snyder, *Signs of the Spirit*, p. 89.

[17]Among many examples, see Harry Blamires, *Where Do We Stand? An Examination of the Christian's Position in the Modern World* (Ann Arbor, Mich.: Servant, 1980); Eric G. Jay, *The Church: Its Changing Image Through Twenty Centuries* (Atlanta: John Knox, 1977, 1978); Hans Küng, *On Being a Christian*, trans. Edward Quinn (Garden City, N.Y.: Doubleday, 1976); Richard F. Lovelace, *Renewal as a Way of Life: A Guidebook for Spiritual Growth* (Downers Grove, Ill.: InterVarsity Press, 1985); Wolfhart Pannenberg, *The Church*, trans. Keith Crim (Philadelphia: Westminster Press, 1983); W. A. Visser 't Hooft, *The Renewal of the Church* (London: SCM Press, 1956).

[18]Snyder, *Signs of the Spirit*, pp. 224, 230. On these societies, see also Howard A. Snyder, *The Radical Wesley and Patterns for Church Renewal* (Downers Grove, Ill.: InterVarsity Press, 1980), pp. 53-64 and passim; Henry D. Rack, *Reasonable Enthusiast: John Wesley and the Rise of Methodism*, 2nd ed. (Nashville: Abingdon, 1992), pp. 237-50; and Robert G. Tuttle Jr., *John Wesley: His Life and Theology* (Grand Rapids, Mich.: Zondervan, 1978), pp. 276-82.

[19]Peter L. Berger, *The Sacred Canopy: Elements of a Sociological Theory of Religion* (New York: Anchor, 1969); Peter L. Berger and Thomas Luckmann, *The Social Construction of Reality* (Harmondsworth, U.K.: Penguin, 1967).

[20]For Canadian examples, see Reginald W. Bibby, *Fragmented Gods: The Poverty and Potential of Religion in Canada* (Toronto: Irwin, 1987), pp. 70-72; for American examples, see George Gallup Jr. and Sarah Jones, *One Hundred Questions and Answers: Religion in America* (Princeton, N.J.: Princeton Religion Research Center, 1989), pp. 42-43.

[21]William Martin, *A Prophet with Honor: The Billy Graham Story* (New York: Morrow, 1991), p. 548. Martin confirmed this judgment with me in personal correspondence dated March 8, 1994.

[22]Arthur F. Holmes, *Contours of a World View* (Grand Rapids, Mich.: Eerdmans, 1983); John R. W. Stott, *Involvement*, vol. 1, *Being a Responsible Christian in a Non-Christian Society*, and vol. 2, *Social and Sexual Relationships in the Modern World* (Old Tappan, N.J.: Revell, 1984-1985); Nicholas Wolterstorff, *Reason Within the Bounds of Religion*, 2nd ed. (Grand Rapids, Mich.: Eerdmans, 1984).

[23]For an introduction to semiotics, see Terence Hawkes, *Structuralism and Semiotics* (Berkeley: University of California Press, 1977), pp. 123-50; and for delightful examples of its use, see Umberto Eco, *Travels in Hyperreality* (London: Pan, 1987).

[24]On the family as a "mission station," see Rodney Clapp, *Families at the Crossroads: Beyond Traditional and Modern Options* (Downers Grove, Ill.: InterVarsity Press, 1993), esp. pp. 149-66.

Chapter 4: Schleiermacher as Apologist/Creegan

[1]John Calvin, *Institutes of the Christian Religion*, ed. John T. McNeill (Philadelphia: Westminster Press, 1960), p. 43.

[2]See the article by Paul E. Capetz, "Calvin, Schleiermacher and Gustafson," *Papers of the International Schleiermacher Society* (Washington, D.C.), 1993, p. 125. Capetz, in referring to the three great foci of the Reformed tradition as "the centrality of God," "an emphasis upon piety" and "the insistence that all of life be appropriately ordered in relation to God," says, "Schleiermacher's work, according to this interpretation, does not constitute a deviation from the pivotal emphases of Reformed theology but illustrates them in exemplary fashion."

[3]George Newlands, "Schleiermacher at Vatican X," *Papers of the International Schleiermacher Society*, 1993, p. 184.

[4]Jaroslav Pelikan, "The Vocation of the Christian Apologist: A Study in Schleiermacher's *Reden*," in *Christianity and World Revolution*, ed. Edwin H. Rian (New York: Harper & Row, 1963), p. 184.

[5]Friedrich Schleiermacher, *On Religion: Speeches to Its Cultured Despisers*, trans. from 1st German ed. by Richard Crouter (Cambridge: Cambridge University Press, 1988), pp. 77-78.

[6]Ibid., pp. 78-79.

[7]Friedrich Schleiermacher, *On Religion*, trans. from 3rd German ed. by John Oman (New York: Harper, 1958), p. 39.

[8]Ibid., p. 36.

[9]Friedrich Schleiermacher, *Christian Faith*, ed. and trans. H. R. Mackintosh and J. S. Stewart (Edinburgh: T & T Clark, 1928), p. 5.

[10]Schleiermacher, *On Religion*, trans. Crouter, pp. 82-83.

[11]See Diogenes Allen, "Christian Values in a Post-Christian Context," in *Postmodern Theology: Christian Faith in a Pluralistic World*, ed. Frederic B. Burnham (San Francisco: Harper, 1989), p. 35.

[12]Schleiermacher, *On Religion*, trans. Crouter, p. 158.

[13]Ibid., p. 153.

[14]Friedrich Schleiermacher, *Christmas Eve: Dialogue on the Incarnation*, trans. Terrence Tice (Lewiston, N.Y.: Edwin Mellen, 1990).

[15]Friedrich Schleiermacher, *On the Glaubenslehrs: Two Letters to Dr. Lücke*, trans. James Duke and Francis Fiorenza (Chico, Calif.: Scholars Press, 1981), pp. 58-60.

[16]Schleiermacher, *Christian Faith*, pp. 12-16.

[17]Friedrich Schleiermacher, *On Human Freedom*, trans. Albert Blackwell (Lewiston, N.Y.: Edwin Mellen, 1992).

[18]Schleiermacher, *Christian Faith*, pp. 62-68.

[19]Ibid., p. 491.

[20]Ibid., p. 525.

[21]See George A. Lindbeck, "The Church's Mission to a Postmodern Culture," and Robert N. Bellah, "Christian Faithfulness in a Pluralistic World," in *Postmodern Theology: Christian Faith in a Pluralistic World*, ed. Frederic B. Burnham (San Francisco: Harper, 1989).

[22]Schleiermacher, *Chistian Faith*, p. 135.

[23]Friedrich Schleiermacher, *Servant of the Word: Selected Sermons*, trans. Dawn DeVries (Philadelphia: Fortress, 1987), p. 87.

[24]Schleiermacher, *Christian Faith*, pp. 479-81.

[25]Ibid., p. 314.

[26]Schleiermacher, *On Religion*, pp. 43-48.

[27]Schleiermacher, *Christian Faith*, p. 27.

[28]Friedrich Schleiermacher, *Hermeneutics: The Handwritten Manuscripts*, ed Heinz Kimme, trans. James Duke and Jack Forstmann (Atlanta: Fortress, 1977), p. 55, no. 91.

## Chapter 5: Politically Incorrect Salvation/Craig

[1]Gordon D. Kaufman, "Evidentialism: A Theologian's Response," *Faith and Philosophy* 6 (1989): 40. For an incisive response to Kaufman see Eleonore Stump and Norman Kretzmann, "Theologically Unfashionable Philosophy," *Faith and Philosophy* 7 (1990): 329-39. (The reader should be aware that the original Stump-Kretzmann article has a page missing between 329 and 330, which was supplied with a later issue of the journal.) They point out that Kaufman's religious agnosticism is in fact less open than Christianity, since he must reject virtually all religious truth claims as (objectively) false.

[2]Allan Bloom, *The Closing of the American Mind* (New York: Simon & Schuster, 1987), p. 26. Calling the conflict between relativism and objectivism "the central cultural opposition of our time," Richard Bernstein reports that as a result of this conflict "there is an uneasiness that has spread throughout intellectual and cultural life. It affects almost every discipline and every aspect of culture" (Richard J. Bernstein, *Beyond Objectivism and Relativism* [Oxford: Blackwell, 1983], pp. 7, 1).

[3]Edward John Carnell, having borrowed this notion from Edgar Sheffield Brightman, popularized it among evangelical apologists (Edward John Carnell, *An Introduction to Christian Apologetics* [Grand Rapids, Mich.: Eerdmans, 1948], pp. 56-64). My explication of this notion is, however, different from Carnell's.

[4]For a good discussion, see Stuart C. Hackett, *Oriental Philosophy* (Madison: University of Wisconsin Press, 1979).

[5]It might be said that when one denies the validity of such logical principles for propositions about God, one is talking in a higher-level metalanguage about propositions expressed in another lower-level language, much as one could talk in German, for example, about the rules for English grammar, and that since the principles of the lower-level language do not apply to the metalanguage, no self-refuting situations arise. But the futility of this response

214 CHRISTIAN APOLOGETICS IN THE POSTMODERN WORLD

is evident in the fact that one could then use the metalanguage itself to describe God, since the restrictions apply only to the lower-level language.

[6]For support for both these claims, see my apologetics text *Reasonable Faith* (Wheaton, Ill.: Crossway, 1994).

[7]John D. Caputo, *Radical Hermeneutics* (Bloomington: Indiana University Press, 1987), p. 156.

[8]For a trenchant critique of postmodern (ir)rationality, as well as attempted responses, see the discussion in James L. Marsh, John D. Caputo and Merold Westphal, *Modernity and Its Discontents* (New York: Fordham University Press, 1992), pp. 18-19, 89-92, 168-77, 199-201. See also the entertaining discussion in Alvin Plantinga, *The Twin Pillars of Christian Scholarship* (Grand Rapids, Mich.: Calvin College and Seminary, 1990), pp. 17-23.

[9]I include annihilation here not because I consider it a biblical alternative to hell, but to underline the fact that adoption of annihilationism does nothing to solve the problem, occasioned by religious diversity, of less than universal salvation.

[10]John H. Hick, ed., *The Myth of God Incarnate* (London: SCM Press, 1977), and *The Metaphor of God Incarnate* (London: SCM Press, 1993).

[11]This is illustrated by Robert Müller's call for "a new universalism" in his plenary address "Interfaith Understanding" at the 1993 Parliament of the World's Religions, August 28-September 4, 1993, in Chicago, a veritable orgy of religious diversity.

[12]Thomas Talbott, "The Doctrine of Everlasting Punishment," *Faith and Philosophy* 7 (1990): 19-42; Thomas Talbott, "Providence, Freedom and Human Destiny," *Religious Studies* 26 (1990): 227-45. For discussion see William Lane Craig, "Talbott's Universalism," *Religious Studies* 27 (1991): 297-308; Thomas Talbott, "Craig on the Possibility of Eternal Damnation," *Religious Studies* 28 (1992): 495-510; William Lane Craig, "Talbott's Universalism Once More," *Religious Studies* 29 (1993): 497-518.

[13]See John W. Sanders, *No Other Name: An Investigation into the Destiny of the Unevangelized*, with a foreword by Clark Pinnock (Grand Rapids, Mich.: Eerdmans, 1992).

[14]For example, Francis Schaeffer held that salvation is available to all persons through general revelation but that no one avails himself of it (Francis Schaeffer, *Death in the City*, in *The Complete Works of Francis Schaeffer: A Christian Worldview*, vol. 4, *A Christian View of the Church*, 2nd ed. [Westchester, Ill.: Crossway, 1982], p. 278).

[15]"Dogmatic Constitution on the Church," in *The Documents of Vatican II*, ed. W. M. Abbott (New York: Guild Press, 1966), p. 34.

[16]"Declaration on the Relationship of the Church to Non-Christian Religions," in *Documents*, pp. 663-66.

[17]Clark Pinnock, "The Finality of Jesus Christ in a World of Religions," paper delivered at the Evangelical Theology Group, American Academy of Religion, November 22, 1992.

[18]Statistics released by the U.S. Center for World Mission indicate that there are now only about nine non-Christian believers per evangelical believer in the world and that the growth of evangelical Christianity per annum far outstrips the world's population growth. About 15-25 percent of the world's population currently lies beyond the reach of the gospel. For more information on the status of world evangelization, see Patrick Johnstone, *Operation World*, 5th ed. (Grand Rapids, Mich.: Zondervan, 1993).

[19]Marilyn McCord Adams, "The Problem of Hell: A Problem of Evil for Christians," in *Reasoned Faith*, ed. Eleonore Stump (Ithaca, N.Y.: Cornell University Press, 1993), pp. 308-11.

[20]Fyodor Dostoyevsky, *The Brothers Karamazov*, trans. Constance Garnett, ed. with a foreword by Manuel Komroff, Signet Classics (New York: New American Library, 1957), bk. 5, chap. 5, pp. 233-40.

[21]Even if one denies that God has such knowledge, the problem still remains that some of the

unreached who are condemned *might* respond to the gospel if they heard it. So how could a loving God fail to bring the gospel to them? Inclusivism offers nothing to solve this problem.

[22]Adams, "Problem of Hell," pp. 313-14; compare p. 319.

[23]Ibid., pp. 315-16. She also alludes to Robert Adams's argument that there is no truth concerning what people would do under different circumstances. But neither she nor her husband has responded to the refutations of his argument in the following essays: Alvin Plantinga, "Reply to Robert M. Adams," in *Alvin Plantinga*, ed. James E. Tomberlin and Peter Van Inwagen, Profiles 5 (Dordrecht, Netherlands: D. Reidel, 1985), pp. 371-82; Alfred J. Freddoso, introduction to *On Divine Foreknowledge*, by Luis de Molina, trans. with notes by A. J. Freddoso (Ithaca, N.Y.: Cornell University Press, 1988), pp. 68-75; William Lane Craig, *Divine Foreknowledge and Human Freedom*, Studies in Intellectual History 19 (Leiden: E. J. Brill, 1990), pp. 247-69. See further Robert M. Adams, "An Anti-Molinist Argument," in *Philosophy of Religion*, ed. James E. Tomberlin, Philosophical Perspectives 5 (Atascadero, Calif.: Ridgeway, 1991), pp. 343-53, and William Lane Craig, "Robert Adams's New Anti-Molinist Argument," *Philosophy and Phenomenological Research* 54 (1994): 857-61.

[24]See the critiques of William Hasker, "Middle Knowledge and the Damnation of the Heathen: A Response to William Craig," *Faith and Philosophy* 8 (1991): 380-89; David P. Hunt, "Middle Knowledge and the Soteriological Problem of Evil," *Religious Studies* 27 (1991): 3-26. For discussion see William Lane Craig, "Should Peter Go to the Mission Field?" *Faith and Philosophy* 10 (1993): 261-65.

## Chapter 6: On Being a Fool for Christ and an Idiot for Nobody/Sire

[1]I wrote this verse high above the Rocky Mountains on a flight from Chicago to Seattle, February 1991. It suggests the focus of this paper: the "invention" of apologetic arguments responding to the *antilogocentric* postmodern posture of today's graduate students and university faculty in the humanities and social sciences.

[2]John Ellis, *Against Deconstruction* (Princeton, N.J.: Princeton University Press, 1989), p. 35. I have found helpful critiques and countercritiques of postmodern literary theory in numerous articles in recent volumes of *The Christian Scholar's Review* and *Christianity and Literature*. I also recommend the following books for their especially helpful analyses: Clarence Walhout and Leland Ryken, *Contemporary Literary Theory: A Christian Appraisal* (Grand Rapids, Mich.: Eerdmans, 1991); Gene Edward Veith, *Postmodern Times: A Christian Guide to Contemporary Thought and Culture* (Wheaton, Ill.: Crossway, 1994); W. J. T. Mitchell, *Against Theory* (Chicago: University of Chicago Press, 1985); Roger Lundin, *The Culture of Interpretation: Christian Faith and the Postmodern World* (Grand Rapids, Mich.: Eerdmans, 1993); and John Ellis, *Against Deconstruction* (Princeton, N.J.: Princeton University Press, 1989).

[3]Friedrich Nietzsche, "On Truth and Lie," in *The Portable Nietzsche*, ed. Walter Kaufmann (New York: Viking, 1954), pp. 46-47.

[4]By contrast, as John Ellis points out, "logocentrism is not a fixation on words as one might expect, but instead a belief that there is an order of meaning existing *independently* of the structure of any given language that is a foundation for all else.... Logocentrism here turns out to be much the same as the more familiar *essentialism*, the belief that words simply label real categories of meaning existing independently of a language" (Ellis, *Against Deconstruction*, p. 35). The entire chapter "Deconstruction and the Nature of Language" (pp. 18-66) is an excellent analysis of antilogocentrism.

[5]Richard Rorty, "Introduction: Pragmatism and Philosophy," in *Consequences of Pragmatism*

(Minneapolis: University of Minnesota Press, 1982), p. xlii.

[6]Quoted by Rorty, "Introduction," p. xx, from C. S. Peirce, *Collected Papers of C. S. Peirce*, ed. Charles Hartshorne, Paul Weiss and Arthur Burks (Cambridge, Mass.: Harvard University Press, 1931-1958), 5:313-14. Echoing this notion, Rorty himself writes: "The world does not speak. Only we do.... But if we could ever become reconciled to the idea that most of reality is indifferent to our descriptions of it, and that the human self is created by the use of a vocabulary rather than being adequately or inadequately expressed in a vocabulary, then we should at last have assimilated what was true in the Romantic idea that truth is made rather than found. What is true about this claim is just that *languages* are made rather than found, and that truth is a property of linguistic entities, of sentences" (Richard Rorty, *Contingency, irony and solidarity* [Cambridge: Cambridge University Press, 1989], pp. 6-7).

One may note that Rorty claims that his view of this matter is "true." Has he not violated his own definition of *truth*? Wouldn't what he said be "true" only if he could get a vast number of people in open dialogue to agree with him? Moreover, I am not convinced that Rorty's view of Peirce does justice to Peirce. Two reviews of Peirce's philosophy take radically different views of Peirce's epistemology. Louis Menand, agreeing basically with Rorty, identifies Peirce as a forerunner of Derrida and Foucault. In contrast, Edward T. Oakes focuses on Peirce's antinominalist stance and never once mentions Derrida, Foucault or any postmodern thinker. See Louis Menand, "An American Prodigy," *The New York Review of Books*, December 2, 1993, pp. 30-35, esp. p. 32; and Edward T. Oakes, "Discovering the American Aristotle," *First Things*, December 1993, pp. 24-33, esp. p. 31.

[7]Ibid., quoting Hans-Georg Gadamer, *Philosophical Hermeneutics* (Berkeley: University of California Press, 1976), p. 18.

[8]Ibid., quoting Martin Heidegger, *On the Way to Language* (New York: Harper & Row, 1971), p. 50.

[9]Rorty, "Pragmatism, Relativism, Irrationalism," in *Consequences of Pragmatism*, p. 165.

[10]Rorty, *Contingency, Irony and Solidarity*, p. 7.

[11]Rorty, "Introduction," p. 173; and *Contingency, Irony and Solidarity*, pp. 52, 67-68.

[12]Quoted in "Deconstruction: The Crisis of Values and Truth in the Academy," *SCP Journal*, Fall 1992, p. 33.

[13]Karen J. Winkler, "Scholars Mark the Beginning of the Age of 'Post-Theory,' " *The Chronicle of Higher Education*, October 13, 1993, p. A9.

[14]Ibid.

[15]Ibid., p. A16. A young professor of linguistics in Zagreb University told me in November 1993 that his field was in theoretical shambles. Two decades ago, linguistics was thought to hold out the best prospect of all the fields of social science of providing a rational and comprehensive theory of language. Today, he remarked, no theory has won its way as dominant. In fact the project itself has been largely abandoned. "It's exciting to be in linguistics," he said. "Anything could happen; no one knows what may come from the ferment in the field."

[16]Winkler, "Scholars Mark the Beginning," p. A9.

[17]Ibid.

[18]See Rorty's discussion of Freud as a "strong poet" in *Contingency, Irony and Solidarity*, pp. 20, 28, 30-34, and his own comments on the power of poetry (pp. 151-52) and on truth as "whatever the outcome of undistorted communication happens to be" (p. 67; also pp. 52, 68).

[19]Thomas C. Oden, *After Modernity . . . What?* (Grand Rapids, Mich.: Zondervan, 1990), pp. 187-90; and Diogenes Allen, *Christian Belief in a Postmodern World* (Louisville, Ky.: Westmin-

ster/John Knox Press, 1989), esp. pp. 1-19.

[20]Allen, *Christian Belief*, p. 6.

[21]See Mark Philip, "Michel Foucault," in *The Return of the Grand Theory in the Human Sciences*, ed. Quentin Skinner (Cambridge: Cambridge University Press, 1985), for a justification of the oxymoron "antipolitical political ideology."

[22]Abductive arguments are a combination of inductive and deductive arguments toward a "best explanation" of some aspect of the world as we perceive it (such as the fact that all people act from some notion of right and wrong). For a superb exposition of this type of argument, see Basil Mitchell, *The Justification of Religious Belief* (Oxford: Oxford University Press, 1973).

[23]George Mavrodes, *Belief in God* (New York: Random House, 1970), pp. 17-48.

[24]This phrase was suggested to me by Brian Walsh. See Os Guinness, "On Remembering the Third Fool and the Devil's Mousetrap," in *The Gravedigger File* (Downers Grove, Ill.: InterVarsity Press, 1983), pp. 227-38.

[25]Rorty recognizes the relevance of a theistic God to issue of logocentricity: "The suggestion that truth, as well as the world, is out there is a legacy of an age in which the world was seen as the creation of a being who had a language of his own" (*Contingency, Irony and Solidarity*, p. 5). But what a paltry reduction of the biblical notion of God as *logos* (Jn 1:1-4), One who spoke the universe into existence (Gen 1) and who spoke to us by his Son (Heb 1:1-3)! Note too how Rorty refers to the notion of even such a reduced theistic deity as a "legacy," as if no one today could possibly believe such a deity existed. This is argument by innuendo.

[26]By "traditional apologetics" I mean those cases for the Christian faith that assume without argument that the human mind is capable of accessing reality, that in principle there can be evidence for historical and religious claims. J. N. D. Anderson, John R. W. Stott, Michael Green, Craig Blomberg and F. F. Bruce are all, in my sense, traditional apologists. *Postmodern* apologetics that would continue basing itself on these traditional assumptions must first establish at least their plausibility.

[27]I have addressed the issue of relativism in chapters 5 and 6 of *Chris Chrisman Goes to College* (Downers Grove, Ill.: InterVarsity Press, 1993), pp. 45-68.

[28]Charles Taylor, "Rorty in the Epistemological Tradition," in *Reading Rorty*, ed. Alan Malachowski (Oxford: Blackwell, 1990), p. 258.

[29]Ibid.

[30]Postmodern thought has received much criticism. Christian apologists do not have to do all the work of discovering major weaknesses in antilogocentrism. Scholars writing in scholarly journals and books are often rich sources of criticism. For example, Bernard Williams's essay "Auto-da-Fé: Consequences of Pragmatism" in *Reading Rorty* (pp. 26-37) is an excellent critique of Rorty's antilogocentrism. Williams identifies a fundamental incoherence in Rorty's work: "Sometimes he seems quite knowing about the status of his own thoughts. . . . At other times, he seems to forget altogether about one requirement of self-consciousness, and like the old philosophies he is attempting to escape, naively treats his own discourse as standing quite outside the general philosophical situation he is describing" (p. 29). Later he points to what he takes to be the impracticability of his philosophy: "It is not very realistic to suppose that we could for long sustain much of a culture, or indeed keep away boredom, by playfully abusing the texts of writers who believed in an activity which we now know to be hopeless" (p. 33).

[31]René Descartes, "Meditations," in *The Philosophical Works of Descartes*, trans. Elizabeth S. Haldane and G. R. T. Ross (New York: Dover, 1955), 1:151-52.

[32]Friedrich Nietzsche, "On Truth and Lie in the Extra-moral Sense" (1873), in *The Portable Nietzsche*, ed. Walter Kaufmann (New York: Viking, 1954), pp. 42-47. See also "How the Real World at Last Became a Myth: The History of an Error," in *Twilight of the Idols/The Anti-Christ*, trans. R. J. Hollingdale (London: Penguin, 1990), pp. 50-51. This is Nietzsche's brief history of philosophy from Plato to his own Zarathustra—that is, from the wisdom and certitude of the pious man to the nihilist, and beyond to the *Übermensch* in whom knowledge is will to power.

[33]Friedrich Nietzsche, "Beyond Good and Evil," in *The Basic Writings of Nietzsche*, ed. Walter Kaufmann (New York: Modern Library, 1969), pp. 213-14.

[34]Lesslie Newbigin, *The Gospel in a Pluralist Society* (Grand Rapids, Mich.: Eerdmans, 1989), pp. 47-48. See also *Discipleship of the Mind* (Downers Grove, Ill.: InterVarsity Press, 1990), pp. 13-24, where I develop this notion in a parallel way.

[35]Lately Kerry Ose told me that she was far more taken with the postmodern project at the beginning of her studies than she is now. She says that she was unaware of how destructive "deconstruction" had actually been. In her words, "I am now more cynical about the postmodern approach to literary study, and to sociological theory as well." But her attitude is, as she admits, still taking form. As we spoke, however, we both saw the "all or nothing-at-all" stance of postmodernism.

[36]Lodge recounts the general pattern of his religious convictions in the 1992 foreword to a republication of *The Picturegoers* (London: Penguin, 1993), p. ix.

[37]"Ten Myths: Campus Is Engaged," a report circulated by Mark and Gwen Potter, IVCF staff at Swarthmore.

[38]Kelly James Clark, ed., *Philosophers Who Believe* (Downers Grove, Ill.: InterVarsity Press, 1993).

[39]Kerry Ulm Ose has herself illustrated this as a graduate student in rhetoric and composition at the University of Illinois in the English Department and the Center for Writing Studies. At the Penn State Rhetoric and Composition Conference, July 13-16, 1994, she delivered a paper entitled "Usable and Transcendent Truths: The Story of One Woman's Subversion of Academic Discourse," in which she analyzed within the framework of current rhetorical theory the way an evangelical Christian student treated her own writing of papers in a philosophy and an English class and how that writing was treated by her instructors. In the process, key elements of a Christian perspective on truth were exposed and shown to be relevant. The paper was recognized by a senior professor as worthy of setting at least part of Ose's agenda for her continued doctoral work.

[40]Robert Bellah et al., *Habits of the Heart: Individualism and Commitment in American Life* (San Francisco: Harper & Row, 1985).

[41]Glenn Tinder, *The Political Meaning of Christianity: An Interpretation* (Baton Rouge: Louisiana State University Press, 1989).

[42]This lecture has recently been expanded and is available in book form as *Why Should Anyone Believe Anything at All?* (Downers Grove, Ill: InterVarsity Press, 1994).

### Chapter 7: Facing the Postmodern Scalpel/Middleton and Walsh

[1]Jane Wagner, *The Search for Signs of Intelligent Life in the Universe* (New York: Harper & Row, 1986), p. 18. The play, written by Wagner, is acted by Tomlin, who has become in effect the play's coauthor through the joint development of the script at the workshop stage.

[2]From the title of his book *Reality Isn't What It Used to Be: Theatrical Politics, Ready-to-Wear Religion, Global Myths, Primitive Chic and Other Wonders of the Postmodern World* (San Francisco: Harper & Row, 1990).

[3]Ibid., p. 75.

[4]N. T. Wright describes this postmodern epistemology as a form of phenomenalism: all I can really be sure of are the phenomena, my own sensory experiences, not anything external to which those sensory experiences correspond. The result is solipsism; private reality is all there is. See the methodological section of Wright's *The New Testament and the People of God* (London: SPCK/Minneapolis: Fortress, 1992), esp. pp. 33-35, 51-53.

[5]Richard Rorty, "Pragmatism and Philosophy," in *After Philosophy: End or Transformation?* ed. Kenneth Baynes, James Bohman and Thomas McCarthy (Cambridge, Mass.: MIT Press, 1987), p. 57. Rorty has this phrase in italics in his text.

[6]See Brian J. Walsh and J. Richard Middleton, *The Transforming Vision: Shaping a Christian World View* (Downers Grove, Ill.: InterVarsity Press, 1984), chaps. 1-2.

[7]For further discussion of "worldview" in relation to Christian higher education see Brian J. Walsh's "Worldviews, Modernity and the Task of Christian College Education," *Faculty Dialogue* 18 (Fall 1992): 13-35.

[8]The recognition of the perspectival character of human knowing has revolutionized the philosophy of science. For example, see Thomas Kuhn, *The Structure of Scientific Revolutions*, rev. ed. (Chicago: University of Chicago Press, 1962); Mary Gerhart and Allan Russell, *Metaphoric Process: The Creation of Scientific and Religious Understanding* (Fort Worth: Texas Christian University Press, 1984); Ian Barbour, *Myths, Models and Paradigms: A Comparative Study in Science and Religion* (New York: Harper & Row, 1974); John Greene, *Science, Ideology and World View: Essays in the History of Evolutionary Ideas* (Berkeley: University of California Press, 1981); and Michael Polanyi, *The Tacit Dimension* (Garden City, N.Y.: Doubleday, 1967). From a more explicitly Christian perspective see Del Ratzsch, *Philosophy of Science: The Natural Sciences in Christian Perspective* (Downers Grove, Ill.: InterVarsity Press, 1986); Nicholas Wolterstorff, *Reason Within the Bounds of Religion*, 2nd ed. (Grand Rapids, Mich.: Eerdmans, 1984); James Sire, *Discipleship of the Mind* (Downers Grove, Ill.: InterVarsity Press, 1990); Langdon Gilkey, *Religion and the Scientific Future* (New York: Harper & Row, 1970); and Walsh and Middleton, *Transforming Vision*, chaps. 11-12.

[9]Rorty, "Pragmatism and Philosophy," p. 60.

[10]Richard Rorty, *Philosophy and the Mirror of Nature* (Princeton, N.J.: Princeton University Press, 1979), p. 325. As the title suggests, Rorty is concerned to debunk the classic notion of the human mind functioning as a mirror of nature. If there is any "mirroring" going on in human knowing, the postmodernist is suspicious that it is a conjuring trick.

[11]Playing with the title of Alasdair MacIntyre's book *Whose Justice? Which Rationality?* (Notre Dame, Ind.: University of Notre Dame Press, 1988).

[12]For a helpful introduction to deconstructionist philosophy see Linda Hutcheon, *The Politics of Postmodernism* (London: Routledge, 1989), esp. chap. 2.

[13]Derrida first used the term regarding Edmund Husserl's phenomenology of consciousness. See especially *Speech and Phenomena*, trans. David Allison (Evanston, Ill.: Northwestern University Press, 1972) and *Edmund Husserl's Origin of Geometry: An Introduction*, trans. John P. Leavy (Stonybrook, N.Y.: Nicholas Hays, 1978).

[14]Berger and Luckmann, *The Social Construction of Reality* (Garden City, N.Y.: Doubleday, 1966), p. 89. In *The Sacred Canopy: Elements of a Sociological Theory of Religion* (Garden City, N.Y.: Doubleday, 1967), chap. 4, Berger describes alienation as forgetting that this world was and continues to be coproduced by humans. He says, "Men then live in the world they themselves have made as if they were fated to do so by powers that are quite independent of their own world-constructing enterprises" (p. 95). The irony of Berger's career is that his later insistence that capitalism needs no legitimation because it has the "normative power

of facticity" on its side falls into precisely the alienated reification he warned against twenty
years earlier. See his *The Capitalist Revolution* (New York: Basic Books, 1986), pp. 207-8. We
are indebted to a former student, Iskandar Saher, for bringing this irony to our attention in
his master's thesis at the Institute for Christian Studies.

[15]Jane Flax, *Thinking Fragments: Psychoanalysis, Feminism and Postmodernism in the Contemporary West* (Berkeley: University of California Press, 1990), p. 34.

[16]From his *Discourse on Method*, chap. 6. See *Essential Works of Descartes*, trans. Lowell Bair
(New York: Bantam, 1961), p. 37.

[17]Jacques Derrida, "Violence and Metaphysics: An Essay on the Thought of Emmanuel
Levinas," in *Writing and Difference*, trans. Alan Bass (Chicago: University of Chicago Press,
1978), p. 91. Although Derrida is at this point explaining Levinas's thought, he is in
agreement with the judgment.

[18]This is Albert Borgmann's description. See *Crossing the Postmodern Divide* (Chicago: University of Chicago Press, 1992), p. 27.

[19]The classic discussion of totalization is found in Emmanuel Levinas, *Totality and Infinity: An
Essay on Exteriority*, trans. Alphonso Lingis (Pittsburgh, Penn.: Duquesne University Press,
1969). This is a very dense and complex philosophical text, but see pp. 17-18 of the
introduction by John Wild for a succinct summary of what Levinas means by "totalization."

[20]James H. Olthuis, "A Cold and Comfortless Hermeneutic or a Warm and Trembling
Hermeneutic: A Conversation with John D. Caputo," *Christian Scholar's Review* 19, no. 4
(1990): 351. This is an important article which attempts to articulate Christian sympathies
with, yet ultimate divergence from, a philosophy of deconstruction.

[21]Kenneth J. Gergen, *The Saturated Self: Dilemmas of Identity in Contemporary Life* (New York:
Basic Books, 1991), p. 252.

[22]Jean-François Lyotard, *The Postmodern Condition: A Report on Knowledge*, vol. 10 of *Theory
and History of Literature*, trans. Geoff Bennington and Brian Massumi (Minneapolis: University of Minnesota Press, 1984), p. 81.

[23]This theme is summed up well by Gary J. Percesepe in his article "The Unbearable Lightness
of Being Postmodern," *Christian Scholar's Review* 20, no. 2 (1990): 118-35.

[24]For Hauerwas's proposals, see *The Peaceable Kingdom: A Primer in Christian Ethics* (Notre
Dame, Ind.: University of Notre Dame Press, 1983) and *A Community of Character: Toward a
Constructive Christian Social Ethic* (Notre Dame, Ind.: University of Notre Dame Press, 1981).
MacIntyre's views may be found in *After Virtue: A Study in Moral Theory*, 2nd ed. (Notre
Dame, Ind.: University of Notre Dame Press, 1984), and *Whose Justice? Which Rationality?*

[25]Lyotard, *Postmodern Condition*, p. xxiv.

[26]Cited by David Harvey in *The Condition of Postmodernity: An Inquiry into the Origins of
Cultural Change* (Oxford: Blackwell, 1989), p. 9, from "Awakening from Modernity," *Times
Literary Supplement*, February 20, 1987.

[27]Fukuyama expanded this essay into a monograph entitled *The End of History and the Last
Man* (New York: Free Press, 1992).

[28]Walsh has discussed and criticized the article at length in chap. 3 of *Subversive Christianity:
Imaging God in a Dangerous Time* (Bristol, U.K.: Regius, 1992/Medina, Wash.: Alta Vista
College Press, 1994).

[29]Fukuyama is clear that this is a metanarrative, citing as his guides G. W. F. Hegel (well
known for his historical scheme of the evolution of world spirit) and the Hegelian scholar
Alexander Kojéve.

[30]Francis Fukuyama, "The End of History?" *The National Interest*, Summer 1989, p. 9. Charles
Taylor accuses Fukuyama of "glaring Western ethnocentrism" in "Balancing the Humours:

Charles Taylor Talks to the Editors," *The Idler* 26 (November/December 1989): 21. William H. McNeill raises similar problems in his review of Fukuyama's *The End of History and the Last Man*, "History Over, World Goes On," *The New York Times Book Review*, January 26, 1992, pp. 14-15.

[31]The oppressive function of the Babylonian metanarrative is evident especially from the sixth century B.C., when neo-Babylonian kings assumed the part of Marduk, the head of the Babylonian pantheon, in the liturgical reenactment of the Enuma Elish at the Akitu festival every new year. In this reenactment Marduk's primordial conquest of chaos was identified with the human king's political conquest of his enemies, thus legitimating Babylonian imperial supremacy. See Paul Ricoeur's insightful analysis of the Enuma Elish in *The Symbolism of Evil*, trans. Emerson Buchanan (Boston: Beacon, 1969), pt. 2, chap. 1.

[32]Note that we are limiting our response to the *ethical* challenge of postmodernity. For the beginning of a response to the *epistemological* challenge of postmodernity (that is, how we are to account for a genuine preconceptual world, a reality given prior to our constructions), see J. Richard Middleton and Brian J. Walsh, *Truth Is Stranger Than It Used to Be: Biblical Faith in a Postmodern Age* (Downers Grove, Ill.: InterVarsity Press, 1995), chap. 7.

[33]See Gerhard von Rad, "The Form-Critical Problem of the Hexateuch," in *The Problem of the Hexateuch and Other Essays* (London: SCM Press, 1966).

[34]MacIntyre, *After Virtue*, p. 216.

[35]On the importance of the lament psalms for the church, see J. Richard Middleton, "Noises from the Ragged Edge: How the Psalms Can Help Us Process Pain," *Canadian Theological Society Newsletter* 14 (November 1994): 4-7. For excellent, accessible summaries of recent scholarship on the psalms of lament, see Walter Brueggemann, *The Message of the Psalms: A Theological Commentary* (Minneapolis: Augsburg, 1984), pp. 54-57, and Claus Westermann, *Praise and Lament in the Psalms*, trans. Keith R. Crim and Richard N. Soulen (Atlanta: John Knox, 1981), pp. 52-71.

[36]For other statements of these two motivational clauses, see Exodus 22:21, 27; Leviticus 19:34; Deuteronomy 5:15; 10:19; 15:15; 16:12; 23:7; 24:19-22. Such statements amply testify to the paradigmatic nature of the exodus story for Israel's ethical life.

[37]Gottwald has argued in many places, but especially in his massive work *The Tribes of Yahweh: A Sociology of the Religion of Liberated Israel, 1250-1050 B.C.E.* (Maryknoll, N.Y.: Orbis, 1979), that the distinctiveness of Yahweh vis-à-vis the gods of Egypt and Canaan is inextricably linked to the distinctiveness of Israel's egalitarian form of social organization. He describes the formation of Israel as "retribalization," a conscious sociopolitical rebellion against the oppressive hegemony of Egypt and the Canaanite city-states. Whether or not the details of Gottwald's historical and sociological reconstruction will stand the test of time, his central insight into the connection between Israel's God and its egalitarian form of life is clearly supported by the biblical data.

[38]Charles Taylor has addressed the centrality of this attitude toward suffering in our Western inheritance, although he traces it only as far back as the New Testament. See his *Sources of the Self: The Making of the Modern Identity* (Cambridge, Mass.: Harvard University Press, 1989), pp. 12-13.

[39]Eloquent testimony to that sensitivity is found in the contemporary tradition of Jewish Passover celebration, the Seder supper, in which the exodus narrative is remembered and rearticulated. During the course of the meal, wine is ritually spilled in compassion for, and solidarity with, the suffering caused to the Egyptians by God's deliverance of Israel at the exodus. While this suffering is realistically recognized as part of the process of historical and political liberation from a brutal regime, it is nevertheless mourned, since God does not

desire that any of his creatures perish. See, for example, Herbert Bronstein, ed., *A Passover Haggadah: The New Union Haggadah*, rev. ed. (New York: Central Conference of American Rabbis, 1975), pp. 48-49.

[40]Walter Brueggemann, "A Shape for Old Testament Theology, II: Embrace of Pain," *Catholic Biblical Quarterly* 47 (July 1985): 395-415.

[41]Walter Brueggemann, *The Prophetic Imagination* (Philadelphia: Fortress, 1978), esp. chaps. 1, 3-4. On the suffering of God in the Prophets, see the seminal work by Abraham Joshua Heschel, *The Prophets* (New York: Harper & Row, 1962).

[42]This indicates that alongside the prophetic trajectory of the embrace of pain (a trajectory that goes back to Moses, regarded in Deut 18:15 as the first prophet), there is another trajectory, which Brueggemann names both the "imperial consciousness" and "structure legitimation," since it is typically the role of kings, at least in the ancient Near East, to enforce order (see Brueggemann, *The Prophetic Imagination*, chap. 2, and "A Shape for Old Testament Theology, I: Structure Legitimation," *Catholic Biblical Quarterly* 47 [January 1985]: 28-46). For some time now it has been widely agreed by biblical scholars that the Old Testament prophets (as far back as Elijah and Elisha in the ninth century and Nathan in the tenth) arose largely in response to the abuses of the Israelite monarchy. In one way or another the prophets all condemn the policies and practices of Israel's kings as essentially a recapitulation of Egyptian bondage. The narrative of 1 Kings 3—11 (in the Hebrew canon, part of the Former Prophets) itself portrays Solomon's grandiose reign in terms similar to the empire of Egypt. Its description of a large harem, a standing army of horses and chariots, the proliferation of wisdom literature rivaling that of Egypt and the introduction of the corvée or forced labor for building the royal palace and the Jerusalem temple portrays, in George Mendenhall's vivid phrase, the beginning of the "paganization" of Israel. Solomon was a new pharaoh, and Israel was returning to Egyptian bondage (see Mendenhall, "The Monarchy," *Interpretation* 29 [1975]: 160).

[43]The vivid accounts of the opposition Jeremiah encountered (from priests, other prophets and the royal establishment) are recorded in Jeremiah 20, 26—28 and 37—38. See also the prophet-priest conflict recorded in Amos 7:10-17.

[44]The substance of our entire analysis of prophecy, exile and the shape of the canon is indebted to J. A. Sanders's important essays "Adaptable for Life: The Nature and Function of Canon" and "Hermeneutics of True and False Prophecy" in *From Sacred Story to Sacred Text: Canon as Paradigm* (Philadelphia: Fortress, 1987).

[45]Prophetic texts that speak of Israel's mission to the Gentiles include Isaiah 42:5-7 and 49:6, while texts that speak of the restoration of the nonhuman creation include Isaiah 55:12-13 and 65:17, 25.

[46]We have benefited tremendously from Lesslie Newbigin's insights in "The Logic of Election," chap. 7 in *The Gospel in a Pluralist Society* (Grand Rapids, Mich.: Eerdmans/Geneva: World Council of Churches, 1989).

[47]This monotheizing insight was also the basis of the so-called prophecies against the nations, collections of judgment oracles found in every major canonical prophetic book (Is 13—21, Jer 46—51, Ezek 25—32) and in some minor ones (besides Amos 1:2—2:3, the entirety of Nahum and Obadiah are directed against foreign nations, while Jonah tells the story of a prophet's mission to Nineveh, the Assyrian capital). Whereas judgments against Israel could cite infringements of the Sinai covenant laws, judgments against other nations could be rooted only in God's purposes and claims as Creator.

[48]For further analysis of the counterideological power of creation in the Bible, see J. Richard Middleton, "Is Creation Theology Inherently Conservative? A Dialogue with Walter Brueg-

gemann," *Harvard Theological Review* 87, no. 3 (1994): 257-77. Brueggemann's response is published on pp. 279-89.
[49]The Former Prophets (Joshua, Judges, Samuel and Kings) and the Latter Prophets (Isaiah, Jeremiah, Ezekiel and the Twelve) together form the Nev'im (Prophets), the second major grouping of books in the Masoretic Text (MT) of the Hebrew Bible. The Septuagint, although grouping and ordering the books differently (an order followed by Christian Bibles), nevertheless agrees with the MT in beginning its next major section (the Historical Books) with Joshua.
[50]It is fascinating that Gerhard von Rad, arguably the greatest Old Testament scholar of the century, disregarded explicit canonical shape and regarded the Hexateuch (Genesis to Joshua), rather than the Pentateuch, as the basic textual unit of the Old Testament (see his "The Form-Critical Problem of the Hexateuch," in *The Problem of the Hexateuch and Other Essays*).
[51]A partial listing of the various and diverse retellings of the story within the biblical text would include Deuteronomy 6:20-25; 26:1-11; Joshua 24:1-15; Psalms 78; 105; 106; 136; Jeremiah 2:5-7; 32:16-38; Nehemiah 9:1-38; Acts 7:1-54; 13:13-41; 1 Corinthians 15:1-11.
[52]Besides Jeremiah 32:17 and Nehemiah 9:5-6, Psalm 136 includes creation as the start of the story. Unlike the Jeremiah and Nehemiah texts, this psalm is not obviously exilic or postexilic, since it ends the story with the entrance into the Promised Land, whereas both Jeremiah 32 and Nehemiah 9 bring the story right up to their contemporaneous exilic or postexilic situation. Nevertheless, the designation of Yahweh as "the God of heaven" in Psalm 136:26 is consistent with a late dating, since this phrase is used for God in Nehemiah (1:4, 5; 2:4, 20), Ezra (1:2; 5:11-12; 6:9-10; 7:12, 21, 23), Daniel (2:18-19, 37, 44) and 2 Chronicles 36:23. Even those occurrences that are set before the exile speak either to pre-Israelite (Gen 24:3, 7) or non-Israelite (Jon 1:9) situations, suggesting that the phrase designates Yahweh as the true God in contexts where Israel confronted other nations with their gods.
[53]It is significant that von Rad not only disregarded the canonical ending of Torah before land possession but also devalued the theme of creation in the Bible and regarded the placement of creation at the narrative beginning of the canon as theologically unimportant (see Gerhard von Rad, "The Theological Problem of the Old Testament Doctrine of Creation," in *Creation in the Old Testament*, ed. Bernhard W. Anderson [Philadelphia: Fortress, 1984], p. 54). By misreading the shape of the canon, von Rad fundamentally misconstrued the point of the story, resulting in his assessment, "presumptuous as it may sound," that the Hexateuch functioned ideologically to legitimate Israel's election and land possession (see von Rad, *The Theology of Israel's Historical Traditions*, vol. 1 of *Old Testament Theology*, trans. D. M. G. Stalker [New York: Harper & Row, 1962], p. 138).
[54]We are not arguing that this interpretation of election *originated* in the exile. Rather, the canonical placing of the creation story at the start of the metanarrative highlights what is already implicit, and often quite explicit, in the Bible and functioned to correct self-serving, nationalistic readings of election which had arisen in Israel. For a "creational" analysis of election, see Terence E. Fretheim, *Exodus* (Louisville, Ky.: John Knox, 1991), pp. 13-14; Terence E. Fretheim, "The Reclamation of Creation: Redemption and Law in Exodus," *Interpretation* 45 (October 1991): 358-59, 363-64; and Terence E. Fretheim, "The Plagues as Ecological Signs of Historical Disaster," *Journal of Biblical Literature* 110, no. 3 (1991): 392.
[55]Other biblical texts that connect these themes include the song of Hannah in 1 Samuel 2:1-10, the exilic pronouncements of Isaiah 40:21-31, and Psalm 22, a prayer of lament that combines the experience of marginality with acknowledgment of God as Creator (vv. 9-11) and as Lord of all nations (vv. 27-28). Not only did Jesus quote Psalm 22 on the cross (Mt 27:46),

but the story of Jesus' death in Mark 15:22-37 contains numerous references and allusions to this psalm.

[56]This is a pronounced tendency in some Reformed or Calvinist theology, with its central emphasis on God's sovereignty. An extreme contemporary example may be found in the Reconstruction movement, which seeks to restore America to an ideal Puritan-like theocracy. For the two most important articulations of this ideal see Rousas John Rushdoony, *Institutes of Biblical Law* (Nutley, N.J.: Craig, 1973) and Greg L. Bahnsen, *Theonomy in Christian Ethics* (Nutley, N.J.: Craig, 1977). For a good brief overview of the movement, see Rodney Clapp, *The Reconstructionists*, rev. ed. (Downers Grove, Ill.: InterVarsity Press, 1990).

[57]This may be seen as a tendency in some early liberation theology from Latin America. It is significant that Pedro Trigo, himself a Latin American liberation theologian, understands faith in God as Creator as an important antidote to both disempowerment and vengeful self-assertion. See Trigo, *Creation and History*, trans. Robert R. Barr (Maryknoll, N.Y.: Orbis, 1991), pt. 2, pp. 69-108.

[58]Marcus J. Borg, *Jesus, a New Vision: Spirit, Culture and the Life of Discipleship* (San Francisco: Harper & Row, 1987), chap. 5; and Marcus J. Borg, *Conflict, Holiness and Politics in the Teaching of Jesus* (New York: Edwin Mellen, 1984), pp. 27-72.

[59]For various lists of despised occupations in first-century Judaism, see J. Jeremias, *Jerusalem in the Time of Jesus* (Philadelphia: Fortress, 1969), pp. 303-12.

[60]See Borg, *Jesus*, pp. 129-42; and *Conflict*, pp. 123-29, 133-34. It is intriguing that even Matthew's parallel to the Luke 6:36 text, which reads "be perfect" (or possibly "mature"), does not use the language of holiness (Mt 5:48). In both cases the context makes it clear that the holiness, perfection or mercy in question consists in loving one's enemies, as God does.

[61]Brueggemann, *Prophetic Imagination*, chaps. 5-6. See also Borg, *Jesus*, pp. 156-65.

[62]Wright made the distinction between "creational covenantal monotheism" and "covenantal monotheism" in a series of public lectures on the Gospel of Mark at the Institute for Christian Studies, July 1988. See also Wright's *The New Testament and the People of God*, pp. 246-52, and *The Climax of the Covenant* (Edinburgh: T & T Clark, 1991), pp. 108, 113-17, 137, 155. James Sanders proposed a similar interpretation of the message of Jesus in "The Bible, Anti-Semitism and the Monotheizing Process," paper given at the annual meeting of the Society of Biblical Literature, San Francisco, 1992.

[63]Although Jesus' ministry was, in the first instance, to the "lost sheep of the house of Israel," he both foresaw the Gentile mission (as is evident in many of his parables, such as those of the vineyard and the banquet) and explicitly commissioned his disciples to bear the metanarrative (the gospel story) to the *goyim*, making disciples of them (Mt 28).

[64]Both Mark 11:18 and Luke 19:47 say that the chief priests and scribes were moved to plot against Jesus' life in response to the temple cleansing. Earlier in Mark (3:6; see the parallel in Mt 12:14) the Pharisees, together with the Herodians, plotted against Jesus because of his healing on the sabbath, an act that anticipated the temple conflict. Matthew also portrays increased confrontational activity between Jesus and the authorities after the temple incident (Mt 21), culminating in the attempt to have him arrested (21:46).

[65]See Hans-Ruedi Weber, *Power: Focus for a Biblical Theology* (Geneva: World Council of Churches, 1989) for an insightful analysis of Jesus as the "convergence" of a number of themes concerning power and justice in the Bible.

[66]Indeed, since both Jacques Derrida and Emmanuel Levinas, the two postmodern thinkers who have raised the strongest *ethical* objections to Western modernity, are Jewish (and self-consciously so), it could be argued that some aspects of postmodernity actually consti-

tute a philosophical articulation of the prior, pervasive biblical concern for justice toward the marginal.

[67]This essay summarizes part of our larger argument in *Truth Is Stranger Than It Used to Be: Biblical Faith in a Postmodern Age* (Downers Grove, Ill.: InterVarsity Press, 1995).

**Chapter 8: There's No Such Thing as Objective Truth, and It's a Good Thing, Too/Kenneson**
I am indebted to James Street, John Hardwig, Frederick Norris and Stanley Hauerwas for their helpful comments and criticisms of an earlier draft of this essay. I began thinking through some of these matters at a conference for new faculty sponsored by the Christian College Coalition. I would like to thank the Coalition and my mentor for that week, Arthur Holmes, for providing an atmosphere for serious theological reflection that helped me clarify several issues.

[1]Ludwig Wittgenstein, *Culture and Value* (Oxford: Blackwell, 1980), p. 27.

[2]Peter C. Moore, *Disarming the Secular Gods* (Downers Grove, Ill.: InterVarsity Press, 1989).

[3]Richard J. Bernstein, *Beyond Objectivism and Relativism: Science, Hermeneutics and Praxis* (Philadelphia: University of Pennsylvania Press, 1983), esp. pp. 16-17.

[4]See, for example, the suggestive article by John Hardwig, "The Role of Trust in Knowledge," *Journal of Philosophy* 88 (December 1991): 693-708.

[5]As Rorty suggests, we should reject the "Cartesian-Kantian picture presupposed by the idea of 'our minds' or 'our language' as an 'inside' which can be contrasted to something (perhaps something very different) 'outside,' " for there is "simply no way to give sense to the idea of our minds or our language as systematically out of phase with what lies beyond our skins." See Rorty's introduction to *Objectivism, Relativism and Truth* (New York: Cambridge University Press, 1991), p. 12.

[6]For a fascinating account of the development of the language of "objective" and "subjective," including the way in which these terms have almost completely reversed their meanings, see Raymond Williams, *Keywords: A Vocabulary of Culture and Society*, rev. ed. (New York: Oxford University Press, 1983), pp. 308-12.

[7]Richard Rorty, *Contingency, Irony and Solidarity* (New York: Cambridge University Press, 1989), pp. 4-5.

[8]See James W. Sire, *Chris Chrisman Goes to College* (Downers Grove, Ill.: InterVarsity Press, 1993), pp. 62-65.

[9]Ibid., p. 63.

[10]Ibid., pp. 63-64.

[11]Sire's strange insistence that Rorty *must* answer the truth question in terms that are satisfactory to Sire suggests that he does not recognize the way in which certain philosophical traditions hold him captive. Rorty is calling for a paradigm shift that would no longer consider the questions raised by the Platonic-Cartesian-Lockean-Kantian tradition as necessary or even fruitful. As Rorty admits, "Pragmatists see the Platonic tradition as having outlived its usefulness. This does not mean that they have a new, non-Platonic set of answers to Platonic questions to offer, but rather that they do not think we should ask those questions anymore" (introduction to *Consequences of Pragmatism* [Minneapolis: University of Minnesota Press, 1982], p. xiv). It is noteworthy that Sire acknowledges Rorty's claim that he is not a relativist but refuses to accept it, commenting that "it is difficult to know what else to call a person who holds that we should be content to call 'true' whatever is accepted by an open society in open conversation" (*Chris Chrisman*, p. 65). Rorty addresses precisely this issue in his article "Solidarity or Objectivity?": "It is not clear why 'relativist' should be thought an

appropriate term for the ethnocentric third view, the one which the pragmatist *does* hold. For the pragmatist is not holding a positive theory which says that something is relative to something else. He is, instead, making the purely *negative* point that we should drop the distinction between knowledge and opinion, construed as the distinction between truth as correspondence to reality and truth as a commendatory term for well-justified beliefs. The reason that the realist calls this negative claim 'relativistic' is that he cannot believe that anybody would seriously deny that truth has an intrinsic nature. So when the pragmatist says that there is nothing to be said about truth save that each of us will commend as true those beliefs which he or she finds good to believe, the realist is inclined to interpret this as one more positive theory about the nature of truth: a theory according to which truth is simply the contemporary opinion of a chosen individual or group. Such a theory would, of course, be self-refuting. But the pragmatist does not have a theory of truth, much less a relativistic one. As a partisan of solidarity, his account of the value of cooperative human inquiry has only an ethical base, not an epistemological or metaphysical one. Not having *any* epistemology, *a fortiori* he does not have a relativistic one. ... For the pragmatist, by contrast, 'knowledge' is, like 'truth,' simply a compliment paid to the beliefs which we think so well justified that, for the moment, further justification is not needed." See Rorty, "Solidarity or Objectivity?" in *Objectivity, Relativism and Truth,* pp. 23-24.

[12]This is my paraphrase of several lines from ibid., p. 30.

[13]Rorty, introduction to *Objectivity, Relativism and Truth,* p. 13.

[14]George Lindbeck offers a pertinent example. In writing about the differences between sentences and propositions, Lindbeck notes that "the sentence 'This car is red,' as it occurs on this page, cannot be a proposition, for it specifies no particular auto and no particular time before or after which the vehicle might be of a different color: it can be neither true nor false. The same point holds *mutatis mutandis* for religious sentences: they acquire enough referential specificity to have first-order or ontological truth or falsity only in determinate settings, and this rarely if ever happens on the pages of theological treatises or in the course of doctrinal discussions. The theological and doctrinal uses of, e.g. 'Christ is Lord' are important, but they are not propositional. For Christian theological purposes, that sentence becomes a first-order proposition capable (so nonidealists would say) of making ontological truth claims only as it is used in the activities of adoration, proclamation, obedience, promise-hearing, and promise-keeping which shape individuals and communities into conformity to the mind of Christ. If this is so, there is a sense in which those unskilled in the language of faith not only fail to affirm but also cannot deny that 'Jesus is Lord.' The reasons for this are formally similar to those which make it impossible to deny the statement 'This car is red' unless one knows the circumstances—for example, the parking lot, ostensively indicated vehicle, and particular time—in which the sentence was uttered. One must be, so to speak, inside the relevant context; and in the case of a religion, this means that one must have some skill in *how* to use its language and practice its way of life before the propositional meaning of its affirmations become determinate enough to be rejected." See *The Nature of Doctrine: Religion and Theology in a Postliberal Age* (Philadelphia: Westminster Press, 1984), p. 68.

[15]This suggests why the proposals of Lesslie Newbigin never quite satisfy: despite his penetrating cultural analyses and his deep desire for a shift in paradigms, he continues too much of the time to operate with the language and assumptions of the old one. For example, Newbigin spends a lot of time deconstructing the dichotomy between public and private, but then holds onto the language of "public truth," insisting that if some-

thing is true, it is true for everyone. But this only follows if one still holds onto the model of truth as correspondence to external and independent reality. See, for example, any of Newbigin's recent works: *Foolishness to the Greeks: The Gospel and Western Culture* (Grand Rapids, Mich.: Eerdmans, 1986); *The Gospel in a Pluralist Society* (Grand Rapids, Mich.: Eerdmans, 1989), or *Truth to Tell: The Gospel as Public Truth* (Grand Rapids, Mich.: Eerdmans, 1991).

[16]The above two paragraphs are a paraphrase of Stanley Fish's argument in "Demonstration vs. Persuasion," in *Is There a Text in This Class?* (Cambridge, Mass.: Harvard University Press, 1980), esp. p. 365. I have changed some of the wording to apply to apologetics, since Fish's immediate concern is literary theory.

[17]Rorty, "The Contingency of a Liberal Community," in *Contingency, Irony and Solidarity*, p. 54.

[18]Ibid., p. 51.

[19]I know that American culture continues to hold science in high esteem because of its putatively pure methodology. This, coupled with its success, has persuaded many people that there is an objective reality apart from human beings and that it can be known and manipulated. But many philosophers of science are themselves questioning the appropriateness of notions like objective truth. People like Rorty remind us that science's much-touted success does not serve as an explanation of anything: "Explaining the success of science . . . by talk of 'fitting the world' . . . is like explaining why opium makes you sleepy by talking about its dormitive power. To say that Newton's vocabulary gets at the truth about the heavens is not an explanation of anything. It is just an empty compliment—one traditionally paid to writers whose novel jargon we have found useful. To say that we should drop the idea of truth as out there waiting to be discovered is not to say that we have discovered that, out there, there is no truth. It is to say that our purposes would be served better by ceasing to see truth as a deep matter, as a topic of philosophical interest, or 'true' as a term which repays 'analysis.' " See "The Contingency of Language," in *Contingency, Irony and Solidarity*, p. 8.

[20]See Rorty's insistence that in the modern period the scientist serves as a kind of priest, as "someone who achieves contact with nonhuman truth by being 'logical,' 'methodical' and 'objective' ("The Contingency of a Liberal Community," in *Contingency, Irony and Solidarity*, p. 52). Compare also Rorty's helpful summary of the work of Hans Blumenberg, who argues, among other things, that "beginning in the seventeenth century we tried to substitute a love of truth for a love of God, treating the world described by science as a quasi divinity." See "The Contingency of Language," p. 22; the reference to Blumenberg is to his *The Legitimacy of the Modern Age* (Cambridge, Mass.: MIT Press, 1983).

[21]After the collapse of the medieval church, whose authority was a *given* in its day, an authority vacuum was created not only for the culture at large but for the church as well. Unfortunately, the candidates that Christians have nominated to fill this office have mirrored the Enlightenment's penchant for putatively bracketing human beings and their interests and convictions. Thus the Protestant Reformation unwittingly encouraged a view of authority that suggested one could locate it externally—in Scripture. Thus it has become commonplace, in good modernist fashion, to appeal apologetically to the authority of Scripture—to some kind of objective revelation—in a way that implies that these Scriptures provide an external, objective authority standing over against the church. They don't. Or more precisely, it's not clear why we want to talk that way. The church is certainly unintelligible apart from its Scriptures, but saying this does not require that we deny that they are *our* Scriptures, that *we* are the ones who claim both to have heard and to continue to hear the voice of God speaking in and through

these human words and human communities.

[22]I think Wittgenstein's conversation with his imaginary interlocutor about mathematics is apropos for those Christians who want to continue to insist that the proposition "Jesus is Lord" is objectively true whether anyone believes it or not: " 'But mathematical truth is independent of whether human beings know it or not!'—Certainly, the propositions 'Human beings believe that twice two is four' and 'Twice two is four' do not mean the same. The latter is a mathematical proposition; the other, if it makes sense at all, may perhaps mean: human beings have *arrived* at the mathematical proposition. The two propositions have entirely different *uses*.—But what would *this* mean: 'Even though everybody believed that twice two was five it would still be four'?—For what would it be like for everybody to believe that?—Well, I could imagine, for instance, that people had a different calculus, or a technique which we should not call 'calculating.' But would it be *wrong*? (Is a coronation *wrong*? To beings different from ourselves it might look extremely odd.)" (*Philosophical Investigations*, pp. 226-27).

[23]See, for example, Stanley Hauerwas and William H. Willimon, *Resident Aliens* (Nashville: Abingdon, 1989), and Stanley Hauerwas, *After Christendom?* (Nashville: Abingdon, 1991).

[24]Because none of us can claim a privileged position or access to truth, all human inquiry is a form of persuasion. This means that all apologetics much be ad hoc apologetics, since there is no way to begin from a theory about truth, justification or belief and from that theory derive an appropriate apologetic strategy. See, for example, the suggestive essay by William Werpehowski, "Ad Hoc Apologetics," *Journal of Religion* 66 (July 1986): 282-301.

[25]Wittgenstein, *Culture and Value*, p. 35.

### Chapter 9: Christian Apologetics in the African-American Grain/Potter

[1]George Kent, *Blackness and the Adventure of Western Culture* (Chicago: Third World Press, 1972), p. 9.

[2]Stanley Grenz, *Revisioning Evangelical Theology: A Fresh Agenda for the Twenty-first Century* (Downers Grove, Ill.: InterVarsity Press, 1993).

[3]W. E. B. DuBois, *The Souls of Black Folk* (New York: Penguin, 1989), p. 5.

[4]Cornel West, *Prophesy Deliverance: An Afro-American Revolutionary Christianity* (Philadelphia: Westminster Press, 1982), p. 24.

[5]See John McDermott, *The Culture of Experience: Philosophical Essays in the American Grain* (New York: New York University Press, 1976).

[6]Cornel West, *Prophetic Fragments* (Grand Rapids, Mich.: Eerdmans/Trenton, N.J.: African World Press, 1988), p. 277.

[7]See Russell Jacoby, *The Last Intellectuals: American Culture in the Age of Academe* (New York: Basic Books, 1987).

[8]Sociologist James Davison Hunter describes this mode of discourse thus: "The culture of critical discourse is a historically evolved set of rules concerning the nature and direction of social discourse. Those imbued with this orientation tend always to justify and legitimate perceptions, assertions, and courses of action solely on the basis of rationally deduced arguments and not on the basis of traditional societal authority—religious, bureaucratic, or familial" (*American Evangelicalism: Conservative Religion and the Quandary of Modernity* [New Brunswick, N.J.: Rutgers University Press, 1983], p. 108).

[9]Michael Green, *Evangelism Through the Local Church* (1970; reprint London: Hodder & Stoughton, 1990), p. 117.

[10]For an insightful discussion of this new phenomenon, see Lerone Bennett Jr., "The Crisis of the Black Spirit," *Ebony*, October 1977. See also Cornel West, *Race Matters* (New York:

Vintage, 1994), esp. chap. 1.

[11]Nicholas Wolterstorff, *Reason Within the Bounds of Religion*, 2nd ed. (Grand Rapids, Mich.: Eerdmans, 1984), pp. 111-46.

### Chapter 10: The Church as Apologetic/Hollinger

[1]Pluralism is of course not totally new, and this is not the first time in history the church has had to face it. In the modern and postmodern world pluralism is, however, experienced with much greater intensity, and it tends to breed a relativism with regards to truth and values. See Robert L. Wilken, "Religious Pluralism and Early Christian Thought," *Pro Ecclesia* 1, no. 1: 89-103.

[2]Peter Berger, *The Homeless Mind: Modernization and Consciousness* (New York: Vintage, 1973), p. 64.

[3]Peter Berger, *The Sacred Canopy: Elements of a Sociological Theory of Religion* (Garden City, N.Y.: Doubleday, 1969), p. 127.

[4]Ibid., p. 45. See also Peter Berger, *The Social Construction of Reality: A Treatise in the Sociology of Knowledge* (New York: Anchor, 1966), pp. 154-63.

[5]Berger, *Sacred Canopy*, p. 46.

[6]Stanley Hauerwas and David Burrell, "From Story to Story: An Alternative Pattern for Rationality in Ethics," in *Why Narrative? Readings in Narrative Theology*, ed. Stanley Hauerwas and L. Gregory Jones (Grand Rapids, Mich.: Eerdmans, 1989), p. 190.

[7]For a helpful analysis of narrative theology and its potential for apologetics, see David K. Clark, "Narrative Theology and Apologetics," *Journal of the Evangelical Theological Society* 36, no. 4 (1994): 499-515.

[8]Alan Jacobs, "Rhetoric and the Task of Apologetics in Contemporary America," *Proceedings of the Wheaton Theology Conference* 1 (1992): 169.

[9]See B. B. Warfield, *Miracles: Yesterday and Today, True and False* (Grand Rapids, Mich.: Eerdmans, 1953).

[10]Robert Bellah et al., *Habits of the Heart: Individualism and Commitment in American Life* (New York: Harper & Row, 1985), pp. 75-76.

[11]Wilken, "Religious Pluralism," p. 103.

[12]Robert W. Jenson, "How the World Lost Its Story," *First Things*, October 1993, p. 21.

[13]Ibid., p. 22.

### Chapter 11: Evangelizing the Church/Webster

[1]Charles J. Sykes, *A Nation of Victims: The Decay of the American Character* (New York: St. Martin's, 1992), p. 11.

[2]Ibid., p. 41.

[3]George Will, "An Evil Act Deserves Swift, Severe Punishment," *Sunday Herald-Times*, April 30, 1989, p. A12.

[4]Paul Ciotti, "If the Menendez Boys Aren't Guilty, Then No One Is," *San Diego Union-Tribune*, January 27, 1994.

[5]Barbara W. Tuchman, *A Distant Mirror: The Calamitous 14th Century* (New York: Ballantine, 1978), p. 101.

[6]C. S. Lewis, *Mere Christianity* (Glasgow: Collins, 1978), p. 180.

[7]E. Ferguson, "Marcion," in *Evangelical Dictionary of Theology*, ed. Walter Elwell (Grand Rapids, Mich.: Baker Book House, 1984), p. 685.

[8]Eugene H. Peterson, *The Message* (Colorado Springs: NavPress, 1993), p. 17.

[9]Portions of this chapter are adapted from *The Easy Yoke* (Colorado Springs: NavPress, 1995).

# Bibliography

**I. Postmodernism**

Anderson, Walter Truett. *Reality Isn't What It Used to Be: Theatrical Politics, Ready-to-Wear Religion, Global Myths, Primitive Chic and Other Wonders of the Postmodern World*. San Francisco: Harper & Row, 1990.

Caputo, John D. *Radical Hermeneutics*. Bloomington: Indiana University Press, 1987.

Connor, Steven. *Postmodernist Culture: An Introduction to the Theories of the Contemporary*. Oxford: Basil Blackwell, 1989.

Fish, Stanley. *Doing What Comes Naturally: Change, Rhetoric and the Practice of Theory in Literary and Legal Studies*. Durham, N.C.: Duke University Press, 1989.

Gadamer, Hans-Georg. *Truth and Method*. 2nd ed. Translated by Joel Weinsheimer and Donald G. Marshall. New York: Crossroad, 1991.

Gergen, Kenneth J. *The Saturated Self: Dilemmas of Identity in Contemporary Life*. New York: BasicBooks, 1991.

Giddens, Anthony. *The Consequences of Modernity*. Stanford, Calif.: Stanford University Press, 1990.

Harvey, David. *The Condition of Post-modernity*. London: Basil Blackwell, 1989.

Hutcheon, Linda. *The Politics of Postmodernism*. London: Routledge, 1989.

Lyotard, Jean-François. *The Postmodern Condition: A Report on Knowledge*. Vol. 10 of *Theory and History of Literature*. Translated by Geoff Bennington and Brian Massumi. Minneapolis: University of Minnesota Press, 1984.

Murphy, Nancey, and James Wm. McClendon Jr. "Distinguishing Modern and Postmodern Theologies." *Modern Theology* 5 (April 1989): 191-214.

Norris, Christopher. *Derrida*. Cambridge, Mass.: Harvard University Press, 1987.

Rorty, Richard. *Consequences of Pragmatism*. Minneapolis: University of Minnesota Press, 1982.

_____. *Contingency, Irony and Solidarity*. Cambridge: Cambridge University Press, 1989.

_____. *Objectivism, Relativism and Truth*. New York: Cambridge University Press, 1991.

Waugh, Patricia, ed. *Postmodernism: A Reader*. London: Edward Arnold, 1992.

*Important Criticisms*

Ellis, John. *Against Deconstruction*. Princeton, N.J.: Princeton University Press, 1989.

Lundin, Roger. *The Culture of Interpretation: Christian Faith and the Modern World*. Grand Rapids, Mich.: Eerdmans, 1993.

Veith, Gene Edward. *Postmodern Times: A Christian Guide to Contemporary Thought and Culture*. Wheaton, Ill.: Crossway Books, 1994.

Walhout, Clarence, and Leland Ryken. *Contemporary Literary Theory: A Christian Appraisal*. Grand Rapids, Mich.: Eerdmans, 1991.

**II. History of Apologetics**

Dulles, Avery. *A History of Apologetics*. New York: Corpus/London: Hutchinson, 1971.

Lewis, Gordon R. *Testing Christianity's Truth Claims*. Chicago: Moody Press, 1976.

Ramm, Bernard. *Varieties of Christian Apologetics: An Introduction to the Christian Philosophy of Religion.* Grand Rapids, Mich.: Baker Book House, 1961.

Reid, J. K. S. *Christian Apologetics.* London: Hodder & Stoughton, 1969.

### III. Apologetics of Modernity

This type presupposes a common ground between the nonbeliever and apologist; however, this common ground assumes several forms, from a universal religious experience to historical facts and evidences.

Berger, Peter. *Rumor of Angels: Modern Society and the Rediscovery of the Supernatural.* Expanded ed. New York: Anchor, 1990.

Corduan, Winfried. *Reasonable Faith: Basic Christian Apologetics.* Nashville: Broadman & Holman, 1993. A contemporary text that includes helpful situations for practicing apologetics.

Craig, William Lane. *Reasonable Faith.* Wheaton, Ill.: Crossway Books, 1994. Currently the best expression of an evangelical apologetics of this type.

Hebblethwaite, Brian. *The Ocean of Truth.* Cambridge: Cambridge University Press, 1988.

Latourelle, René, and Gerald O'Collins. *Problems and Perspectives of Fundamental Theology.* New York: Paulist Press, 1982.

Nash, Ronald H. *Worldviews in Conflict: Choosing Christianity in a World of Ideas.* Grand Rapids, Mich.: Zondervan, 1992.

Robinson, John A. T. *Honest to God.* London: SCM Press, 1963.

Sproul, R. C., John Gerstner and A. Lindsley. *Classical Apologetics: A Rational Defense of the Christian Faith and a Critique of Presuppositional Apologetics.* Grand Rapids, Mich.: Zondervan, 1984.

#### Important Criticisms

Frame, John M. "Van Til and the Ligonier Apologetic." *Westminster Theological Journal* 47 (Fall 1985): 279-99. A review of R. C. Sproul, John Gerstner and A. Lindsley, *Classical Apologetics,* 1984.

Kaufman, Gordon D. "Evidentialism: A Theologian's Response." *Faith and Philosophy* 6 (January 1989): 35-46.

Topping, Richard R. "The Anti-foundationalist Challenge to Evangelical Apologetics." *Evangelical Quarterly* 63 (January 1991): 45-60. Addresses Carl F. H. Henry's and S. C. Hackett's foundationalism.

Zemek, George J., Jr. "Classical Apologetics: A Rational Defense." *Grace Theological Journal* 7 (Spring 1986): 111-23. Another review addressing R. C. Sproul, John Gerstner and A. Lindsley, *Classical Apologetics,* 1984.

### IV. Apologetics Between Modernity and Postmodernity

In addition to arguments grounded in a universal common ground, this apologetic strategy argues that Christianity's plausibility must also be established. Like the apologetic strategy above, this one also retains the language of objective truth.

#### Establishing Plausibility

Brent, John S., and Douglas E. Chismar. "Person-Centered Apologetics: An Empathetic Approach." *Journal of Psychology and Christianity* 3 (Spring 1984): 18-26.

Clark, David K. *Dialogical Apologetics: A Person-Centered Approach to Christian Defense.* Grand Rapids, Mich.: Baker, 1993. Clark revisions apologetics in terms of the individual's concerns and needs, successfully integrating plausibility and credibility.

Green, Michael. *Evangelism Through the Local Church.* Nashville: Oliver-Nelson, 1992. Excellent resource exploring our multifaith society (pp. 45-82), the secular challenge (pp. 113-230) and appropriate responses that enhance the church's plausibility (pp. 425-43).

_____. "How to Use Apologetics: Secular Background." In *The Work of an Evangelist: International Congress for Itinerant Evangelists*, pp. 697-704. Edited by J. D. Douglas. Minneapolis: World Wide Publications, 1983.

Jacobs, Alan. "Rhetoric and the Task of Apologetics in Contemporary America." *Proceedings of the Wheaton Theology Conference* 1 (Spring 1992): 163-73.

McGrath, Alister E. *Intellectuals Don't Need God and Other Modern Myths: Building Bridges to Faith Through Apologetics.* Grand Rapids, Mich.: Zondervan, 1993. Excellent advice on establishing and retaining plausibility.

### Integrating Plausibility and Credibility

Alexander, John F. *The Secular Squeeze: Reclaiming Christian Depth in a Shallow World.* Downers Grove, Ill.: InterVarsity Press, 1993. Illustrates an effective use of narrative in apologetics.

Clark, Kelly James. *Return to Reason: A Critique of Enlightenment Evidentialism and a Defense of Reason and Belief in God.* Grand Rapids, Mich.: Eerdmans, 1990. Provides a helpful introduction to developments in Reformed epistemology—which rejects modernity's understanding of foundationalism—and some of its implications for apologetics.

Moore, Peter C. *Disarming the Secular Gods: How to Talk So Skeptics Will Listen.* Downers Grove, Ill.: InterVarsity Press, 1989.

Morris, Thomas. *Making Sense of It All: Pascal and the Meaning of Life.* Grand Rapids, Mich.: Eerdmans, 1992.

Newbigin, Lesslie. *Foolishness to the Greeks: The Gospel and Western Culture.* Grand Rapids, Mich.: Eerdmans, 1986.

_____. *The Gospel in a Pluralist Society.* Grand Rapids, Mich.: Eerdmans, 1989.

_____. *Truth to Tell: The Gospel as Public Truth.* Grand Rapids, Mich.: Eerdmans, 1991.

Roberts, Robert. "Theology and Personal Maturity in Christianity and Carl Jung." *Proceedings of the Wheaton Theology Conference* 1 (Spring 1992): 56-73.

Roxburgh, Alan J. *Reaching a New Generation.* Downers Grove, Ill.: InterVarsity Press, 1993.

Sire, James. *Chris Chrisman Goes to College.* Downers Grove, Ill.: InterVarsity Press, 1993.

_____. *Why Should Anyone Believe Anything At All?* Downers Grove, Ill.: InterVarsity Press, 1994.

### Important Criticisms

Hauerwas, Stanley. *After Christendom?* Nashville: Abingdon, 1991.

_____. *A Community of Character: Toward a Constructive Christian Social Ethic.* Notre Dame, Ind.: University of Notre Dame Press, 1981.

### V. Apologetics of Postmodernity

This apologetic strategy accepts at least some of the major postmodern criticisms of modernity—(1) totalizing is oppressive, (2) objectivity is a false category, (3) foundationalism is false—and thus attempts to shift the paradigm away from claims about objective truth. One common form of this apologetic approach is called postliberal or "ad hoc" apologetics.

### Theoretical Foundations

Berger, Peter, and Thomas Luckmann. *The Social Construction of Reality: A Treatise in the*

*Sociology of Knowledge*. Garden City, N.Y.: Anchor, 1966.

Bernstein, Richard J. *Beyond Objectivism and Relativism: Science, Hermeneutics and Praxis*. Philadelphia: University of Pennsylvania Press, 1985. Attempts to transcend the dualism between objectivism and relativism.

Hauerwas, Stanley. *A Community of Character: Toward a Constructive Christian Social Ethic*. Notre Dame. Ind.: University of Notre Dame Press, 1981.

_____. *The Peaceable Kingdom: A Primer in Christian Ethics*. Notre Dame, Ind.: University of Notre Dame Press, 1983.

Kierkegaard, Søren. "Communication." In vol. 1, A-E, of *Søren Kierkegaard's Journal and Papers*, pp. 252-319. Edited and translated by Howard V. Hong and Edna H. Hong. Bloomington: Indiana University Press, 1967. Kierkegaard's idea of indirect communication needs to be mined for apologetics.

Middleton, J. Richard, and Brian Walsh. *Truth Is Stranger Than It Used to Be: Biblical Faith in a Postmodern Age*. Downers Grove, Ill.: InterVarsity Press, 1995.

*Postliberal or "Ad Hoc" Apologetics*

Handspicker, Meredith B. "Toward a Postliberal Apologetics." *Journal of the Academy for Evangelism in Theological Education* 7 (1991-1992): 72-83.

Placher, William C. *Unapologetic Theology: A Christian Voice in a Pluralistic Conversation*. Louisville, Ky.: Westminster/John Knox, 1989.

Tilley, Terrence W. "Incommensurability, Intratextuality and Fideism." *Modern Theology* 5 (January 1989): 87-111.

Werpehowski, William. "Ad Hoc Apologetics." *Journal of Religion* 66 (July 1986): 282-301.

Whittaker, John. *Matters of Faith, Matters of Principle*. San Antonio, Tex.: Trinity University Press, 1981.

*Important Criticisms*

Clark, David K. "Narrative Theology and Apologetics." *Journal of the Evangelical Theological Society* 36 (1994): 499-515.

Netland, Harold A. "Apologetics, Worldviews and the Problem of Neutral Criteria." *Trinity Journal* 12 (Spring 1991): 39-58.

**VI. The Church Within Culture**

Colson, Charles, with Ellen Santilli Vaughn. *The Body: Being Light in Darkness*. Dallas: Word, 1992.

Guinness, Os, and John Seel, eds. *No God But God: Breaking with the Idols of Our Age*. Chicago: Moody Press, 1992.

Hauerwas, Stanley. *After Christendom?* Nashville: Abingdon, 1991.

Hauerwas, Stanley, and William Willimon. *Resident Aliens*. Nashville: Abingdon, 1989.

Horton, Michael Scott, ed. *Power Religion: The Selling Out of the Evangelical Church?* Chicago: Moody Press, 1992.

Jenson, Robert W. "How the World Lost Its Story." *First Things* 36 (October 1993): 19-24.

Newbigin, Lesslie. *Foolishness to the Greeks: The Gospel and Western Culture*. Grand Rapids, Mich.: Eerdmans, 1986.

_____. *The Gospel in a Pluralist Society*. Grand Rapids, Mich.: Eerdmans, 1989.

_____. *Truth to Tell: The Gospel as Public Truth*. Grand Rapids, Mich.: Eerdmans, 1991.

Wells, David F. *No Place for Truth*. Grand Rapids, Mich.: Eerdmans, 1993.

# Name Index

## Subject Index

# List of Contributors

**William Lane Craig** is currently a visiting scholar at Emory University, after working at the Higher Institute of Philosophy, University of Louvain, for the last seven years. Holding earned doctorates from the University of Birmingham and Universität München in the areas of philosophy and theology, Craig publishes widely in these fields. Among his more recent works are *The Historical Argument for the Resurrection of Jesus During the Deist Controversy* (Edwin Mellen), *Assessing the New Testament Evidence for the Historicity of the Resurrection of Jesus* (Edwin Mellen), *Theism, Atheism and Big Bang Cosmology* (coauthored with Quentin Smith; Oxford University Press) and *Reasonable Faith* (Crossway Books).

**Nicola Hoggard Creegan** is currently an adjunct instructor in religion at North Carolina Wesleyan College. After graduating from Gordon-Conwell Theological Seminary, she earned her Ph.D. from Drew University. She has been book review editor for the *Ellul Studies Form* and a participant in the International Schleiermacher Society. Currently she is writing a book on evangelicalism and feminism.

**Dennis Hollinger** is a pastor at the Washington Community Fellowship, Washington, D.C. He also serves as an adjunct professor at Eastern Baptist Theological Seminary and Trinity Evangelical Divinity School (Washington, D.C., extension). He earned his Ph.D. from Drew University and has published in periodicals ranging from *Urban Mission* to *Journal of Religious Ethics*.

**Philip Kenneson** is assistant professor of theology and philosophy at Milligan College. His Ph.D. is from Duke University. His articles have previously appeared in *Modern Theology*, *Discernment*, *Asbury Theological Journal* and *Soundings*.

**Roger Lundin** is professor of English at Wheaton College. He is widely published. His latest work is the acclaimed *The Culture of Interpretation: Christian Faith and the Postmodern World* (Eerdmans). Lundin has also coauthored *Literature Through the Eyes of Faith* (with Susan Gallagher) and *Responsibility of Hermeneutics* (with Anthony Thiselton and Clarence Walhout; Eerdmans) and coedited *Voices from the Heart* (with Mark Noll; Eerdmans).

**J. Richard Middleton** teaches at and is completing Ph.D. studies at the Institute for Christian Studies in Toronto. He has coauthored, with Brian Walsh, *The Transforming Vision* and *Truth Is Stranger Than It Used to Be: Biblical Faith in a Postmodern Age*. He has contributed to *The Harvard Theological Review*, *Christian Scholar's Review* and *The Crucible*.

**Dennis Okholm** is associate professor of theology at Wheaton College. After master's work at Trinity Evangelical Divinity School, he completed the Ph.D. at Princeton Theological Seminary. His articles have appeared in *Christian Scholar's Review*, *The Proceedings of the American Benedictine Academy*, *The Complete Library of Christian Worship* (Star Song) and the

*New Dictionary of Christian Ethics and Pastoral Theology* (InterVarsity Press). He is a coauthor of *Invitation to Philosophy: Issues and Options* (Wadsworth) and a co-organizer of the annual Wheaton Theology Conference.

**Timothy R. Phillips** is assistant professor of theology at Wheaton College. After master's work at Gordon-Conwell Theological Seminary, he completed the Ph.D. at Vanderbilt University. His articles have appeared in *Christian Educator's Handbook on Spiritual Formation* (Victor Books) and *Through No Fault of Their Own? The Fate of Those Who Have Never Heard* (Baker Book House). He is a member of the Theology Committee of the National Association of Evangelicals and co-organizer of the annual Wheaton Theology Conference.

**Ronald Potter** is assistant professor of Christian thought and contemporary culture at the Center for Urban Theological Studies, Philadelphia. His articles have appeared in *Urban Family, Christianity Today* and *The Other Side*. He authored the chapter "The New Black Evangelicals" in *Black Theology: A Documentary History, 1966-1979* (edited by James H. Cone and Gayraud S. Wilmore; Orbis Books). He has lectured at Westminster Theological Seminary, Harvard Divinity School, Union Theological Seminary and the Candler School of Theology. He is on the ministerial staff at the Mount Tabor AME Church in Philadelphia.

**James W. Sire** serves as senior editor and campus lecturer for InterVarsity Press and InterVarsity Christian Fellowship. His Ph.D. is from the University of Missouri. His books include *The Universe Next Door, Discipleship of the Mind* and *Why Should Anyone Believe Anything at All?* (all InterVarsity Press).

**John G. Stackhouse Jr.** is associate professor of religion at the University of Manitoba. After his master's work at Wheaton Graduate School, he earned the Ph.D. from the University of Chicago. He publishes regularly in *The Christian Century, Christianity Today, Perspectives* and *Crux*. His latest book is *Canadian Evangelicalism in the Twentieth Century: An Introduction to Its Character* (University of Toronto Press).

**Brian J. Walsh** is a senior member in worldview studies at the Institute for Christian Studies in Toronto. He did his Ph.D. work at McGill University. He is coauthor, with J. Richard Middleton, of *The Transforming Vision* and *Truth Is Stranger Than It Used to Be: Biblical Faith in a Postmodern Age*. He has also written *Subversive Christianity* and frequently writes for journals.

**Douglas D. Webster** earned his Ph.D. in theology at the University of Toronto. He has several years' experience of pastoring in Indiana, Colorado and California. His books include *Finding Spiritual Direction* and *Selling Jesus: What's Wrong with Marketing the Church*.